SAGE was founded in 1965 by Sara Miller McCune to support the dissemination of usable knowledge by publishing innovative and high-quality research and teaching content. Today, we publish over 900 journals, including those of more than 400 learned societies, more than 800 new books per year, and a growing range of library products including archives, data, case studies, reports, and video. SAGE remains majority-owned by our founder, and after Sara's lifetime will become owned by a charitable trust that secures our continued independence.

Los Angeles | London | New Delhi | Singapore | Washington DC | Melbourne

Sadhus in Indian Politics

Sadhus in Indian Politics

Dynamics of Hindutva

Koushiki Dasgupta

Los Angeles | London | New Delhi
Singapore | Washington DC | Melbourne

First published in 2021 by

SAGE Publications India Pvt Ltd
B1/I-1 Mohan Cooperative Industrial Area
Mathura Road, New Delhi 110 044, India
www.sagepub.in

SAGE Publications Inc
2455 Teller Road
Thousand Oaks, California 91320, USA

SAGE Publications Ltd
1 Oliver's Yard, 55 City Road
London EC1Y 1SP, United Kingdom

SAGE Publications Asia-Pacific Pte Ltd
18 Cross Street #10-10/11/12
China Square Central
Singapore 048423

Published by Vivek Mehra for SAGE Publications India Pvt Ltd and typeset in 10.5/13 pt Berkeley by AG Infographics, Delhi.

Library of Congress Control Number: 2021941441

ISBN: 978-93-91370-93-0 (HB)

SAGE Team: Rajesh Dey, Satvinder Kaur and Megha Dabral

To Ma and Baba

Contents

Preface and Acknowledgements

The ideas and views expressed in this book were first conceptualized as part of my research on the changing patterns of Hindu politics in post-independence India. Though my research spanned the rise and development of the Hindu rightist forces mostly in a regional setting, I have had the opportunity to examine how different individuals and groups have attempted to appropriate the discourse of Hindutva over the years. Sadhus, or ascetics, contributed hugely in building the edifice of Hindutva through using multiple expressions on different political and non-political platforms. To what extent can we outline a common theme that developed in the communication with the sadhus in politics in regard to the spiritual accomplishments of the 'self'? This particular question helped me think about the actual framework of identifying sadhus as 'individual', 'conscious' actors offering an alternative reading of the Hindutva politics in India. My foremost intention is to deconstruct the misconceptions and confusions around the ideology of Hindutva over the ages. Hindutva has travelled a long way from the late 19th century to the present, held different connotations and combined the ideas of freedom and dominance in certain contexts. Sadhus, or ascetics, as conscious agents of social change, enjoy a unique sense of freedom in contemplating their Hindu-ness or Hindutva but are forced to deal with the dominant language of political Hindutva that has displaced some of their original perceptions towards the ideology. I discuss the stories of a few sadhus here as case studies to reflect the essential patterns of ascetics' involvement in politics to show how the modalities of their involvement have been anticipated under different contexts from the early 20th century to recent times. The quintessential divergence between Nehruvian secularism and political Hindutva produced conditions of anxiety and tension within the boundaries of ascetic politics without keeping the sadhus away from making important political decisions.

I am happy to acknowledge the support I have received from different spiritual–philanthropic organizations and the wide range of information I have received from the sadhus who opened their minds to me on several occasions. They helped me develop my perception of the many worlds of 'sadhudom' in a meaningful manner. Some of them answered my questions in a reluctant way and repeatedly requested me not to disclose their names in the book. They love to celebrate their Hindu-ness/Hindutva in their own ways but believe in the importance of Hindu consolidation in India. I pay my sincere gratitude to these anonymous sadhus wholeheartedly.

I am immensely grateful to Professor Peter Flügel of the Centre for Jain Studies, SOAS University, London, for providing me the necessary assistance to carry on with my research at the institution for some period of time. I am also indebted to the Honourable Vice Chancellor of Vidyasagar University, Professor Ranjan Chakrabarti, for his kind support and encouragement all through my academic career. I pay my sincere gratitude to the anonymous reviewers of the manuscript for their thoughtful comments and suggestions. I am also deeply grateful to the editors and staff of SAGE Publications for their kind interest and help in the preparation of the book.

I am thankful to the staff at the India Office section at British Library, London, SOAS Library, London, National Library, Kolkata, National Archive, New Delhi and Nehru Memorial Museum and Library, New Delhi. I will always cherish my interactions with my learned friends, colleagues and members of different religious organizations in India and the United Kingdom for making this project possible.

My friends and well-wishers Subodh da, Sudhirji, Virendra, Rano-kaku and Bikash da have had an overarching influence on my life for several years. I will be grateful to them forever. Dr Swapan Kumar Roy and Mrs Roy stood with my family during difficult times and helped me in one way or the other to take my work forward. I thank them too.

Lastly, I pay my gratitude to my dear father, who always stood firm with me in all possible ways.

Introduction

I

In the wake of the so-called post-secular turn in global politics, the boundary between the religious and the political has become a peeving embarrassment for those who hardly recognized the so-called revival of the 'religious' in the post-Cold War era, hardly paying attention to the global metamorphosis of the approaches to secularism.[1] The Westphalian fetishism of keeping religion out of the purview of the state has long dominated the philosophy of secularism in colonial and post-colonial nations as a global teleological model of human development; however, the readings of post-secularism eventually brought out a radical critique of the concept that modern democratic principles could best be pursued only with a secular framework. The secular could also be conducive to violence and injustice, and by intentionally ostracizing religion from politics, as Jürgen Habermas mentioned, modern society has lost one of its powerful moral resources.[2] Now, in the case of non-Western societies that are different from the highly industrialized–urbanized societies and are traditional and hierarchical, the possibilities of religion being the prime component of change whipped up controversies over the relationship between religion and economy, that between religion and politics and religion as an instrument of social control. Marx Weber's thesis of capital accumulation leading to a process of rationalization/secularization in the modern Western societies could not get a match in the conditions created by the traditional societies, because here a shared framework of religious ethics, social behaviour and economic practices determined the dynamics of politics (Weber 1930). Charles Taylor, in his book *A Secular Age*,[3] talked about the people in these societies who did not live in a secular age ever, rather experiencing a society deeply implanted in sacred practices and dealing with the so-called secular issues of human rights, women's rights, identity crisis and social justice through their traditional belief-oriented outlooks. We may relate this alternative framework to the perspective of multiple modernities, which sanctioned society-specific and nation-specific constellations of religious/secular formations against the regnant imposition of the Western type of secularism on traditional societies.

Importantly, one must never look for a revival of religion or return of religion in a traditional society like India. Religion, forming the essential pillar of traditional belief systems and knowledge systems, never withdrew from the public domain, rather continued to stay strong within the web of community consciousness. Simultaneously, the self-observing–unsettled attributes of religion made it the most volatile category of innovation, manipulation and mobilization through a series of narratives, myths, rituals, experiences and others. The symbolic values added to religion thus made it malleable to identity formation, winding up with categories of race, ethnicity or culture. Through these interrelated categories, religious ideas muscled in on politics far more strongly that merely standing as a transcendental experience. Interestingly, in certain situations, any one of these categories may appear overruling and paramount to religion and create conditions for dilating the implications of politics. In that case, religion penetrates politics through identity-specific channels and makes it a plausible site of further peregrination. My intention in this book is to see politics mainly as *janaseva*, not as *rajniti*, because politics as *rajniti* does not bear anything symbolic to *raj* dharma in modern India. *Raj* dharma denotes the responsibilities/duties of the kind that a ruler would have towards his/her subjects or citizens, because the word dharma retains concerns about ethics, morality, law and governance. The real implications of the term *raj* dharma have been replaced by new ideas and connotations with the shifts in modern democratic politics, and the word *niti* came into circulation instead of dharma. Interestingly, sadhus associated with politics exercised a more spontaneous expression like *janaseva* for politics. This particular connotation is highly connected with imaginative possibilities and performative actions, with a deep sense of engagement with spirituality, ethics and moral judgement.

It could be viewed as an alternative discourse of politics but very much attached with power plays, mobilizations and manipulations. This domain creates possibilities of politics being driven by religion or dharma, not the other way round. Unfortunately, politics as *janaseva* also falls into the pit of making everything party-centric and activity-oriented. The moment *janaseva* becomes autonomous or free from party politics, it opens up a critical discourse that acknowledges the modalities of ascetic intervention in public affairs.

The phenomenal rise of the so-called Hindutva[4] movement in India serves as the quintessential example of that ideological construction where religion sinks into politics by means of a powerful rhetoric of Hindu culture and Hindu race. It is claimed that had not the semantics of Hinduism stood so strong in popular perception the word 'Hinduness' as a near parallel to 'Hindutva' would have been a better word for 'Hinduism'. According to this logic, the word 'Hindutva' makes the ideal reference to delineate what can be considered a Hindu race or Hindu culture.[5] The challenge of reading Hindutva as the complete understanding of Hindu thoughts and ideas makes it difficult to understand each of its constituencies separately. Since the presence of the 'religious' in Hindutva got reflected mainly by identity-specific notions, Hindutva proponents thoughtfully cultivated the basic traditions of Hinduism over decades to make it a bit feasible for their own narratives. Ascetic traditions or nationalist asceticism, for instance, have been valorized by Hindutva primarily to counter colonial vilification of the Hindu sadhus[6] as otherworldly and apolitical. With the ascendency of the Hindu rightist forces since the 1980s, a large number of sadhus have appeared influential over the Hindu electorate, and a few others have simply fought elections by themselves.

Conceptual Underpinnings

The evolution of the ideology of Hindutva in India remained multifaceted and multidimensional. With the breaking down of the capitalist consensus in the late 20th century and the rise of the neoliberal economic structure, Hindutva became a tool of electoral mobilization, as well as a component of development politics in India. It travelled through a muddled path of spirituality, democratic progress and caste mobilization and, more importantly, projected itself as the bastion of popular development under the new-generation leadership of a particular political party. What makes the subject unique to Indian history is the sheer disconnection or lack of communication between today's Hindutva and its past incarnations. The ways it was conceived and projected in the past does not make any real historical sense in its present context. The word 'Hindutva' itself flung its users into indecision. It is the sloppiest jargon thus far, misinterpreted to the point of total confusion. The state or quality of being Hindu carries the finest aspects of one's social, cultural, spiritual and intellectuals attributes, and overall a nuanced engagement with Hinduism. Hindutva is set on a journey of self-evolution, and anything that disrupts this journey simply reduces Hindutva into mere identity politics.

The many histories of Hindutva in India were constructed rhetorically in the late 19th century around multiple networks, and at each stage of its evolution, the ideology moved through sustained interaction with different spiritual/religious, social and political forces, encompassing a wide range of connotations, aptitudes, forms and expressions. What is being conceived as Hindutva today differs largely from its conception when it started its journey and created its own intellectual framework in the early 20th century. Hindutva, in each of its incarnations, has remained truthful to the idea of restoring the Hindu culture in its unadulterated form and more or less constructed Hindutva as tantamount to *Bharatiyatva* or Indianness. With the dramatic rise of the right-wing forces, Hindutva appears to be a dynamic instrument of tactical manoeuvrings against the potential threats to the power base. It has generated strategic appeal to attract the electorate mainly through systematic use of certain cultural–economic discourses based on the Hindu majoritarian world view. It left enough scope for speculations by the minorities and other socially disadvantaged groups about the actual intentions of the Hindutva propaganda. It is highly problematic to find out how Hindutva, being a social ideology, transformed into a political instrument and how a certain political force established its sole hegemony over that ideology. Let me be clear on this point: Hindutva was never solely occupied by any political party or any individual or group as far as its initial history is concerned. It might have carried different meanings and connotations for different people, but it had never been associated with a power structure. It is quite misleading to associate Hindutva with V. D. Savarkar only. He popularized the subject and especially denoted the characteristics that validate the Hindu-ness of a Hindu. However, though he had his own explanations, which might have been well circulated and politicized on a wider scale, he was not the only one who defined Hindutva. It would be disingenuous to history if we overlook the construction of Hindutva in regional terms at a given time period.

In a general setting, Hindutva or Hinduness could be described in a self-distancing mode of identity formation which denies Hindu-hood to be a birth right. One individual who claims to be a Hindu by birth must prove his worth of being a 'true' Hindu after attaining and nurturing certain attributes in life. These attributes could be defined in terms of what does not make a Hindu and what makes a Hindu, simultaneously. It is an open-ended discourse of speculations, belief systems and sociopolitical convictions explored at the level of ideology because of its tremendous potential to create a sense of group solidarity with a vision of the past, and a vision of the future as well. Hindu religiosity or spirituality, for instance, in no case delivered less of the message of Hindu-ness in a self-critical, tolerant mode. In the same way, one could claim to be a good Hindu without having any interest in Hindu religious practices. All six schools of Hindu philosophy declared their believes in the existence of the 'atman' or soul; however, a few of them rejected the existence of a personal God or a God with attributes. There is no yardstick to define who is a true Hindu and who is not, and as a natural corollary to these propositions, Hindutva must be understood as a way of life or a state of mind, and it should not be tagged with anything related to Hindu fundamentalism. It has nothing to do with the non-Hindus or the religious 'others', and any political party, media, intelligentsia or the civil society should not indulge in addressing Hindutva merely as a communal propaganda. Unless one comes out of the spell of Savarkarian notion of Hindutva, one would continue to be entrapped by the racial–ethnic connotations of Hindutva based on the requirements of the Hindu–identity formation project in the early 20th century. The racial–ethnic model of Hindutva had been built as a challenge to the orientalist construction of Indian inferiority and British superiority. It stigmatized the 'other' religions as threatening, especially those 'Pan-isms that are struggling forth from continent to continent. After independence, with the establishment of a democratic–secular type of a nation in India, the ideology suffered greatly from imprecision and ambiguity. However, after the birth of a separate Muslim majority state, it settled on its narrative of being identified only with Indian culture, Hindu nationalism and religion. The more it appealed to the insecurity of a communally threatened Hindu population, the more it grew as a political ideology.

It took time for Hindutva to get fully transformed into an instrument of political mobilization in favour of the Hindu majority, which happened once the Bharatiya Jana Sangh turned into the Bharatiya Janata Party (BJP) and strategically deployed a vast network of organizations for the cause of electoral achievements in the 1980s. The Babri Masjid demolition in 1992 could be identified as a turning point insofar as the evolution of Hindutva is concerned, under the changed economic and political settings in the 1990s when the gross predicament of the ruling Congress also marked the end of the commitments of a socialist economy in the country. The new model of Hindutva was exclusively constructed in contrast to how it developed in the early decades of the 20th century. The universal–liberal spirit of enlightenment present in early-20th-century Hindutva offered a unique value system to the project of Hindu identity formation during the phase of the nationalist struggle, and it substantially smashed any attempt to defend an exclusive Hindu identity as a separate nation. However, the problem is that leading intellectuals in contemporary India hardly acknowledge the fact that Hindutva is neither a political doctrine nor a religious dogma and that India would never be a Hindu Pakistan, because Hindutva is not the substitute of Islamic radicalism and could never become such. Senior Congress leader and author Shashi Tharoor pointed out in an interview that the Hindutva movement is the mirror image of the Muslim communalism of 1947 and that it would convert India into a mono-religious state. Even though he made such flimsy statements in the context of criticizing the BJP and making Hindutva out to be precisely the Modi model of political maneuvering, Tharoor and his friends turned a blind eye to the fact that by harping on one single narrative of Hindutva for long, they gave power and legitimacy to a politically manufactured idea over its authentic alternatives. The BJP model of Hindutva might have established its dominance within a short period of time, but is it possible to hijack the democratic tradition of Hinduism from the Hindus and force them to believe in a dictatorial system so fast? The analogy that the Modi model of Hindutva would convert India into a Hindu Pakistan lacks the very simple understanding that Hinduism is not a monotheistic religion like Islam established by a specific founder. It is a tradition, often referred to as Sanatana Dharma, that originates in eternity and encompasses a range of philosophies, practices, beliefs, concepts and sectarian ideologies. Even if a particular political force attempts to bring out the principles of fundamentalism out of Hinduism, it would become a half-hearted, meaningless effort, since Hinduism does not and cannot produce anything similar to fundamentalism. Religious orthodoxy and Hinduism are contradictory in nature, even though caste oppression and idealization of the Brahmins has often put Hinduism in evil light throughout history. When Chandranath Basu first used the term 'Hindutva', he used it in the context of writing an authentic history of the Hindus and used Hindutva as the quality of being Hindu. In a real terminological sense, the distinction between Hindu and Hindutva is ludicrous, and those who project Savarkar's pamphlet on Hindutva as the central text on the subject simply play with the facts. There are millions of Hindus who have not heard of the term or the pamphlet yet. Pertinently, the term Hindutva has no business with Savarkar or his text, because Hindus in general define their Hindu-ness or Hindutva mainly on the basis of their own experiences and preferences, and no one can force them to follow a single text, a particular sect or even a few basic rituals.

The proposition that Hinduism is a better choice in opposition to Hindutva only creates fallacies and ratifies the claim of Hindutva being a subject of political construction. Undoubtedly, one political cult of Hindutva has been at work within the democratic fabric of the country, but what is interesting to note is that the Congress and other leftist groups contributed hugely in hyping up this political project based on the idea that Hinduism and Hindutva are different and mutually opposing to each other. I use the term Hindutva in this book in two different ways—in its original incarnation and also in its constructed political avatar—to identify how the latter employed its energy in identity politics and power plays and ultimately enjoyed a position of dominance over the other experiences and expressions of Hindutva. To be precise, the Hindutva of a Bengali is not the same as that of a Tamilian or Punjabi, and a so-called secular–non-practising Hindu could observe his/her Hindutva separately from the rest of the community. For a certain period of time, it seemed like a dream to manipulate or attract a great section of the Hindus for the electoral success of a political party or to make them aware of some common political interests in future India. The electoral success of the National Democratic Alliance (NDA), in which the BJP came up as the single largest party in the 1998 elections, indeed marked a new journey for political Hindutva and anti-Congressism in the country, and in the 2014 elections, the BJP for the first time meticulously sewed up a unique coalition accommodating a range of historically marginalized groups. It was high time the BJP started mainstreaming the high tides of political Hindutva in Indian politics. The construction of a Ram temple in Ayodhya, the repealing of Article 370 and the assurance to introduce the Uniform Civil Code all signalled BJP's Hindutva agenda with promises of economic rejuvenation. The Babri Masjid demolition affair and the Ram temple agitation provided the BJP the necessary impetus to use Hindutva as a powerful tool for mobilizing support in favour of the party. Hindutva was exclusively construed in contrast to how it evolved in the nationalist context immediately after India's independence. The new model of political Hindutva looked far more strategic and aggressive than its previous incarnations and tactically aimed at spreading its appeal among the low-caste poor. It is all about power, not about renunciation, spirituality, religiosity or self-realization. It has nothing to do with art and literature, creativity or philosophy. Because it deals only with unconditional power, this new model of Hindutva chooses to follow a checks-and-balances policy in all of its supporting constituencies. The sadhus are not an exception here. While some have been tempted to see the sadhus as an extravagant force in the new model of 21st-century Hindutva, I argue that doing so would undermine the importance of the missing link between Hindutva in its actual pedagogical incarnations and Hindutva in its most recent political avatar.

The sadhus consistently played a pivotal part in the Hindutva discourse. They created a salient shared identity of Hindu-ness through imageries, rituals, practices, speeches and others. They are the ones who justified the socio-religious implications of political Hindu-ness to a greater audience. Their presence in the Hindu nationalist–Hindutva discourse in the colonial and post-colonial time helped political Hindutva settle its score with its critics in later years. The idea that Hinduism is good and Hindutva is bad seems to be scrawny and fragile because of the continuous support Hindutva proponents have received from saffron-clad sadhus over the years. Despite being a minority, the sadhus have developed the image of true and trustworthy protectors/ guardians of the Hindu religion and society, the reason why Hindutva proponents have always drawn on them to justify a distinct socio-political priority, even though it runs counter to what informed the principles of asceticism or 'sadhudom'. It is problematic to decode the complex relationship between 'sadhudom' and Hindutva in its non-political incarnation, because political power comes with violence, forceful persuasion and hatred, while asceticism rejects each of these obnoxious attributes of power politics. This is not to deny that the sadhus also hold a substantive amount of 'power' in Hindu society. They personify the spiritual authority and the power of wisdom, and their status as 'gurus' helps them to lead others on the path of righteousness. The power of sadhus exists not in their exercise of control but in their ability to influence. Unlike political leaders, they do not subject others to their control or limit others' freedom but convince them in some ways that it is to their 'advantage to perform (or withhold) the act in question' (Walter 1964, 351). Simultaneously, the sadhus themselves experience an amount of power in their own lives, because in general practice they choose to follow asceticism according to their own will and reject material possessions—the so-called symbol of the highly masculine urban societies.

Following this logic, the interesting question remains: did political Hindutva fully absorb the sadhus, or did the latter manage to enjoy their 'power' and authority even when they participate in the

Hindutva project voluntarily? The question did not arise until the VHP (Vishva Hindu Parishad) played a critical role in cementing the bond between the sadhus and the political bosses championing an exclusive Hindu identity. The sadhus' presence in the Kumbh Mela congregation as a united block or the *akhara* type of their organizational entity helped them wield a kind of distinctive command over the political developments in the country, such that for the first time the sadhus acquired the necessary agency to be an exclusive political force after independence. The objective was to recover and protect the 'Hindu' past from the potential threats gaining strength under a secular regime. As long as the Congress was in power, the political activism of the sadhus remained restricted. With the decline of the Congress, and especially with the rise of the BJP, sadhudom evolved as a distinctive political category breaking the hitherto influential citadel of secularism into pieces. With the Babri Masjid affair in 1992, one circle of the story ended. We have reasons to see it as the success of 'dissent' in democracy, because the emergence of a handful of latent sadhus challenged the existing structure of secularism in the country and also generated series of controversies on the nature of the future state in India. Keeping aside the stories of mob violence and destruction during the Babri Masjid affair, the involvement of the sadhus in the rise of the BJP became evident; however, their mutual differences and the lack of enthusiasm on the part of the BJP on the issue of constructing the Ram temple crafted a kind of tense relationship between the sadhus and the BJP afterwards. The irony was that the small but vocal group of socially engaged sadhus who lent their support to the Ram Janmabhoomi movement did not appear all of a sudden; rather, they had been involved in the claims of Ram Janmabhoomi since the pre-independence time. Sadhus from the Nirmohi Akhara claimed ownership of the Babri Masjid site early in 1853, and the administration even permitted the Hindus to access the site for prayer. Following a number of lawsuits, the matter received sufficient public attention, causing severe protests since independence, and the Rajiv Gandhi government tried to mollify the protesters demanding concessions on the Ayodhya dispute. The unlocking of the gates to the mosque in Ayodhya through a judicial order and the permission to do *shilanyas* at the disputed site provided the VHP–RSS (Rashtriya Swayamsevak

Sangh) duo the most awaited opportunity to demand a Ram temple in Ayodhya, while the Congress government viewed the reopening of the gates as part of its political strategy to get a hold over Hindu votes, especially after the revocation of the Shah Banu verdict. The latter did not happen, because the RSS–VHP–BJP trio launched a serious campaign to make Hindus believe in their efforts to induce the government to concede to their demands; the Congress, on the other hand, lost a great segment of its Muslim support base in Uttar Pradesh, leading to a point of no recovery in the near future. It was in the late 1980s that the sadhus literary stepped into the Ram Janmabhoomi movement in an organized way, and both the VHP-affiliated sadhus and others took over the *shilanyas* ceremony in Ayodhya with passion and chivalry. This marked the beginning of a new journey for Hindutva. Despite claiming to maintain a safe distance from power politics, these sadhus stood strong with the narratives of the VHP–RSS–BJP; however, they got disillusioned at a later stage when Indian politics became more polarized than before. The moral universe of these sadhus crumbled with the coming of the liberal economic transformations followed by the rise of a communalist spiritual culture in the country. They struggled to survive the waves of socio-economic changes leading to the erosion of traditional community allegiances, and the traditional *akhara*-oriented 'outdated' sadhus no longer remained useful for the new urban classes who looked for solace and comfort only in spirituality in a fast-moving world. India was changing, as was the popular discourse on religion, spirituality and politics.

II

In common perception, sadhus in India have been described as religious ascetics or holy persons. They may live jointly in a monastery or may wander from one place to another. In this discussion, the word 'sadhus' is used mainly to signify the institution-based ascetics from a particular religious order, because the fundamental narrative of Hindutva mainly entertained these sadhus either as a subject category or as active participants in the discourse. Examining the roots of the word asceticism[7] makes it clear why modern ascetics in India connect well with systematic training exercises, including physical and spiritual training programmes, to realize the highest purpose of life. It is a journey of self-realization through self-regulatory practices, like renunciation and abstinence. 'Asceticism...may be defined as a voluntary, sustained, and at least partially systematic program of self-discipline and self-denial in which immediate, sensual, or profane gratifications are renounced in order to attain a higher spiritual state or a more thorough absorption in the sacred' (Kaelber 1987, 441). Adding to this explanation, Kaelber identified five categories of asceticism in relation to ascetics' interactions with the existing culture. Out of these, two are important for an understanding of asceticism that does justice to this discussion: (a) asceticism and culture in paradox; and (b) asceticism as a transformer of culture. In the first category, the spiritual seeker or the ascetic is in conflict with the existing norms. He is not a typical nonconformist but an individual actor who looks for his own autonomy within the mundane world but questions the prevailing practices. In the case of the second category, the ascetic enthusiastically engages with worldly affairs with an intention to transform the practices towards a desired direction. In the political discourse of Hindutva in India, one can trace these two types of ascetics or sadhus who operated within the personal and social domains 'by consciously developing an alternative symbolic universe'.[8] In this alternative universe, the ascetic looks for a 'more true and real, reconstructed, ascetic understanding of power outside the dominant social structure' (Valantasis 1995, 796, 807). The realization of power or authority in the alternative symbolic universe of an ascetic is always contested.

> Two different societies, two different worlds compete for the definition, articulation and modulation of power. This contestation reveals the duality of power in asceticism, a duality that revolves around the constellation of old world and new, old person and new, old society and new, and the various ways in which different systems of power operate in each of these dual environments. (Valantasis 1995, 810)

Did the politics of Hindutva in India ensure an 'alternative universe' to the sadhus oscillating between two identities and two subjectivities? The Hindutva movement as a creative space for exerting power enabled the sadhus to orient themselves towards a unique collective through integrating different ascetic traditions and sectarian orders.

It in fact opened up the context through which the sadhus might have found meaning in the alternative symbolic universe and constructed an alternative reality of their own. The problem is, Hindutva as a theoretical proposition did not hold a fixed meaning for all. There were sadhus who performed within their alternative universe of politics while staying at the margins of the Hindutva movement initiated by the Sangh Parivar. They seemed reluctant to work for its objectives but at the same time continued to make references to their reluctance and denial only to legitimize their own consciousness of the subject. They rejected the dominant version of Hindutva and criticized different nuances of the Hindu nationalist movement but stayed close to the discourse. This is why major discussions on sadhus' involvement with politics begin with the sophistry of the Hindu nationalist ideology and end with the Hindutva movement.

In the spirit of framing one cognitive category of Hindutva in India, perceptions portray sadhus as having their own political authority as independent individuals and remaining dormant within the Hindu nationalist movement. Standing on the porous boundary of the two adverse-seeming worlds of politics and asceticism, sadhus often lost the agency of being accepted as an autonomous force that could help a political party grow or even shape their own brand of politics. What explains this position, the dominance of a majoriterianism form of nationalism; especially in this case, Hindu nationalism turned Hindutva, creating a transcendental mythical essence of unity among the political and religious leaders mostly with the intension of organizing a monolithic configuration of leadership against the religious 'other'. Along with this understanding, the proponents of Hindutva, especially those who believed V. D. Savarkar to be sole authority on the subject, fashioned an illusion that these 'divine men' would always be in support of the programmes adopted by the official mouthpiece of Hindutva, that is, the BJP and its allied organizations, while the parochial differences between the sadhus themselves would never be a real impediment for the success of the so-called homogeneous/monolithic Hindutva movement. In reality, the sadhus who had worked within the bigger framework of Hindu nationalism never conformed to the popular patterns of Hindu politics, rather preferred to opt for transient alignment with the network. This network operated mostly through the use of religious symbols in electoral politics, not explicitly for making the Hindu vote a profitable category of political mobilization. With the coming of the VHP, the politicization of the ascetic space started with an explicit objective to make Hindutva some kind of a divine project.

Hindutva in post-independence India had always been a contested domain that fought with the waves of secularism and leftist liberalism with an aim to settle on its ideological boundaries. Far from being fixed as a definite ideological category in the nationalist literature, the project of Hindutva always clashed with the embodied politics of community building in the larger society. Despite lacking a self-critical understanding of what the Hindu-ness of a Hindu entails, the Hindutva proponents sought legitimacy from competing ideas by maintaining a glorified supremacy over them. The conflicting strands of thoughts encompassing the problematic underpinnings of Hindutva have been swaddled into the web of accounts enunciating the fallacy of reproducing the present as a direct consequence of the past. Asceticism, or to be precise 'sadhuism',[9] portrayed as the central aspect of Hinduism, received critical appraisal in the colonial documents that criticized ascetic renunciation[10] as being akin to social mendicancy, indolence and political inactivity. Renunciation makes for an antinomian way of life in which the ascetics leave behind every worldly concern. The early colonial accounts[11] suspected Hindu ascetics to be camouflaging scoundrels engaged in plundering, looting or making provocative actions against the East India Company government. The historical importance of ascetics as nationalist warriors or asceticism as symbolizing masculinity and power became evident only when systematic studies were done on the subject by nationalist writers and thinkers in subsequent years. Bankim Chandra Chattopadhyay, Swami Vivekananda, Aurobindo Ghosh, Bal Gangadhar Tilak, and M. K. Gandhi—all participated in building up the ascetic–nationalist understanding mostly within a shared notion of indigenous history and presented asceticism as an ideology of greater sociopolitical implications.[12] Chattopadhyay's ascetic nationalism drew its inspiration from the context of the crisis of masculinity which emerged from the British critique of the effeminate Bengalis (used simultaneously with effeminate Indians/Hindus) employed to describe the upper-caste, upper-class Hindu men. Challenging this notion of effeminacy, Chattopadhyay put religion, or the spirit of a resurgent Hinduism, at the centre of ascetic nationalism. The configuration of an ascetic warrior belonging to indigenous Hindu traditions was in tune with the idea of Hindu masculinity—the fundamental prerequisite for the construction of a Hindu nation. Chattopadhyay's upholding of the ascetic–nationalist warrior as an ideal example of nationalist articulations proved worthy of political implications, and a bunch of thinkers pursued the path of masculinized spirituality as the model of nationalist regeneration. A unique blend of karma yoga and selfless service or *seva*[13] defined the nuances of ascetic nationalism since the late 19th century.[14] Concurrently, this opened up the possibilities of virtue politics, or politics as the subject of ethical concern. This is the particular terrain where spirituality and action met and transformed the individual quest for *moksha* into the collective desire for freedom. Asceticism generated raw debates on modernity's claim to produce political subjects as self-governing individuals. Nationalist writers and thinkers in fact galvanized the self-liberating attributes of renunciation into self-governing accolades of modernity, thereby relocating the entire discourse of asceticism to within the sociopolitical realities of the colonial society.

In the Hindutva project of the 20th century, these nationalist perceptions of asceticism received a new lease of life to authenticate the visions of Hindu nationalism as similar to Indian nationalism. The stereotypes of an outwardly indolent holy man as the symbol of nationalist wisdom invented the importance of spiritualism and renunciation—something that of a constant source of inspiration for the Indian society—a potential marker of protest and resistance to imperial ideology. The imperialist affirmation of imposing subjecthood on the Indians stood in sharp contrast to the spirit of asceticism which explored the idea of the ascetic as a social transformer, a champion who speaks for society as a whole. Thus, ascetics, when speaking for the society or talking of nationalist regeneration, produced spontaneous avenues for Hindu identity formation. Hindu identity, or to be precise the identity of upper-caste Hindu males, which always faced the colonial criticisms of effeminacy or impotency, found in these newly explored ascetic principles a sense of liberty, a unique way of self-recovery—a set of self-motivating principles for defining their true Hindu self. I want to call this principle the highest manifestation of cultural Hindutva, which infused the spirit of renunciation and celibacy into the sociopolitical fabric to rejuvenate the Hindus with a sense of pride and responsibility.

As long as these self-motivating principles of Hindu-ness operated as means of self-transformation or self-articulation, the frozen binaries of 'inner' and 'other' did not make any difference to their overall approaches to society. The dichotomy of manly Britishers and effeminate Indians long influenced the self-discovery of the nationalist Hindu elites who found in the new ascetic–nationalist principles an opportunity to challenge the existing stereotypes. Therefore, the ascetic principles of self-restraint, sexual abstinence, selfless service, physical strength and dissemination of traditional knowledge—all contributed to the nation building process, as well as to Hindu identity formation since the late 19th century. Constructed cosily over a series of approaches to stimulate selected cultural traits from the past, they negotiated with the upper-caste Hindus' passion for reviving Sanatana Dharma,[15] drawing on the text of the Bhagavad Gita in nationalist discourses and creating a spiritual–moral understanding of politics. As long as the project of Hindu identity formation moved within the ascetic–nationalist parameters of self-articulation and self-rejuvenation, it appeared to be a critical response to the West, if not resistance. The moment it endeavoured to focus on the Hindus as the majority community embodying the Indian identity, bearing the uninterrupted legacy of the Aryans and upholding a sacred territory, the entire narrative of Hindu identity formation suddenly shifted to a separate zone. This was the ideology of Hindu nationalism, organized and codified mainly around the 1923 publication 'Hindutva: Who is a Hindu' by V. D. Savarkar. Its primary incarnations, the Hindu Mahasabha and the RSS, crystallized the ideology into a mere political creed against the 'threatening others', that is, the Muslims in specific. Hindutva, or the very qualities of what makes one a Hindu, strictly implied the criteria of a common territory, a common language and a common racial status. Savarkar provided the theoretical understanding of political Hindutva, while K. B. Hedgewar, the founder of the RSS, transformed it into a movement.

Undoubtedly, the Savarkarian RSS legacy in general provided one monochromic pattern of Hindutva in India. The assimilating principles in Hindu nationalism, what Christophe Jaffrelot has called 'strategic syncretism',[16] prepared an egalitarian, monolithic structure where individual aspirations were hardly acknowledged. Unlike cultural Hindutva, which believed in investing much on individual ideological propositions on Hindu identity formation, the proponents of political Hindutva built a codified structure, leaving little or no scope for alternative understandings. Interestingly, asceticism had never suited the category of a codified monolithic Hindutva, because asceticism itself is self-liberating and irrepressible by existing social norms or narratives. It fitted well with the flexible framework of cultural Hindutva where different sets of sectarian believes,[17] traditional knowledge systems and moral–ethical principles essential for self-articulation involved critical engagement with the past. It was a far more complex process that developed partially as a response to the West and partially in response to the call for nation building in the late 19th century. Eventually, this 'nation' turned into a Hindu nation not because it followed any strict majoritarian principle but because of the growing involvement of Hindu revivalism and cultural nationalism.[18] These two streams of thoughts moved in parallel, shared similar religious symbols, took inspiration from common spiritual traditions and proposed similar programmes. In the case of Bipin Chandra Pal and Aurobindo Ghosh, for instance, nationalism itself became a religion—a creed that demanded completes submission.[19] Marxist critics might have charged these early nationalists with mixing religion with politics, especially for the latter's efforts to Hinduize nationalist politics at the turn of the 19th century, but one must not miss the spiritual–cultural resources present in the Hindu revivalist rhetoric for negotiating an approach for living together peacefully.[20]

It should be noted here that the Hindu–Muslim question was never an apolitical question for the early nationalists but instead was a national problem of supreme importance. Undoubtedly, it was an unfortunate mistake on the part of the early nationalists that they never presented any solution to the Hindu–Muslim fiasco. The Hindu revivalist essence of a syncretic culture, as referred to in the message of Advaita Vedanta, provided the best possible answer to the question of nationalist regeneration at that point of time, and the task of defining Hindu-ness also became a nationalist proposition in a synthetic value system. This is why revivalism and nationalism, when placed together on a cultural–spiritual domain, made way for the development of cultural Hindutva as an ideological category flexible to individual perceptions and opinions. This is the domain where ascetic–nationalist practices flourished and set the patterns for how ascetics or sadhus would be involved in politics. Indeed, the waves of Savarkarian Hindutva slowly took over the space of cultural Hindutva under tense political circumstances; the former hardly caused any replacement as such. It is important to acknowledge that shades and patterns of alternative Hindutva were present in the dominant discourse of political Hindutva, which in reality appeared to be a draconian affair not only for its opponents but also for those who had registered their individual dissent from within. The text and subtext of the so-called political Hindutva also changed over time depending on the views of Savarkar, M. S. Golwalkar, S. P. Mookerjee, Deendayal Upadhyaya and others. Caging this ideology in one static monolithic structure simply does not do justice to its long-developed history in the pre- and post-independence time. Asceticism, when explored as part of cultural Hindutva, displayed a strong essence of self-discipline and self-restraint central to the task of nation building in colonial India. The labyrinthine interplay of culture and religion present in cultural Hindutva kept the ball rolling further in political Hindutva, which basically educed two mutually corresponding praxis of culture/religion and nation/state.[21]

Despite facing the fundamental dilemma of whether to portray Hinduism as a religion or as a culture, or simply as both, Hindutva forces gradually shifted all their attention to culture, because culture turned out to be a broader category than religion, like a nation in relation to its states. Hindutva's greater emphasis on culture boosted the possibilities of making the religious and caste-wise 'others' an indivisible part of the Hindu society, while its hankering for a nationhood set in opposition to the notion of statehood laid down the principles of a Hindu Rashtra where each and every religion and caste would submit to the broad category of a Hindu culture, not to the Hindu religion. It was Savarkar who located Hinduism mostly in the cultural realm and restricted Hindu nationality to Indian religions only. M. S. Golwalkar, the first *sarsanghchalak* of the RSS, however provided two options before the foreign races. They

> must either adopt the Hindu culture and language, must learn to respect and hold in reverence Hindu religion, must entertain no ideas but those of glorification of the Hindu race and culture—or may stay in the country, wholly subordinated to the Hindu nation, claiming nothing.... (Golwalkar 1939, 47–48)

Despite these subtle differences in approach, both of them strongly advocated for the cause of an encompassing Hindu culture that would evolve common to each and every formulation of the Hindutva ideology in India. In the whole trajectory of the Hindutva movement, the Hindu religious identity remained dormant to the Hindu cultural identity—a Hindu way of life that structured the fabric of social behaviour, as well as the patterns of political behaviour, though to a lesser extent.

Importantly, Hindutva's political involvement could never arrive at a definite conclusion on how a Hindu Rashtra should look like in response to a secular state or in what ways Hindu interests could best be protected from the 'threatening others', especially from the Muslims and the Christians. Several strategies and symbols were invented to defend the 'dying Hindus'[22] in an era of competitive demography when the numerical strength of the Muslims appeared to be a danger for the Hindus under representative politics. Partly substantiated by the British policy of separate electorates and mostly by their own apprehensions of a possible Islamic domination in the near future, the Hindutva forces emerged as far more reactionary and aggressive in the 1930s. This made the self-articulating dimensions of cultural Hindutva indisposed to have a check on the growing sense of enmity against the 'religious others' inside the political circle. Political Hindutva, being reactionary and suspicious in nature, thus keyed in on a spurious form of Hindu unity, drawing others into its fold. Obscured by the interplay of the self and the other, the 'we' in Golwalkar's Hindutva thus identified a 'they' as the oppositional 'other', and this particular praxis of opposition backed political Hindutva to take a hold over the spirits of individualism, alternative voices and multiple Hinduisms reciprocated through greater or lesser degrees of dissent.

III

In my efforts to uncover the quirky relationship shared by the sadhus with Hindutva, I station them primarily in the domain of cultural Hindutva, but as those eventually endorsed by political Hindutva after independence. Despite developing a thorough understanding of the patterns of their involvement with politics, this book explores the zest of 'individualism' reflected by the sadhus in both the organized and unorganized domains of politics. Central to my argument evolves a crucial understanding of what political involvement means for the sadhus who had operated from the associational space of ascetic Hinduism or from an exclusive political party of their own. The entire morphology of Hindu politics drew on new meanings and expressions by the sadhus, while the sadhus themselves reflected patterns of freedom and autonomy within the political constructs of Hindutva. The paradoxical position shared by the sadhus in regard to Hindu identity formation and Hindu consolidation portrays the nuances and modalities of cultural Hindutva, which in turn functioned as a site for alternative knowledge production, crucial to the construction of a non-confrontational pan-Hindu identity. In this book, a few case studies are projected to reveal the dialectics of Hindutva as a flexible category that in turn confronted with the meta-narratives of a Hindu Rashtra offered by the RSS, Bharatiya Jana Sangh, VHP and others. Interestingly, almost all the sadhus under discussion have operated from the ideological structure of cultural Hindutva and helped to propagate the ideology for social recognition and social legitimacy but continued to invest much on the spirit of ascetic autonomy. This particular aspect of autonomy of the sadhus clashed vehemently with the VHP—a much younger offshoot of political Hindutva—even though the VHP claimed its sole authority over the Hindu sadhus devoted to the cause of building a Hindu nation in India. Apart from analysing the 'troubled' relationship between the sadhus and the VHP in general, this book puts forward the issue of conflicts encountered by the VHP in regional settings. The regional functioning of the VHP has never been a subject of scholarly scrutiny, while its tribal projects and environmental projects in different states often outline the fundamental conflicts of interest present in the Hindutva movement.

Opening up these spaces permits us to explore the frameworks of Hindutva in the non-political traditions, embedded in cultural and social practices. Moving away from the approaches so far discussed, through the prism of communalism or militancy, the ascetic's discourse of Hindutva has raised important questions about the political functions of religion in contemporary India. The notion that within politics 'the effect of religion can be detected in every facet'[23] relates to a set of uncomfortable points that clarify the fact that religion or religious practices do not essentially contradict secularism; rather, in traditional societies, like India, religion plays its role as the source of insightful spiritual experiences.[24] Hindutva, when studied as part of a political statecraft or as a primary site of high politics, excludes sombre engagement with the merits of religious practices as a source of spiritual strength but produces frameworks explicit to a strategy of knowledge production solely on the trajectory of the 'insider–outsider' status towards the understudying of the racial–cultural parameters of being a Hindu. In doing so, the dominant form of Hindutva excludes or manipulates the spiritual strength of religion but keeps coming back through multiple actors to a relevant context in different layers of politics. The sadhus or ascetics displayed their strength of spirituality through bodily discipline, celibacy and scholasticism to construct one austere, courageous and self-sacrificing narrative of the Hindu race that could effectively use its moral vigour, virility and righteousness for nationalist regeneration in India. The word 'Hindu' here denotes not a member of a particular religion or community but is a universal floating concept used to address all Indians (Sen 2000). Religion minus spirituality would have provided further implications for Hindutva as a political project, but it failed to impress the early nationalists and the ascetics who had challenged the colonial stereotypes of Indian effeminacy and moral predicaments. The spiritual approach to strength and masculinity motivated almost all sadhus when they were active in the public domain. A Vedantin like Swami Vivekananda, a Shaiva yogi like Swami Pranavananda or a Dasnami monk like Swami Karpatri—all picked up the notion of ascetic masculinity to create an alternative discourse of Hindutva dedicated to the task of nation building in one way or another. In this book, the taxonomy of this 'alternative discourse' is explored from different perspectives, while the RSS version of Hindutva, by virtue of its being strictly defined and sectioned by thoughtful endeavours, claims a kind of authority over the ascetic–spiritual formulations of Hindutva. Despite bearing a similar antipathy to the Western stereotype of effeminate Hindus, the RSS shaped masculinity as an ardently militant category placed against the potential enemies of the nation. Building on this model of enmity against the 'others', the RSS-led Hindu militancy made a critical departure from the spiritual–ascetic–nationalist premise of Hindutva. This latter premise of Hindutva fell short of meeting the imaginations of the people, while RSS's political–militant Hindutva managed to stay in popular imaginations in colonial and post-colonial times.[25]

Divided into four chapters, this book examines the patterns, networks and modalities that allowed the sadhus entry into the world of politics. Some of these sadhus deployed the arts of *seva* and *sangathan* as primary sites for political mobilization, and some others stepped into the world of electoral politics after contriving a unique mosaic of Hindu 'traditionalism' (Sanatana Dharma), leading to some conflicts and tensions in the modern democratic structure, whereas the rest developed a critique of the Hindutva movement while staying within the institutional premises of Hindu nationalism. This book pays special attention to sadhus who worked beyond the organizational purview of Hindu nationalism and the BJP but often engaged, knowingly or unknowingly, in promoting the cause of the Hindutva movement on transnational platforms. Mostly gathering momentum among the urban–professional classes and the Hindu diaspora, these spiritual leaders espoused a unique techno-religious world of Hindutva and appropriated a new set of vocabulary for the creation of a Hindu nation. The first chapter explores the potentials of *seva* as a normative domain for reflecting greater political interests through numerous avenues and projects. Keeping its focus mainly on Swami Pranavananda and the Bharat Sevashram Sangha as study cases, this chapter provides original insights into the nuances of Hindu identity formation and Hindu consolidation through *seva* networks in India and abroad. It offers an analysis of how the spiritual–*seva* organizations addressed and encountered issues of politics different from the familiar patterns.

The second chapter brings into focus the problems of locating the world of 'traditionalism' in the modern democratic structure and its subsequent clash with the dominant right-wing version of Hindutva in India. In this chapter, a thorough discussion is offered on the North Indian yogi-turned-politician Swami Karpatri Maharaj and his party Ram Rajya Parishad as a classic example to understand the trends of orthodoxy and its conflict with modern democratic politics. Starting his journey primarily as an ally of the Bharatiya Jana Sangh, Swami Karpatri gradually voiced his dissent over the RSS brand of Hindutva and espoused the cause of Ram Rajya for the revival of Sanatana Dharma and Brahmanical supremacy. The third chapter ventures into the fragments of interests emerging strong within the VHP through questioning its so-called authority over the sadhus with an institutional affiliation. This chapter brings out the inner tensions of the VHP, travels through the muddled relationship the VHP shared with the sadhus and puts up the conflicts of interests present in the organization's visions of a Hindu Rashtra in India.

Adding to the understanding of what makes a sadhu important on national and transnational platforms, the last chapter outlines the rise of universal gurus who have promoted Hindutva in a transnational setting, especially among the Hindu diaspora abroad. This chapter analyses the shifting status of Hindutva as a movement in an age of information and technological boom and reveals the many ways the new-age gurus negotiated with the changing face of politics in a neoliberal India. The sustained importance of Hindutva in neoliberal India presented the paradox of transnational networks promoting the hypernationalist ideology. Shaped largely by the new-age gurus as partners of the technological boom in urban cities, this new format of Hindutva displayed irreducible character through aiding the new media and multiple commercial interests. Mostly attracting the tech-savvy Hindu diaspora in India and abroad, these sadhus have developed new idioms for one techno-religious Hindutva. Here the commercial, cultural and political discourses of Hindutva meet on a transnational platform, combined with the method of direct communication with their recipients. Divided into two operational terrains, one in India and the other abroad, this new formulation of transnational Hindutva has ensured an opportunity for the new-age gurus to get involved with the clusters of high politics in an upright manner. In sharp contrast with their earlier positions of taking part in politics either as individual spiritual influencers or as interactive agents of Hindutva nationalism, now these sadhus have turned into strategic partners for political mobilization. Despite having the advantage of entering inside the drawing rooms of the new urban–professional classes, through electronic media channels or microblogging sites, these gurus have reached the other sections of the population through the innovative channels of Ayurveda, yoga and lifestyle activities.

They have served to build a transnational network of Hindus with the spread of the smartphone culture, playing up the notion of *guru-bhakti* with market-specific interests. These sadhus might not have delved into any engagement with the votaries of political Hindutva or operated independently from an autonomous domain, but they have infused the most influential vision of Hindutva into the body politic of the nation. Backed by media platforms, commercial partners, corporate partners and Hindu philanthropic organizations, the new-age gurus have been offering a highly mediated space of Hindu politics developed over the last few decades. They have developed the notions of a class friendly Hindutva which synchronously served on feeding the interests of the nation by providing them life-style tips, health remedies, self-comforting spiritual messages through numerous social-service programmes. The appeal of this new service approach, or the commoditization of spirituality, is different from that of the social service approaches that the VHP and the RSS used as an electoral tactic to attract Dalits and *adivasis*. Mostly targeting the urban professional classes, this new brand of Hindutva promoted the interests of the pro-market middle classes but also sustained its mass appeal to a large extent. The gurus taking part in this problematic space used vocabularies and expressions familiar with the neoliberal model that stressed much on the essentials of individualism. They inculcated correct values and moral values of 'good Hindus'—a normative vision of society where the 'utility-maximising' individuals, to use Shankar Gopalakrishnan's phrase, would form the Hindu Rashtra.[26] In this project, the social service approaches conceptualized mainly for the lower-caste Hindus as target recipients have been relegated to a point of civilizing discourse where the elites take part in the social upliftment agenda or even the state approves the reservation policies as charity, not as social justice.[27]

'Sadhuism', or Hindu asceticism, occupied multiple imaginations throughout history. 'Sadhuism' as a social, religious or political phenomenon facilitated multiple interpretations of a historical trajectory that reinvented nationalism, contested colonialism and provided the essential rationale to induce the ideal of individual self-aggrandizement within the systematically outlined boundary of a distinct political culture. With the rise of a Hindu militant culture since the 1980s, the debate around sadhus and Hindu nationalism became highly symbolic. The common perception that the BJP has mobilized sadhus and their followers for electoral gains has been dismissed not on flimsy grounds but on its failure to explain why the BJP and its predecessor, the Bharatiya Jana Sangh, did not systematically plunge into the world of sadhus for electoral gains. The BJP, for instance, has organized rallies, processions and religious pilgrimages in the presence of saffron-clad sadhus on selected occasions to show Hindutva's ideological solidarity with Hinduism. The sadhus often were included in a quixotic show where everything was transformed into a spectacle of politics displaying the 'greatness of Hindu culture'.[28] These 'spectacles of politics' bring down religion and religious actors to a certain level of equality, convenient for having a reciprocal dialogue—but the problem is, religious actors or sadhus always have a hold over this dialogical paradigm by virtue of their being entrusted with a sense of superiority on each and every thought and action entrenched in worldly affairs. This is why 'religion becomes a tool rather than on an equal level with politics', and sadhus 'use their powers to shape politics'.[29]

The idea that religion would be knocked off from politics as secularism turned up died a premature death—at least in India—when the majoritarian version of nationalism, or Hindu nationalism in India's case, seriously faced the threat from the 'religious others' and the 'caste/class others' when these 'enemies' claimed their rightful representation not only in policymaking processes but also in history—in that past that has so far been incarcerated in the aphorism of one homogeneous-golden age structure. Liah Greenfeld called it the majoritarian anxiety of the traditional nationalist elites against a 'manly', 'intolerant other' (the Hindu elites against the Muslims and the lower castes in the case of Hindu nationalism)—and this is the anxiety that feeds on the ideology of Hindutva as an elite-driven political project.[30] The psychoanalytic diagnosis of Hindutva thus makes it an overtly volatile affair where sadhus participate either as agents or as freelance aficionados who could be fundamentalists, liberals or simply innocent observers. They can help in generating the sense of anxiety shared by the majority using their special ability to infuse desired meaning into myths, anecdotes or events from history, but only if they wish to do so. This autonomous space of sadhu activism is identified and explored in this book, with careful attention to the fact that the sadhus did not form any compatible group or segment but rather showed their commitment to a preternatural spiritual authority that sanctioned them the liberty and freedom to overpower politics or to come to an adjustment with it.

By the late 1980s, the public emergence of a bunch of sadhus created a buzz among the English-speaking intellectuals, including a section of the media. Sadhus asking for votes and speaking at political rallies caused enough discomfort among these people, who found the deployment of sadhus in mainstream politics highly disturbing and alarming for the secular fabric of the country. Debates surrounding the involvement of sadhus in Hindutva politics often overlook the particular point that there exist different patterns and methods of their involvement in political decision-making processes which solely depend on how particular individuals relate to the discourse of Hindutva. What I suggest here is that Hindutva does not rely upon one singular source or interpretation; instead, it may have different formulations based on one's individual perception. Whereas the existing literature on the subject provides sufficient attention to one dominant version of political Hindutva espoused by a group of political and pseudo-political organizations, sadhus often explored the fallacy of having one constructed territory of Hindutva which knowingly or unknowingly contested the alternatives. The 'unpredictable' sadhus generated immense tensions in the ideological circles, and both political and non-political strategies were employed to address the sadhus in an amicable manner. The flag-bearers of Hindutva in India registered some amount of success in muzzling the dissidents; however, on most occasions, they opted for adjustment with the sadhus. The ever-expanding horizon of religion in Indian politics led to the phenomenon of sadhus participating in politics developing different meanings but ended up joining the trajectory of a nationalist past that claimed Hindutva to be synchronized as *Bharatiyatva* and identified sadhus as the most trustworthy agents of Hindutva in modern Indian history. This book unveils these questions and reveals the conflicting stands taken by the sadhus while making sense of the shifting and competing patterns of Hindutva in contemporary India. Through examining individual sadhus and their activities as study cases, this book takes into account the ephemeral relationships shared by sadhus from specific operational zones with the Hindutva movement. This book also delves into the variable status of Hindutva as a fluid category with contradictory thoughts and identities that trotted out the aspects of religion, spirituality and politics in India.

NOTES

1. Mark Juergensmeyer, *Terror in the Mind of God: The Global Rise of Religious Violence* (Berkley: University of California Press, 2003); Partha Chatterjee, *Nationalist Thought and the Colonial World* (Delhi: Oxford University Press, 1986).
2. Jürgen Habermas, 'Secularism's Crisis of Faith: Notes on a Post-Secular Society', *New Perspectives Quarterly* 25, no. 4 (2008): 17–29.
3. Charles Taylor, *A Secular Age* (Cambridge: Harvard University Press, 2017).
4. According to the *Oxford English Dictionary,* Hindutva is a state or quality of being Hindu; (Hindu-ness)—the ideology of establishing the hegemony of Hindus and the Hindu way of life. *Encyclopaedia of Hinduism* refers to Hindutva as the culture of the Hindu race where Hindu dharma, not Hinduism, has been valorized and practised by Hindus, as well as Sikhs and Buddhists. The term 'Hindutva' first appeared in the novel *Anandamath* by Bankim Chandra Chattopadhyay and came into use through the Bengali intellectual Chandranath Basu in the 1890s. Hindu-ness has evolved into the most relatable form of Hindu nationalism in India. Despite having multiple meanings and connotations, the term received popular attention mostly through the writings of V. D. Savarkar in 1923. Hindu nationalism, for instance, has been denoted as the manifestation of the

spiritual and cultural traditions of the Indian subcontinent. Eventually developing as a movement, the cause of Hindutva has been propagated by the Hindu nationalist volunteer organizations Rastriya Swayamsevak Sangh (RSS), Vishva Hindu Parishad (VHP), Bharatiya Jana Sangh, Bharatiya Janata Party (BJP) and other auxiliary organizations.

5. V. D. Savarkar, *Hindutva: Who is a Hindu*? (Bombay: Pandit Bakhle Publications Division, 1923) (1999 edition).
6. 'The term *sadhu* is commonly translated as "holy man" or "ascetic." *Sadhu* denotes a male; a holy woman would be a *sadhvij* and so in some ways I find the word "ascetic" preferable since it is gender-free. Yet as a historic category, the word "ascetic" misleads even as it communicates. Asceticism conjures up images of hair shirts, flagellation, and deprivations of all bodily appetites. While some *sadhus* do undergo severe austerities, this is certainly not the case for all of them. Most broadly, *sadhu* means "good man" or "virtuous man." Among its fan of Sanskrit meanings, *sadhu* denotes "straight" and "to hit the goal": a *sadhu* is someone who aims for the goal of salvation. More specifically, *sadhu* stands for someone who has been initiated into an ascetic sect to devote himself to achieving release from the cycle of death and rebirth. *Sadhus* are ideally celibate. They do not work for wages but are rather dependent on alms and donations. They do not identify with ties of blood or caste. *Sadhus*, then, are seen as fundamentally different from lay householders (*grahmthi*) caught up in the world of social enterprise (*samsar*). This difference is also dramatized in the use of the term *sadhu* for lay people who do not behave in conventionally expected ways, such as those who are selfless, or celibate at an inappropriate stage of life'.

   Narayan Kirin, *Storytellers, Saints, and Scoundrels: Folk Narrative in Hindu Religious Teaching* (Philadelphia, PA: University of Pennsylvania Press, 1989), 63–64.
7. In Western discourse, 'ascesis referred to training for athletic events. The root metaphor of ascesis is taken from sport and connects the definition of power with the subject's empowering training for success'. For details, see, O. Hardman, *The Ideals of Asceticism: An Essay in the Comparative 1924 Study of Religion* (New York: Macmilan, 1924); Walter O. Kaelber, 'Asceticism', in *The Encyclopedia of Religion*, ed. Mircea Eliade (New York: Macmillan, 1987); R. Margaret Miles, *Fullness of Life: Historical Foundations for a New 1981 Asceticism* (Philadelphia, PA: Westminster, 1981).
8. Richard Valantasis discussed in detail how the symbolic universe of the ascetics explored the implications of power. The works of Peter Berger and Thomas Lockmann are equally important to decode in what ways the 'ascetic symbolic universe legitimates the regimes of power in ascetic subjectivity and ascetic social relations'. Richard Valantasis, 'Constructions of Power in Asceticism', *Journal of the American Academy of Religion* 63, no. 4 (winter, 1995): 775–821; Peter L. Berger and Thomas Lockmann, *The Social*

Construction of Reality: A Treatise in the Sociology of Knowledge (Garden City, New York: Doubleday, 2011).

9. The puzzling category called 'asceticism' raised several controversies over its origin and development through the course of Indian history. Involving a spectrum of practices and traditions, asceticism invokes the notion of lifestyle training that requires sexual abstinence, renunciation from material possessions, dietary restrictions and an abstinent lifestyle meant for spiritual revelation. Either as a part of monastic traditions or as lone practitioners, Hindu ascetics took the path of sanyasa or renunciation. These ascetics, in colloquial parlance, are called sanyasis or sadhus. The sadhu connotes basically the practice of sadhana or a path of spiritual discipline. In Sanskrit, the term sadhu (*sadhvi* for females) refers to those with certain qualities and virtues living a life of an ascetic away from or on the edges of society. Those who want to become a sadhu must submit to a guru, and the guru decides if the former is eligible to be a sishya, and only then does the person transform into a sanyasi or sadhu. 'The academic and hagiographic literature on renunciation has often privileged the world-denying model of the Brahmanical texts for representative imaginings of this way of life'. Antoinette E. DeNapoli, 'A Mandal of Their Own: Gender and the Reimagining of Community by Hindu Renouncers in Northern India', in *Modern Hinduism in Text and Context*, ed. Lavanya Vemsani (London: Bloomsbury Academic, 2018). (Bloomsbury Collections Web, 8 May 2020, p. 170).

   For the discussion on the semantics of 'sadhuism', see, Monier Williams, *Sanskrit English Dictionary with Etymology* (Oxford: Oxford University Press, 1990), 1201; Gavin Flood, *An Introduction to Hinduism* (Cambridge: Cambridge University Press, 1996), 92; Gavin Flood, *The Blackwell Companion to Hinduism* (Chester: John Wiley & Sons, 2008), 212–13; Harvey J. Sindima, *Introduction to Religious Studies* (Lanham, MD: University Press of America, 2009).

   Brahmanical texts have adopted a conspicuous position on the eligibility of women leading a life of celibacy. According to Indologist Patrick Olivelle, 'early Sanskrit grammatical literature records several names for female ascetics, although it is unclear whether such references imply recognition of the legitimacy of female asceticism on the part of the Brahmanical elite'. Patrick Olivelle, *The Āśrama System: The History and Hermeneutics of a Religious Institution* (New York: Oxford University Press, 1993), 189.

10. 'Renunciation represents an alternative worldview and way of life to the dominant institution of house holding, ritual practice, and a mode of existence that emphasizes the importance of life- in- the- world'. DeNapoli, 'A Mandal of Their Own', 168.

11. The colonial understanding of Indian asceticism has been flooded with a plethora of writings. For the early accounts on Indian asceticism in the imperial imagination, see, John Campbell Oman, *Mystics, Ascetics and Saints*

of *India* (London: Fisher Unwin, 1905); William Henry Sleeman, *A Report on the System of Megounnaism*; James Mill, *History of British India* (Calcutta: Sreampur, 1839); Rudyard Kipling, *Plain Tales from the Hills* (Oxford: Oxford University Press, 2001). Apart from the early accounts, there are anthropological studies on ascetic orders. To name a few, William R. Pinch, *Warrior Ascetics and Indian Empires* (New Delhi: Foundation, 2006); William R. Pinch, *Peasants and Monks in British India* (Berkley, CA: University of California Press, 1996); John N. Farquhar, 'The Fighting Ascetics of India', *Bulletin of the Royal Rylands Library* 9, no. 2 (1925): 431–52.

12. The stereotypes of Bengali effeminacy against British manliness have been discussed by Mrinalini Sinha as a construction to run down the waves of protests and discontents of the subject population in the 19th century. For details, see, Mrinalini Sinha, *Colonial Masculinity: The Many Englishman and the Effeminate Bengali in the Late Nineteenth Century* (Manchester: Manchester University Press, 1995), 16–17; Also see, Chandrima Chakraborty, *Masculinity Asceticism, Hinduism: Past and Present Imaginings of India* (Ranikhet: Permanent Black, 2011), 42–52.
13. To understand the qualitative differences between *seva* as social service and *seva* as sadhana or *seva* as a secular enterprise carried out by non-governmental organizations (NGOs) and charity organizations in the West or *seva* as part of Hindu traditions, see, John H. Ehrenreich, *The Altruistic Imagination: A History of Social Work and Social Policy in the United States* (New York: Cornell University Press, 1985).
14. Chandrima Chakraborty, *Masculinity Asceticism, Hinduism: Past and Present Imaginations of India* (Ranikhet: Permanent Black, 2011), 40.
15. 'Dharma in Hinduism has multiple meaning, but in all cases as a moral term, dharma bears semantically on "what ought to be done (kartavya)," and by implication (negatively), on "what ought to be avoided (akartavya)" or "what ought not to be done." Dharma as a moral term presides over the domains of "oughtness" and "prohibition."' Julius Lipner, 'The Truth of Dharma and the Dharma of Truth: Reflections on Hinduism as a Dharmic Faith', *International Journal of Hindu Studies* 23 (7 December 2019): 217.

    According to Bimal Krishna Matilal, 'In various contexts, the word dharma may mean: law, justice, custom, morality, ethics, religion, duty, nature, or virtue', to which we may add 'propriety' and 'righteousness'. Bimal Krishna Matilal, 'Elusiveness and Ambiguity in Dharma-Ethics,' in *The Collected Essays of Bimal Krishna Matilal: Ethics and Epics*, ed. Jonardon Ganeri (New Delhi: Oxford University Press, 2002b), 37.
16. Christophe Jaffrelot, *Religion, Caste and Politics in India* (London: C. Hurst Co. Publishers, 2011), 26.
17. Louis Dumont explained what constitutes a 'sect' for an ascetic. 'The Indian sect is a religious grouping constituted primarily by renouncers, imitates of the same disciple of salvation, and secondarily by their lay sympathesizers any of whom may have one of the renouncers as a spiritual master or guru....

In theory, for the man-in-the-world adherence to a sect is an individual matter, superimposed on caste observances, though not obliterating them, and the sect respects these observances even though it relativisms them and criticizes worldly religion from the point of view of individualistic religion. Moreover, the sect, springing from renunciation, has the power to recruit irrespective of castes'. Louis Dumont, *Homo Hierarchicus: The Caste System and Its Implications* (Delhi: Oxford University Press, 1966).

18. Peter Heehs, 'Bengali Religious Nationalism and Communalism', *International Journal of Hindu Studies* 1, no. 1 (April, 1997): 118.
19. Heehs, 'Bengali Religious Nationalism and Communalism', 121.
20. Partha Chatterjee, *The Nation and Its Fragments: Colonial and Postcolonial Histories* (Delhi: Oxford University Press, 1994[1993]), 237–38.
21. Arvind Sharma, 'On Hindu, Hindustān, Hinduism and Hindutva', *Numen* 49, no. 1 (2002): 27.
22. Colonel U. N. Mukherjee, in 'Hindus: a Dying Race', (1909), develops his argument by 'comparing a monolithic Hindu society with equally singular conceptions of Muslim and English societies'. This is an important text in analysing the early growth of Hindu communitarian interests in Bengal. See, Pradip Datta, 'Dying Hindus': Production of Hindu Communal Common Sense in Early 20th Century Bengal', *Economic and Political Weekly* 28, no. 25 (19 June 1993): 1305–19.
23. G. Moyser, *Politics and Religion in the Modern World* (London: Routledge, 1991), 18–19.
24. R. A. Emmons and R. F. Paloutzian, 'The Psychology of Religion', *Annual Review of Psychology* 54 (2003): 377–402.
25. Walter K. Andersen and Sridhar D. Damle, *Brotherhood in Saffron, The Rastriya Swayamsevak Sangh and Hindu Revivalism* (New Delhi: Westview Press, Vistaar Publications, 1987); van der Veer, *Religious Nationalism: Hindus and Muslims in India* (Berkeley, CA: University of California Press, 1994).
26. Shankar Gopalakrishnan, 'Neoliberalism and Hindutva: Fascism, Free Markets and the Restructuring of Indian Capitalism', *Radical Notes* (29 October 2008): 21–22.
27. Tariq Thachil, *The Saffron Wave Meets the Silent Revolution: Why the Poor Vote for Hindu Nationalism in Indian* (Faculty of the Graduate School of Cornell University, 2009, 24.
28. Rajesh Pradhan, *When the Saints Go Marching in: The Curious Ambivalence of Religious Sadhus in Recent Politics in India* (New Delhi: Orient BlackSwan, 1989), 20.
29. Ibid.
30. Liah Greenfield, *Nationalism: Five Roads to Modernity* (Cambridge, MA: Harvard University Press, 1992), 487–90; Pradhan, *When the Saints Go Marching in*, 24–25.

Seva, Sangathan and Hindutva

Locating the (A)Political Sadhus

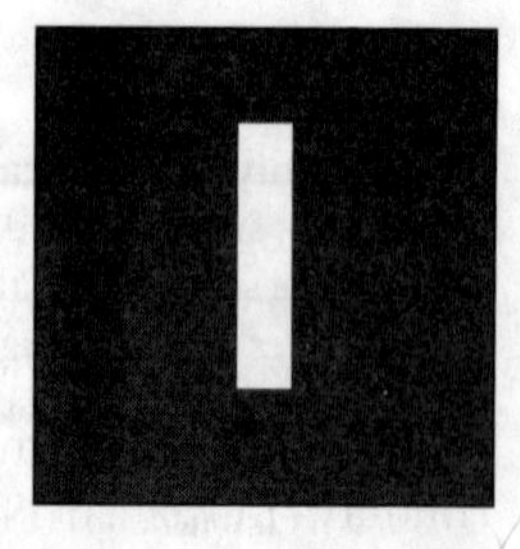

As far as the interpretive shifts in the scholarship on asceticism in South Asia are concerned, Hindu sadhus have been evolved as a critical symbolic element of nationalist politics. Despite their popular reputation as spiritual ascetics divorced from all worldly affairs, sadhus have remained active as traders, moneylenders, mercenaries, landlords or leaders in social and religious reform movements. The multiple patterns of their involvement in public affairs challenged the notion of an 'apolitical' sadhu reflected in the orientalist literature on India. Interestingly, the assumptions that sadhus entered party politics and held power positions by their own will did not get legitimacy from any corner; rather, their association with the so-called 'impure' world of politics has been justified on the grounds of a situational compulsion to protect the Hindu religion and culture from both internal and external threats. I have used the term '(a)political sadhu' here to denote the tensions present in the perspectives of ascetic engagement with public affairs, which refer to the sadhu as an outsider working at the boundaries of mainstream politics. Because of their unique relation to the public domain, they offered a critical approach to the political developments and took corrective measures to show the right path of action. Therefore, all they had done, or practised, should be taken as part of a larger scheme of nationalist regeneration motivated by the spirit of collective welfare. The veracity of this explanation laid in the historical topography of asceticism has changed with the growing politicization of Hindu religion and culture since the early 20th century. The ways the (a)political sadhus addressed and responded to the rising waves of Hindu nationalism contributed to the understanding of an innovative and alternative model of Hindu politics. In this category, *seva*, or selfless service, has been picked up as one of the most promising sites for imparting the alternative model of Hindu politics, where spatiality, cultural resurgence and the ideas of Hindu identity formation correspond mutually within the larger territory of a Hindutva movement. This chapter positions the notion of 'politics' as a newly invented category of self-recovery and self-regeneration which called for a Hindu *sangathan* through the philanthropic associational spaces, evolving as the symbolic manifestation of an inherited culture and history. Furthermore, this chapter chooses to bring out the subtle interplay of cultural Hindutva with political Hindutva—an interesting equilibrium of flexibility and rigidity thus far pushed away in the array of chosen narratives. Having outlined these approaches, this chapter takes cognizance of how the notion of apolitical sadhus fits well with these patterns of Hindutva and highlights a range of issues with regard to the idea of caste consolidation at an ethno-religious–cultural space.

Existing ideas that highlight the modalities of Hindu nationalism in the non-political space often use Hindu identity formation as an entry point to the world of politics.[1] There were instances when philanthropic–spiritual organizations deployed the art of *seva* (volunteering) for reviving/constructing the 'true' Hindu 'self' of a Hindu (Hindu-ness) to develop a modern Hindu identity conducive to the ideas of a Hindu nation in India.[2] It seems to be a challenging project, since what makes a 'true' Hindu self (Hindu-ness) has never been appropriated or negotiated at the psychosomatic space of its contenders; rather, a series of arguments and assumptions have been orchestrated to determine who is fit to be called a Hindu in the real sense of the term. The art of providing *seva* in the traditions of Hinduism evolved as an influential space for exploring the 'true' Hindu self of an individual (Hindu-ness), mostly because of its twin attributes: *seva* as an act of spiritual enlightenment and *seva* as a wider project of social transformation. In the organizational space of modern Hinduism, both these attributes remained strong and overlapping and brought into focus one interesting framework to trace how performative traditions of *seva* helped in Hindu subject formation—one of the principal hypotheses of the Hindutva movement in India (Beckerlegge, 2000).[3] Additionally, the act of *seva* also generated possibilities of a secular mode of functioning among the marginal poor irrespective of their religious affiliations.[4]

Most of the educational, cultural, tribal-oriented, relief care and healthcare initiatives of the Hindu religious *seva* organizations were aimed at ameliorating the problems of the subaltern poor in general. All these efforts might have fetched greater social legitimacy for those organizations in the long run. In almost all the organizations, the 'guru', or a spiritual figure,[5] remained thoroughly influential for the public representation of *seva* mainly as a performative act of selfless service to boost the morale of making a 'true' Hindu, defined in terms of his/her dedication, devotion and sense of fellowship with the society at large. Etymologically, the word 'guru' is indicative of one who dispels the darkness of ignorance and constitutes a charismatic personality in social standards.[6] The term charisma is suggestive of

> certain qualities of an individual's personality, by virtue of which he is set apart from ordinary men and treated as endowed with supernatural, superhuman, or at least specifically exceptional powers or qualities. These are not accessible to the ordinary person, but regarded as of a divine origin and on the basis of them the individual concerned is treated as a leader. (Weber 1947, 329)

On virtue of his being a healing agent and a source of divine enterprise, the guru creates his own sphere of influence and a guru–follower network, which in turn substantiates the divine existence of the guru at a wider level, especially in the context of *seva*.

The inner dynamism of the divine presence in the social sector of *seva* did not essentially claim its legitimacy in regard to the sense of dharma, referring to the moral duty of an individual to the greater society, but mostly did so in simple religious terms of worshipping the God in the form of suffering humanity. When placed in a wider social spectrum, however, the entire morphology of *seva* became far more powerful in commutating and reaching the masses quickly than other ways or means.[7] When explored as a cultural approach to reach the masses, the act of *seva* could have transformed into one normative domain of politics, but it is not imperative that all sorts of selfless–devotional *seva* acts would land up in a political space. It solely depends on the world view of the organizer or the leader—how he would like to locate his organization in the world of politics; however, in reality, the ethical–social attributes of *seva* had shown tendencies of showcasing its political leanings by virtue of its being an influential medium to reach the masses, cutting across caste and class boundaries. Did political proclivity remain inherent to the act of *seva* espoused by the guru-based spiritual organizations? If not, then how did the gurus relate to the 'political' world? Were they pseudo-political? These questions remained crucial to decipher the patterns of their involvement in politics while seeking freedom from all worldly actions. Before driving deep into these ideas, I would like to make some quick references to the theoretical perceptions of *seva* as a subject of spiritual sadhana and public utility.

LOCATING *SEVA* IN THE SPIRITUAL PREMISE

The sadhu, or a guru in this case, could be cited as a potential source of spiritual authority in Indian society. While transmitting the highest spiritual knowledge among his disciples and followers, the guru creates a network of power, authority and faith which upholds the guru lineage (Mckean 1996, 1–2) from one regeneration to the other. The ideal of guru lineage and the patterns of authority shared by the guru generate a sense of security among the disciples, while the guru-based institutions manifest a paternalist responsibility to their followers (Kakar 1978, 124). The paternalist imageries of a guru conform to an alternative family structure for the society concerned; it elaborates the model of dependence and devotion in a scrupulous manner. Interestingly, the spiritual knowledge and authority acquired by the guru are transcendental in nature, and Hindu spirituality, as believed and practised, is far more democratic and secular than others. The guru lineage or the guru–*sishya* networks could have had their own sectarian preferences, especially in terms of rituals, customs and practices. The ideology of *seva*, when reflected in the popular domain, remained far more tolerant, democratic and even 'universal' to its beneficiaries.[8] The secular spirit of universal *seva* imparted an amount of social legitimacy to the guru-based organizations and authenticated the authority of a Hindu guru as the upholder of indigenous secularism, and thus no danger was felt in mixing religion with politics.[9] The proponents of indigenous secularism remained highly critical of the so-called Western mode of secularism,[10] which refers to the complete separation of the state and religion, or politics and religion. What makes a Hindu guru self-assured of not being misguided by the world of public actions, since the life of a sanyasi needs to be protected from the so-called 'contaminated' space of *sansara*, or worldly actions? It does not resonate with separating religion from politics or keeping faiths and beliefs in the private domain, secluded from the public world. It is the strength of spirituality or *adhyatmika* which provides the ideological underpinning of an 'abiding concern with the world without letting go of the metaphysical quest' from the self (atman) of the being. (Srinivasan 2014, xii)

The sense of practical wisdom embedded in spirituality serves to gain a self-understanding of the private and the public as an integrated, holistic construction, where the political/public is subordinate to the spiritual/private. Furthermore, it privileges the universal notions of a Hindu world view existing over the traditions of Vedantic, Tantric, Puranic or any such other sectarian perspectives. The pedagogic formulations of a universal spirituality might have many shades of meanings, which somehow sounds problematic.[11] The Hindu world-view of spirituality dealt with the 'union of the individual atman (self) to the universal supreme soul (*Paramatma/Brahman*) though sadhana'.[12] The spirit of this sadhana constitutes spirituality, which leads to *moksha* or liberation from the circle of birth and death. Since spirituality or supreme wisdom has been assigned the highest value in the life of a Hindu, and especially in the life of a guru or *sadhak*, gurus hold the ability to nullify the worldly sufferings. As a result, when they face challenges and conflicts in the public domain, they can take resort to their supreme wisdom and interpret the problems from a different angle. Spiritual revelations work as a liberating force in the life of a sadhu, a positive energy that supports him or protects him from the sloppy realities of the public domain muddled with desires and worldly expectations. The strength of spirituality also explains why a good number of Hindu sadhus followed a liberal–independent path, despite being attached to the framework of Hindu nationalism, and constantly suggested how Hindu ideals could complement liberal politics in India. Drawing upon the indigenous sources of freedom and equality, these Hindu sadhus presented an alternative to the metanarratives of Hindutva ideology; those who failed to do so simply lost their individual agency for ever.

Practising universal *seva* as spiritual sadhana emerged as a creative option for the Hindu sadhus who wanted to reach the masses through various resourceful means. The idea of 'universal seva', when reflecting the capacity to move beyond the limitations of caste, class and religion, provides a unique opportunity for the sadhu to prove his social credibility not simply as a spiritual leader but also as a *jana sevak*, or someone devoted to public service. The term *jana seva* or *lok seva* or public service resonates well with the ethics of democratic politics which believes in politics being a selfless service to the nation. Politics, when judged in the light of selfless service, makes no room for the desire to hold office or have formal power; rather, it focuses on the ideal of *tyag*, or abstention from worldly attractions. According to this logic, the sadhus or spiritual gurus who have been committed to the act of *seva* for social welfare may easily get into the world of politics, because politics provides them an ostensibly rich structure to articulate the *jana seva* mission across the country. But it does not look viable considering the complicated relationship between these two domains. These complications could have resulted mostly from the fundamental confusions between religion and politics present in classical Indian philosophical thinking, where the notions of *artha* and dharma have been assigned to politics and *moksha* and dharma to religion. One strand of thought emphasized the continuity of dharma and moksha, and the other viewed them in opposition. Both these perception date back to the pre-colonial period but keep on influencing the porous boundaries of religion and politics even in modern time.

In the view of the Dharmasastras and the Arthasastra, *artha* serves dharma, and dharma leads to *moksha*.[13] In the Bhagavad Gita too, dharma has been depicted in terms of political action and one's caste duty, that is, *swadharma*, executed with the attributes of *niskama karma*, or detachment, leading to *moksha*. The Advaita Vedantins, on the other hand, accepted the importance of dharma only for those who dealt with worldly affairs, not for those who went on the path of renunciation or *sanyasa*. For an ascetic who has achieved *moksha* or the non-duality of the atman and the Brahman (*advaita*), the action-oriented rules of dharma do not carry any meaning, since in the state of *moksha* no action prevails. The realization of the non-duality of the self ends the legitimacy of dharma. Denying any continuity between dharma and *moksha*, Adi Shankara proposed the fundamental dichotomies of religion and politics. The other Vedantins like Ramanuja, however, emphasized the continuation of restricted actions performed as divine worship. The mutually conflicting positions of these two streams of thought influenced the key understanding of religion and politics in modern times. M. K. Gandhi, for instance, accepted the position of the Gita and the Dharmasastras and preferred to see politics as closely interlinked with religion.[14] Swami Vivekananda attempted to synthesize these two positions, while the individuals like Sri Aurobindo simply marked a departure from the world of politics only to pursue the life of a yogi.

The gurus operating from the domain of *seva* might have encountered the inner tensions of dharma and *moksha*, because *seva* as a normative space of selfless service and public welfare highlighted the attributes of worldly action and spiritual enlightenment. To avoid an immediate clash between these mutually conflicting terrains of engagement, Swami Vivekananda and Ramakrishna Mission brought the message of *niskama karma* into practice. Emanating from the ideal of *karma* yoga, *niskama karma* advocates engagement in worldly actions while giving up the fruits of the actions. While practising *niskama karma*, involvement in the public domain should not count as a threat to the status of the sadhu, because selfless karma helps one renounce internally, and such a state of mind, if attained, makes the individual confident enough to tackle worldly issues in a proper manner. Swami Vivekananda's reading of the Bhagavad Gita[15] made him suggest *niskama karma* to be highest ethics of life; he implied that abstention from worldly actions, or *sanyasa*, would not bring *moksha*; rather, working incessantly without attachment and without the expectations of rewards would bring the *niskama karmi* eternal happiness. When applied in politics, *niskama karma* could generate the 'pure' conscience of the nation. Unlike Bal Gangadhar Tilak, who interpreted karma yoga as a specialist craft for those have the mental strength to follow the path of *niskama karma*, that is, *sthitaprajnas*[16]—mostly the new Brahmins, well versed in philosophy and religion—Vivekananda suggested *niskama karma* to be a mass craft that could be practised by all, irrespective of caste and class. That is why in his understanding of *niskama karma* the idea of charity or '*dana*' is absent. Here, the poor and the rich, the sadhu and the householder, the Brahmin and the non-Brahmin, all are equal and mutually connected.[17] In this framework of universal *seva*, no one is giving or receiving, no one is superior to others, but all reflect the essence of the truth in one way or the other. In the realm of politics, application of the ideal of *niskama karma* is highly problematic, because if all are equal and nobody is placed at a superior position, then how should the leader–follower relation look like? What should be the modalities of authority and power in politics for a *niskama karmi*? These are the incongruent issues that produced the fundamental paradox of situating the sadhus in the public domain, or in the realm of active politics.

HINDU NATIONALISM, HINDUTVA AND *SEVA*

The ideology of Hindu nationalism, while expanding beyond the limits of being a narrow political craft, accommodated the cultural–ethical sprit of *seva* in its periphery and utterly smudged the inner tensions of ethics and politics, culture and politics and, overall, religion and politics. Both Hindu nationalism and the philanthropic act of *seva* jointly coordinated the fundamental premises for creating a 'true' Hindu identity out of a range of false identities and, when settled on this mission, made Hindutva (Hindu-ness) a subjective category with greater political implications. Interestingly, far from coming out as a homogenous project, the Hindutva movement scraped out different implications of its practices, and the actors involved in the project responded differently to the call for identity formation. Crucial here is the fact that Hindu nationalism primarily functioned as a political ideology with fixed objectives, and when hooked up with the space of *seva*,[18] it unleashed conflicts and discomforts for those who entered into this political space from the ethical–spiritual space of *seva*. The latter might have shown loyalty to the cause of Hindu nationalism and joined the Hindutva movement in their respective domains.

The spirit of conflict and discomfort present in the porous boundaries of *seva* and politics gave rise to the dialectics of Hindutva. The gurus or spiritual leaders who had participated in the Hindutva movement tried their level best to carve out a middle path of adjustment but finished in sheer discomfort in the long run.

One may ask why the gurus of the *seva* organizations failed to come out as autonomous agents of Hindu identity formation, beyond the purview of Hindu nationalism, but it must be taken into cognizance that the spirit of assimilation and integration present in this ideal of identity formation spontaneously worked in favour of Hindu consolidation or Hindu *sangathan*.[19] The Hindu *seva* originations might have shown orthodox or reformist tendencies in the course of their historical developments. They hardly demonstrated any essential intention to utilize *seva* as a politically motivated instrument deployed purposely for articulated gains.[20] Rather, *seva* depended mainly on how a particular organization or guru had conceptualized its public role and intended to exercise its power over the followers and the beneficiaries. In most cases, the marginal poor emerged to be the primary beneficiaries of *seva* works and participated in the subject formation of the Hindutva project. The elites, especially the middle class, enjoyed a kind of power position in this trajectory of *seva*, since charity or service always flew from the top to the bottom and the bottom itself provided the fundamental contours for outlining Hindutva as a modern type of sociopolitical movement. The idea of subject formation for Hindutva through *seva* might not have provided any agency to the marginal poor. The latter lacked spontaneous participation in the project, rather remaining at the receiving end, allowing Hindutva to be an elitist project all through its journey.

Orientalist scholarship working on re-imagining the religious landscape in India in the late 19th century had produced new theories of understanding a modern Hindu identity with approaches related to social upliftment, Hindu organization and rejuvenation of the ideas and meaning of what constitutes a modern nation. These aspects had outlined the ways and means of practising *seva* towards the socially marginalized, those who had been denied agency in the so-called mainstream of Hinduism's boundaries. The orientalist observers and the Christian missionaries might have developed an interesting site for inscribing meanings onto the hitherto fragmented contours of a Hindu identity; in a self-serving manner, they disapproved of the ritualistic, donation-oriented, private imagination of *seva* prevalent in India in contrast to the much-civilized, society-oriented, organized attributes of *seva* manifested in the Western mode of charity.[21] The orientalist perception of public utility through charity received greater impetus in the state-sponsored projects of social philanthropy in the 19th century and created the context for re-asserting the existing Indian tradition of *seva* manifested mostly in the form of *dana* or giving. The practice of *dana* or donation has deep-rooted meanings in Indian philosophical traditions;[22] however, it had never been interpreted within an organized space of *seva* inscribed with the spirit and essence of public utility.

A few scholars who saw the rise of a new organized space of *seva* as an outcome of the Indian encounter with the West often looked for a re-appropriation of the philosophy of Advaita in this new context to ensure a palpable presence of the Hindu society within the process.[23] Each living being is unadulterated and a component of the almighty with the same divine substance—this message of Advaita, when relegated to the organize space of *seva*, opened up the debates on whether the transformation of *dana* to *seva*, from private to public, from unorganized to organized, was conducive to the much-anticipated influence of the West over the Indian traditions or if it emerged as a hybrid process of interaction between the East and the West in shaping the ideology of *seva* in the public domain. It became a moot point in the discourse of *seva* in the late 19th century. The central focus of the question, however, gradually moved on to how *seva* had been evolved as an alternative space for Hindu identity formation in the consecutive years.

Together with the process of a nationalist self-assertion by the Hindu reformers against the imperialist stereotypes of a backward India, the Vedantins like Swami Vivekananda stepped into the world of organized *seva* with the ideas of Advaita (*jive seva* is similar to worshipping the God) but at the same time elevated this project to the level of a response to the imperialist assumptions of a 'backward–fatalist–feminine' India. Beaming with the spirit of masculinity, positivity, rationality and, above all, utility, the new language of *seva* challenged the so-called backward-looking elements of Indian society and continued to inculcate the spirit of nationalist self-evaluation. This nationalist self was very much in tune with the Hindu traditions—the two had a shared past, a shared ancestry and a shared culture. Cultivation of the self in the making of a new Hindu identity resonated the contexts for organizing one unified universal category of Hinduism which could infuse a collective Hindu feeling in a community of varied traditions and simultaneously brought the caste group of 'others' into the boundaries of a homogeneous Hinduism. *Seva* organizations, especially those that were styled as capable of meeting the needs of public utility, fitted nicely with this new connotation of identity contraction and social integration, because *seva*, as mentioned earlier, evolved as a unique space of negotiation between culture, race and religion—three primary components to inscribe an identity onto a particular community. This study does not offer any scope to discuss how modern *seva* organizations had been formed following the model of the missionary networks in the latter half of the 19th century,[24] but it takes note of the fact that the idea of 'social reform' initiated the endeavours of social upliftment through organized community movements much before organized *seva* practices arrived at a larger scale. What was particularly innovative in the new language of *seva* was a spirit of community bonding and a sense of responsibility to the marginal 'others' of the society—two important themes dispensing an amount of effervescence to the dynamism of group solidarity.

The emergence of a complex, non-linear pattern of nationalism in the 19th century and its deep investment in unfolding a high-caste Hindu culture caused a critical interest in the compatibility of spirituality and politics. Swami Vivekananda was probably the first important Hindu leader who brought spiritualism closer to politics, but he kept his political engagements independent of classifications. He could have influenced an entire generation of revolutionary nationalists, swadeshi youths, young entrepreneurs and nationalists, but he himself stood away from any political activism as such. Despite representing the bhadralok perception of nationalist politics and Hindu resurgence, Swami Vivekananda engineered the spirit of intellectual freedom and individuality in organized endeavours to uplift the condition of the suffering masses through *seva* practices. This indicated a paradigm shift in contemporary nationalist politics, because the involvement of celibate monks in nationalist reconstruction through *seva* appeared to be innovative and path-breaking. The bhadralok perception of bourgeoisie charity which asserted its agency mostly in the social reform movements of the 19th century faced stiff challenge from Vivekananda, who evoked the message of universal *seva* based on equality, fellowship, solidarity and nationalist regeneration. Now, nationalist regeneration as Hindu unity suggests severe problems in the world of active politics, if judged from a post-colonial, neoliberal perspective, since the votaries of soft Hindutva invested much on the inadequate model of Hindu unity parallel to national unity but distanced themselves from the transcendental universal appeal of a spiritual quest for salvation embedded in the context of resurgent nationalism (Sharma 2015, 84–86).

One needs to take into account the fact that Swami Vivekananda died in the year 1902, much before the so-called ideology of Hindu nationalism had emerged as crucial to the understanding of Indian politics. Faced with multiple political realities and identities, India was struggling to define a new language of nationalism, which was full of difficulties and differences at the turn of the century. Vivekananda might have visualized this new nationalism though a Hindu lens, because Hinduism offered him a unique space for celebrating the differences intrinsic to Indian society. It was a space full of contradictions and complexities where orthodoxy and freedom/elitism and *lokavidya*/tradition/modernity could grow and evolve at the same pace. When manipulated in opposition, all these contradictions and dichotomies could fabricate the spirit of Hinduism in a desired direction; however, the sense of spirituality then emerged as the quintessential approach towards assimilation and unification.[25] Spirituality, as mentioned earlier, always stood superior to the inherent contradictions of religion and channelized its essential energy in the early construction of nationalism.

Late-19th-century nationalism in India declared its 'sovereignty' from the outer domain of the colonial and championed the cause of a resurgent Hinduism that claimed its autonomy from colonial interventions. Vivekananda was strongly appreciative of this nationalism that made the nation speak for itself and searched for a shared past of the collective self. Hinduism granted him the affordable choice to look for a foundation of that nationalism. The idea of a Hindu nation or Hindu way of life produced the context for an ideological basis to the construction of a nationalist identity, if not a monolithic homogeneous identity. *Jata mat tata path* ('there are as many ways of reaching the goal as there are ideologies'), the message from Vivekananda's guru Ramakrishna, rightly supported the hypothesis of Hinduism being a flexible, all-embracing concept that could act as a cementing force for the nation.[26] Hinduism's capacity to accommodate all shades of thoughts, beliefs and ideas makes it different form the other religions but do not encourage opposition or hostility to others. This catholic spirit of Hinduism, Vivekananda believed, would form the basis of a common indent for the Hindus and merge into a larger Indian identity. Within the caste-ridden bourgeoisie world of 19th-century Bengal, the syncretism spirit of resurgent Hinduism infused the essential impetus to visualize the strength of a future Hindu nation; however, portraying nationalism in the light of a shared Hindu past or shared Hindu identity did not provide Vivekananda a clean chit at all. He might have given Muslims an unintentional miss in most of his speeches and lectures, but his profound admiration for a Hindu way of life, history, culture and spirituality often brought him closer to the Hindu nationalist paradigm. Appropriating Vivekananda into the *mata* structure of Hindu nationalism could have been a dubious project, because in his imaginings, Hinduism had never been a monolithic construction with ethno-territorial–political attributes, and the act of *seva* in no occasion demonstrated any tendency to make India a Hindu nation/'Hindu Rashtra'. The interpretations of to what extent the act of *seva* as *niskama karma* proved to be conducive for Hindu consolidation set an essential edifice for the understanding of: (a) *seva* leading to spiritual salvation; (b) *seva* leading to Hindu identity formation; and finally (c) *seva* as an entry point to politics for the sadhus or the sanyasis. The third aspect emerged central to the understanding of the conflicts and disagreements present in Hindu nationalism, especially in the Hindutva movement.

HINDUTVA REDEFINED: THE ALTERNATIVES

To make my point, I take the case of one less discussed Hindu *seva* organization, Bharat Sevashram Sangha (BSS), and its central spiritual guru, Swami Pranavananda, to reveal an interesting pattern of cultural–spiritual Hindutva absorbed by the metanarratives of the RSS–VHP (Rashtriya Swayamsevak Sangh–Vishva Hindu Parishad)-led political Hindutva. Interestingly, developed in the ethno-linguistic boundaries of Bengali middle-class nationalism of the early 20th century, the BSS built up its own critique of the Ramakrishna Mission in a restricted manner and shared a kind of mixed response to Swami Vivekananda. Despite that, the Hindutva proponents spared no effort to situate both Swami Vivekananda and Swami Pranavananda on a predictable platform, and especially in the absence of a macro-analysis of the varied ideological viewpoints, one unstipulated discourse of ascetic politics was determined to bear out the underpinnings of the Hindutva movement. The all-inclusive appetite of this dominant version of Hindutva wrapped up each single thought and idea that flourished around some Hindu organizations in a regional setting. The sadhus/sanyasis always occupied a central position in the Hindutva discourse, even though they had shown resistance to any monolithic construction of Hindutva or remained apolitical and uncommitted to any specific brand of politics. One could call this not a kind of strategy from the part of the Hindu nationalists to gain social validity to a limited extent but a well-designed approach to get the popular mandate from the larger part of the society. Sadhus involved in *seva* activities might not have conformed to the norms of active politics or engaged in political disputes, fighting of elections or patronization of a political party, but they possessed immense authority to influence the public culture of a society. The inscribing of political connotations onto that sense of 'authority' thus revealed the travesty of mass mobilization in an impatient manner.

In the Hindutva literature in India, the name of Swami Pranavananda has been referred frequently in relation to the 19th-century legacy of Hindu nationalism, along with Dayananda Saraswati, Swami Vivekananda and others. Born in a Bengali village to a Kayastha family in 1896, *brahmachari* Binode, renamed as Swami Pranavananda established the BSS in the year 1923. The history and development of the BSS implied the regional cultural entrenchment of Hindutva in Bengal, outside the North Indian geographical circles (Voix 2011, 210). Unlike the Ramakrishna Mission, the BSS evolved primarily as a Bengali Hindu organization committed to the cause of Hindu nationalism in the countryside of Bengal. From its very inception, one can trace the history of the BSS as part of the Hindutva movement embedded in the ethno-cultural space of Bengal. It could be shown as the first instance of a *seva*-oriented organization that contributed independently to the undercurrents of Hindutva movement and tried hard to keep a safe distance from the RSS-led Hindi–Hindu nationalist narratives. The uneven relationship shared by the BSS and the RSS in fact identified the dilemmas of Hindu politics at a regional setting and displayed the conflicting contours of the Hindutva movement, tantamount to the understanding of a collaboration–completion syndrome in between. Currently spread over different countries all over the world, the BSS symbolized the epitome of service, spirituality and Hindu *sangathan*; however, its essential equation with the mainstream Hindutva forces still remain unsettled and complicated. To elaborate my point in detail, I cite three important themes from the array of thoughts on the BSS: (a) reconfiguring the caste society through *seva* programmes; (b) reverberating the facades of Bengali–non-Bengali identities in the manifestation of Hindutva; and (c) reflecting the tensions faced by the RSS–VHP in Bengal—the 'troubled' zone of Hindu politics.

Greatly appreciated by both the government and the masses, the BSS built up its image as being the foremost *seva* organization to arrive on the spot at the time of a natural calamity or national emergency. Swami Pranavananda, in fact, started his relief *seva* works amid the devastating cyclone in Bengal in 1919, followed by the Sundarbans famine of 1921, the black fever epidemic of 1925, the famine of 1927 at Khulna, the flood in Tangail in 1939, the malaria fever of 1931 at Asashuni and so on. In the riverine delta of East Bengal, flood, famine and other natural calamities had been a regular feature, and Swami Pranavananda jumped at the opportunity for providing relief services rapidly through supplying necessary commodities, food and healthcare to the suffering population. In the remotest areas of the Bengal countryside, where government-run relief services were limited in number or almost non-existent, partly because of poor transportation facilities, Swami Pranavananda and groups of young *brahmacharis* started all-round *seva* activities under extreme hardship. At times, inadequate resources, lack of communication networks, shortage of expert volunteers, etc. turned out to be real impediments for the swami. Nevertheless, his *seva* efforts earned him respect and reputation among all sections of the common Bengali masses.[27]

This empowered the BSS with a certain amount of command over the poor populace and allowed Swami Pranavananda to be looked up to as a natural leader of the common masses. After being reported in the reputed dailies from the cities, the swami received donations and appreciation from the then-prominent Bengali intellectuals such as Acharya Prafulla Chandra Ray, Dinesh Chandra Sen, Shyam Sundar Chakravarty and many other renowned personalities—those who had come in close contact with the swami at different points of time. Acharya Prafulla Chandra Ray, an eminent nationalist and the father of Indian chemistry, actively participated with the swami in village reconstruction programmes with an objective to establish Gandhian visions of khadi *charkha* and hand-crafted cotton industries. At Bajitpur, poor Hindu and Muslim families started working on *charkhas*, while Swami Pranavananda initiated the process of providing peasants with agricultural credit as part of his rural reconstruction programme.[28]

While expanding his *seva* activities in urban areas, Swami Pranavananda took keen interest in the reformation of the Hindu pilgrimage sites all over India, especially to nurture a feeling of security and belongingness in the Hindu pilgrims who were being threatened and harassed by the *pandas*, or priests, at the popular pilgrimage sites. During his lifetime, a number of ashrams, *jatri niwas* facilities and rest homes were built all over India through the large amount of donations received from both Bengali and non-Bengali businessmen, industrialists, zamindars, members of the princely families and others. Raphael Voix overtly represented the pilgrimage activities of the BSS as travel agency networks created mainly for the service of Bengali pilgrims. The success of BSS's pilgrimage programme, Voix mentioned, depended largely on making all the communications in a non-Bengali-speaking area in Bengali. The Bengali pilgrims felt at home within the ashram premises, and accordingly, fellowship developed among them spontaneously (Voix 2011, 218–219). Simply calling the pilgrimage service of BSS a travel agency programme does not serve the historical purpose at all, because it undermines the palatable part of the story called identity formation. Second, the implications of BSS-led *seva* programmes had their own scopes and insights in a regional setting different from the national one. Negotiating with the Bengali identity through pilgrimage programmes outside of Bengal allowed the BSS to calibrate the potentials of an ethno-linguistic variation of Hindutva, while in Bengal it impacted reasonably the non-Bengali-Hindi speaking communities, especially the Marwaris.

The latent spirit of Bengali culture and language might have helped in the promotion of a Bengali Hindu identity, but in no case did it supersede the supra-local idea of Hindu integration, because the ethics of service and Hindu identity formation were always negotiated in universal and pan-Indian realities. Hindu nationalism might have been mobilized in specific contexts (Menon 2012, 165), but when viewed as a larger existential reality, it appears to be transcendental and crucial to the spirit of nation building. The transformative possibilities of Hindu nationalism as an ideology and Hindutva as a movement hold up the stamp of their origin in the devotional functioning of Swami Pranavananda, both in the margins and in the mainstream, both among the monks and among the household devotees. The pilgrimage programmes initiated by Swami Pranavananda did not endorse any Bengali–non-Bengali divide but employed their own version of Hindutva on an alternative praxis. This alternative praxis coincided with the ideal of Hindu Samaj Samannay at both the rural and urban sectors simultaneously, and the pilgrimage programmes of Swami Pranavananda afforded him the best possible channels to reach the Bengali bhadralok, far more swiftly than any others means. Going on a yearly pilgrimage tour had always been a choice to the Bengali bhadralok, and finding a familiar ambience with free food and accommodation at the BSS ashrams infused them with a sense of security and belongingness with other pilgrims away from Bengal. Impressed by the services provided at the ashrams, these pilgrims were easily convinced in the BSS and its activities and ultimately ended up becoming disciples of the guru. Swami Pranavananda successfully brought a good number of middle-class devotees within the fold of the BSS through large-scale pilgrimage programmes, while at home he much preferred to operate *seva* programmes among the subaltern poor in the villages.[29]

At home, the swami's Hinduizing objectives remained highly critical of those modernist concerns that had re-articulated themselves in the nationalist framework through one middle-class public space. He completely rejected that bhadralok sense of 'colonial' modernity and discarded any kind of debate or discussion on such issues as Western education, women's education, domesticity, conjugality, political representation of women and others.[30] In his project of Hindutva, this anti-Western critique held an important position, and instead of taking refuge in modern symbols, ideas or anecdotes, Swami Pranavananda went on reviving and perpetuating the imageries of the 'past' as an integrated whole, only to articulate the 'Hindu-ness' of a Hindu, at a time when one hegemonic middle-class culture had already nudged the metanarrative of nationalist modernity in India. Did he mean that the 'Hindu-ness' of a Hindu should be revived or reconstructed away from the middle-class public space? Perhaps not, because Swami Pranavananda, when operating from a *seva*-based public organization, had already submitted to a colonial public space created on the networks of *sabhas*, samitis, *samajs*, *sanghas*, societies and others. These were the platforms representing people's rights to the state, as well as to claim legitimacy within the larger society—supposed sites for 'being public' in the public domain.[31]

Contrary to this middle-class culture of public representation, the BSS managed to survive as an apolitical organization with overtly political objectives. The so-called hegemonic presence of the colonial state had been negotiated through structural reformation of the religion in regard to its affiliation to the Hindu society—in particular, the real authority of Hinduism was imparted to the texts, scriptures and practices embodied in the wisdom of the popular sources. These were the ideologies mediated by the middle classes[32] and essentialized by the lower-class masses, and it was the perception of a Hindu *sangathan* through which the ideology of Hindutva was formulated. However, the fundamental problem with a Hindu nationalist organization sprang from the fact that the attributes of a lived religion or popular practices did not always manifest the textual or scriptural documents' ideas of what makes one a true Hindu; rather, the intellectual accounts of Hinduism differed ostensibly from what was practised in the lived experiences.[33] Therefore, Swami Pranavananda's perception of Hindutva developed mostly based on what he had practised and realized through his own life experiences, not solely through textual intellectual interpretations. For example, Swami Pranavananda, being a Shaiva and a yogi, adopted select references from the Vedas but dismissed the claims of the Vedas being the ultimate authority. He never appreciated the Samhitas like Dayananda Saraswati or imparted high value to the Upanishads like Ram Mohan Roy, but he pinned down certain cognitive views on character building, guru *bhakti*, patriotism and *seva*. Swami Vivekananda's ideas on what it meant to be a Hindu fortified the perceptions of Swami Pranavananda to a great extent, but the non-dualist model of Advaita Vedanta that constituted the world view of Swami Vivekananda did not survive as a validating point of self-articulation in the ideas of Swami Pranavananda. The intellectual remaking of Hinduism in the 19th century might have had given a doctrinal coating over the multiple perceptions of what makes a Hindu, but it hardly created an absolute identity of the Hindu-ness of a Hindu.

Under the changed political circumstances in the early 20th century, when the value of number became far more crucial to the cause of identity making, the Hindu–non-Hindu binary led to a process called 'othering' of the others. It impetuously perpetuated the Hindu identity and subsequently made the Hindus conscious of their self-perception. Visualizing and romanticizing the notions of an uninterrupted, 'timeless'/changeless past supported the self-perception of the Hindus as being an inseparable part of a shared tradition that is sacred, pure and authentic. These traditions were not in opposition to the modern but were uninterrupted by the modern, and that was what was required: a revival of that pure, authentic past as an integrated whole imparting a Hindu way of life—a transcendental collective identity and an integrated pattern of thoughts. Disquieting faults could be traced out of this formulation of identity making, since Hinduism, as it is referred to, represents multiples sectarian sensibilities, philosophical narratives and fragments of practices stretched over regions and cultures in a discreet manner. Even the term Hindutva makes room for further explanations, if taken away from its politics of what makes a Hindu separate from a non-Hindu and how a Hindu could invest on his self-perceptions of being a Hindu under sociopolitical compulsions.[34]

The Savarkarian inertia of asphyxiating the multitudes of Hinduism and Hindu-ness influenced a whole generation of Hindu nationalists in India.[35] This is the reputation and 'aura of Savarkar',[36] that he dared to make a comparison between Hinduism and Hindutva and declared,

> The ideas and ideals, the systems and societies, the thoughts and sentiments which have centred around this name [Hindutva] are so varied and rich, so powerful and so subtle, so elusive and yet so vivid that the term Hindutva defies all attempts at analysis. Forty centuries, if not more, had been at work to mould it as it is. Prophets and poets, lawyers and law-givers, heroes and historians, have thought, lived, fought and died just to have it spelled thus. For indeed, is it not the resultant of countless actions—now conflicting, now commingling, now cooperating—of our whole race? Hindutva is not a word but a history. Not only the spiritual or religious history of our people, but a history in full.[37]

Despite this, the meta-discourse of Savarkarian Hindutva failed to acknowledge the other patterns of the Hindutva movement which flourished at the regional level but continued to share a tepid relationship with the so-called mainstream. The other variations of the Hindutva movement gathered momentum in reaction to the macroscopic space of a Western mode of renaissance, or in response to a demographic number politics within the margin of the colonial state but conceived in the spiritually motivated space of *seva* being the most meaningful site for Hindu identity formation and social reconstruction. Bringing people close to one structure of self-affirmation generated one Hindu way of looking at the differences that also sought to look for solutions both within and outside the Hindu society. Furthermore, the political connotations of an 'enemy other' (especially denoting Islam) remained absent in the pattern of cultural Hindutva; rather, the process of self-invention in this case occasionally involved searching for certain values and ideas in the 'other' culture, thereby confirming the accommodative pursuits of Hinduism, in opposition to its fundamental variants.

Despite this, the BSS has been charged of fanning communal undercurrents in the Bengal countryside, and its so-called apolitical affiliations have often encouraged the critics to look for an undisclosed agenda behind its *seva* programmes. I will come back to this point later. Before that, I would like to focus on Swami Pranavananda's visions of *seva*, whether judged as an entry point to politics or simply as the means to spiritual salvation. The connotations of politics in the Bengal of the early 20th century were different from what we speculate today. Thus, assuming politics or *jana seva* as part of the larger scheme of nation building or *jatigathan* hardly called for any conflict of interests; nevertheless, Swami Pranavananda's frequent prefixing of the term 'Hindu' before 'nation' was likely to obscure the project at a wider context.

In the publications of the BSS, Swami Pranavananda has been addressed as the 'yugacharya' or the ultimate teacher of the time (*yuga*). Soon after he finished his *brahmacharya* sadhana, Swami Pranavananda got initiated from the Natha yogi Swami Gambhiranathji, and in 1916, the enlightened swami revealed four fundamental messages to his followers. He declared his 'time' (*yuga*) to be 'the *yuga* of great awakening, great unification, great assimilation and great liberation' (Swami Vedananda 1385 BS, 62). In order to achieve *mahamukti* or great liberation, he declared, one should walk on the path of dharma, which remains not in rituals or in temples or mosques but in meditation, sacrifice, self-control, truth and *brahmacharya* (Swami Vedananda 1385 BS, 45–46). He repeatedly emphasized the revival of 'Sanatana Dharma', which he believed could be evoked through *brahmacharya* or self-restraint—a key to character building and nation building (Swami Nirmalananda 1382 BS, 21).

Swami Pranavananda desired his followers to practise the dharma that would make them enlightened of his real self and aware of their duties and responsibilities towards the society and the nation (Swami Vedananda 1385, 179). Then, inheriting the legacy of the resurgent Hinduism of the late 19th century, Swami Pranavananda posed a counter-challenge to colonial modernity and attempted to infuse the Indian values of spirituality, *seva* and *sangathan* into the psyche of the Hindu society.[38] Historically, there have been confusions over the idea of a Hindu resurgence in the organizational space of modern Hinduism in 20th-century Bengal, especially when the waves of the Ramakrishna movement had already overwhelmed a section of the Bengali Hindus with the ideas of reform, revival, selfless service, spirituality and yoga, combined with the knowledge of Advaita Vedanta (Gupta, 1973; Basu 2002; Basu, 2002; Beckerlegge,1995, 2007). The powerful presence of the Ramakrishna Mission in the sociocultural milieu of modern Bengal surpassed the existence of the BSS to an extent; however, the latter crafted its own patterns of 'Hindu revival', partly in addition and mostly as a challenge to the Ramakrishna Mission.

The spiritual paradigm of *seva* and the nationalist paradigm of Hindutva, central to the Hindu resurgence project, had been developed by Swami Pranavananda. Both these paradigms kept nurturing a unique sense of Hindu *jatigathan* (nation building)—a jargon used by Swami Pranavananda in the early 1930s. Accordingly, the swami launched the Hindu Samaj Samannay movement (the word *samannay* stands for assimilation, consolidation, integration and overall solidarity across the castes and classes), or a Hindu consolidation movement, both at the level of caste integration and for the nationalist awakening of the Hindu *jati* through large-scale *seva* activities.[39] *Seva*, as a means of Hindu consolidation, presented one unique blueprint of understanding the paradox of caste in Bengal of the early 20th century and acted as a site for inscription of meanings onto the hitherto fragmented contours of Hindu identity. Essential to the concept of *seva*, this idiosyncratic space of Hindu *jatigathan* added to the framework of reviving the Sanatana Dharma (eternal religion) from centuries of customized corruption. Reviving the Sanatana Dharma—a much hyped project of the Hindu nationalist organizations—appeared to be a palpable template for the BSS when combined with the spirit of ascetic masculinity[40] and Hindu Samaj Samannay. Contrary to this, the dialectic of upper-caste hegemony and lower-caste assertion of subjectivity provided the BSS different possibilities of social mobilization.

IN THE WHIRLPOOLS OF CASTE: THE BENGALI INERTIA

In Bengal, Hindu *sangathan* seemed to have been a subject of contestation mainly because of the hegemonic preoccupation of the upper caste with the construction of a public space.[41] This space was not autonomous in nature, since most of the Hindu reformist/spiritual–humanitarian organizations worked here for the transformation of the Hindu society, and even the colonial state effectively translated the contours of this public domain for so long. Caste identities—one of the most powerful expressions of popular aspirations in the early 20th century—occasionally asked for preferential treatment from the colonial state and responded quietly to the hegemonic arrangements of the upper castes. Gradually, the spirit of defiance towards the social authority of the higher castes led to the development of several caste organizations.[42] The question of class looked fragile and weak at this point of social convergence because the caste members, at least in certain cases, formed greater unity on the lines of only caste. Staying within a caste group seemed to be beneficial, since the colonial government also distributed official patronage based on the principle of the caste status of an individual. However, the question here is: did the lower-caste masses always imbibe the spirit of colonial patronage and respond to the caste leaders accordingly? Perhaps not, because the caste movements and the policies of the colonial government hardly brought anything promising that could nullify the grievances of these people and make them free from age-old social embarrassments.

Undoubtedly, a few movements were organized by specific caste associations, ensuring the participation of the masses of their respective communities through addressing their political ambitions on effective platforms.[43] In general, the social gap between the caste elites and the masses continued to exist, and the deadlock in social interactions resulted in the weakening of the possibilities of horizontal unification of the society. It also indicated towards the existence of a separate world of consciousness of the lower-caste masses. This is the space where the *seva*-oriented/spiritual Hindu organizations aspired to intervene, and the BSS entered into this lower-caste world of consciousness with the baggage of nationalist reconstruction. The ideological impetus behind these endeavours was derived mainly from the universal ideal of salvation, or what is described as *mahamukti*, through providing *seva*, or moral, spiritual and material service, to the 'dying Hindus', irrespective of their caste (Swami Vedananda 1385 BS, 128–132; Swami Advaitananda 1364 BS, 19).[44]

The metaphor of Hindus being a 'dying race' denoted the colonial binary of the hyper-masculine Muslims and effeminate Hindus who were projected to be unfit for any greater responsibilities (Datta 1993, 1305–1308). Uncontrolled sexual practices and lack of moral vigour constituted the key aspects of this Hindu effeminacy according to British scholarship (Boehmer 1995, 71; Fanon 1967, 73). Lack of masculinity was seen as the primary cause underlying the so-called decline of the Hindus. The publications like *Hindu Sangathan: Saviour of the Dying Race* by Swami Shraddhanand[45] and *Hinduism and the Coming Census: Christianity and Hinduism* by U. N. Mukherjee[46] openly addressed different Hindu interests to meet at a point of agreement to counter the numerical superiority of the religious 'others' through constructive means. Interestingly, much before the Bengali Hindus took an interest in the idea of *sangathan*, the Arya Samaj and Hindu Mahasabha started campaigning to popularize the Sangathan movement against the myths of a united Islam in North India.[47] However, it was only after the failure of the non-cooperation–Khilafat liaison in Bengal that the idea of a competitive demography claimed serious attention from the educated Hindus. The 19th-century notion of Aryanism might have had a great influence on Swami Pranavananda; however, he had rightly realized that the Arya Samaj of North Indian origin might not be in tune with the Hindu resurgence in Bengal.[48] This idea of Hindu Samaj Samannay inculcated Swami Pranavananda's visions on the caste question separately from the other Hindu nationalist thinkers.

As a direct consequence of these developments, the Sangathan propaganda in Bengal asked for an early reinstatement of Hindu masculinity and also called for Hindu solidarity on an urgent basis. Other than checking uncontrolled sexual practices (essential for *brahmacharya* sadhana), removal of untouchability, maintenance of proper diet, spread of education and eradication of poverty were included as important components of the Hindu solidarity movement. It seemed to be a matter of political survival for the Hindus; however, the success of the movement depended largely on to what extent the socially marginalized classes could respond to this ideological–political syndrome. The 19th-century modernizing project of the colonial state even fell short of the challenges set by traditional modes of casteist self-sufficiency. The census statistics, though not very trustworthy reflections of the social reality, provided an indication of the extent to which human resources were wasted in the name of tradition and social autonomy. Moreover, the native defenders of the system did not ever entertain any interference of the colonial state into those subjects they believed to be 'exclusive' and 'unique' to the Hindu society.

The 19th-century social reform movements, or even the spirit of Hindu resurgence, shared the same dilemma in dealing with the issues of caste. Now in an environment of competitive demography, the Hindu leaders for the first time took the issue of the Depressed Classes[49] sincerely. This was partly because of the fact that they truly realized that as long as untouchability was practised in the Hindu social order, the lower-caste Hindus would remain vulnerable to the vested interests. Side by side, the lower-caste Hindus, especially the *adivasis*, came out as more masculine and physically stronger than the upper-caste Hindus. Thus, integration of these people into the mainstream now became the first and foremost priority for the overall well-being of the Hindu society. No doubt, this approach was unlikely to bring any massive change in the mindset of the Depressed Classes, for whom political empowerment was much more important than mere social recognition. For long, there had been a desire among the lower castes to rise up the social ranks. As Hitesh Ranjan Sanyal pointed out, their capacity to adjust towards upward social mobility helped the system stay alive even through some awkward situations.[50] Unless the Depressed Classes[51] were welcomed into or adjusted in the upper-caste political process, the Hindu solidarity movement would become a rootless orchid in the near future. On a deeper analysis, Swami Pranavananda's Hindu Samannay did not completely reflect the Brahmanical doctrine of *adhikari-bheda*; rather, the individuality and identity of a caste was appropriated in selective manner (Professor Sumit Sarkar has elaborated this doctrine of *adhikari-bheda* as a 'formal doctrine from above' which 'tended to signify not fluidity and openness but neat compartmentalization, the drawing up of definite boundaries and the arrangement of differences in a fixed hierarchy').[52] The idea of Brahmanical domination was missing in the framework of the Hindu Samaj Samannay, and even the principles of power relations—the chief component of a caste society—remained weak and inactive. It was unique in character, exclusive in its approach. It was a flexible model of cultural homogenization without disturbing the status quo of caste. Very neutrally, Swami Pranavananda rejected any radical social transformation, especially the abolition of the caste system. Emphasis was placed on a mode of adjustment and agreement between the castes without encouraging any drastic change (Swami Vedananda 1395 BS, 347).

At different Hindu conferences,[53] the *sangha* raised proposals for the establishment of schools for celibates, hostels for pupils, charity night schools, training schools for Hindu campaigners, free libraries, gymnasiums, charitable medical centres, agricultural gardens, museums for village crafts, etc. Mainly in the districts of Jessore, Khulna, Bakarganj, Faridpur and 24 Parganas, Swami Pranavananda started all-round works among the Namasudras, Paundra-Kshatriyas, Yugis, Rajbanshis and Kaivartas. Interestingly, almost all these castes had already shown strong aspirations for rising high up the social ladder; however, the Namasudras[54] for the first time expressed their independent desire to have more exposure in the political field. The Depressed Classes, those who agitated for special social and economic treatment from the colonial government, also demanded a higher *varna* status to prove their Hindu-ness. Hindu organizations, which had always been in a kind of denial about the modern colonial space, obviously found this trend of the Depressed Classes seeking upward mobility a tricky prospect. For Swami Pranavananda, the lower castes' demands for upward mobility and related aspirations were very much alarming, since all these tendencies were coming out of the colonial package. However, the ideological hegemony of caste did not disappear with the changes. The growth of an autonomous public space or the leanings towards occupational mobility might have resulted in some subsidiary changes in the normative structure of caste, but the issues of cultural divergence remained safely ingrained in the narratives of tradition and practice.

It is also important to note that most of the respondents of Swami Pranavananda were from the lower-caste peasantry, particularly untouchables from remote villages. They had very restricted avenues of mobility in the industrial city space[55]; however, they did not remain entirely untouched by the new ideas generated by the waves of colonial modernity. By 1935, more than 20 Milan Mandirs had been established to facilitate large-scale *seva* programmes by the BSS, especially at places where the Depressed Classes were residing in large numbers. In the districts of Khulna, Jessore, Barisal and 24 Parganas, BSS centres were opened. Hadi, Muchi, Poundra-Kshariya, Namasudra, Bagdi, Kapali—all these castes were simply addressed as 'Hindu' (*Pranav* 1342 BS, 226–227, report 4–8) and brought under initiatives for economic self-dependence or self-help. The *seva* projects of the BSS aspired to impart social citizenship to the Depressed Classes. However, the idea of social citizenship might have been a puzzle for those living in a stagnant world of poverty, illiteracy and superstitions. In most of the cases, any movement for social mobility and creation of avenues for social acceptability was initiated only by a group of caste members who were wealthy and aspired for power; the rest of the community remained mostly silent or indifferent. In the villages, one could see how the interdependence between caste and economic conditions indicated the actual tensions of unequal land distribution and indebtedness. The articulate sections of these castes had access to the nationalist political domain, but the backward sections failed miserably in this regard. The BSS attracted large numbers of lower-caste disciples from the Bengal countryside, where the popularity of the caste associations and the nationalist appeal of the so-called upper-caste bodies, like the Congress, were very poor.[56] Surprisingly, the urban upper-caste Hindus remained more or less reluctant to join the BSS for a considerable period of time. The ideal of the Hindu Samaj Samannay might have appeared less impressive, since the movement did not offer any agency to these people. However, cross-sections of the urban middle-class Hindus responded to the call of the *sangha* at a later date under forced political circumstances. It must be mentioned here that Swami Pranavananda happened to be an ardent Hindu nationalist but not in the regular sense of the term. He did not speak on the popular themes like 'threatening Muslims' or 'alien Christians' ever, but he rather preferred to make the Hindus think in terms of a 'real' unity with the Muslims.

Espousal of the cause of Hindutva in a Muslim-majority province might have encountered difficulties in regard to defining Hindutva's relation with the Muslims. Talking about Hindu–Muslim relations without being flattered by any political interest seems challenging; however, the early nationalists in Bengal did not pay any serious attention to the question. Such men as Sri Aurobindo, Bipin Chandra Pal, Bankim Chandra Chattopadhyay and Swami Vivekananda were confident enough to carry on the nationalist mission within the spiritual–cultural worldview of Hinduism. As noted by Partha Chatterjee (1994),[57] the Indians asserted their superiority in the inner-spiritual domain and continued to dream of hegemony, if not dominance, in the inner-spiritual sphere. Nationalism for them did not mean engaging in a political battle against imperialism but meant preserving their cultural–spiritual intelligence, and politics, therefore, firmly resembled a voluntary discourse to defend and protect these resources. Until and unless the Hindu–Muslim question clashed with this interest, the early Bengali nationalists took a more or less sceptical position on the issue.[58] The same interplay of thoughts fortified the Hindu nationalist visions of Hindutva in Bengal. Such visions were developed not in response to the political uncertainties faced by the Hindus under a separate electorate system or in agreement with the 'enemy other' theory to validate one's identity against the other[59] but through an urge to preserve the civilizational resources to provide a common nationality, a cultural inheritance to all Hindus, irrespective of sectarian and casteist affiliations. The territorial–racial substance of a Hindu nation[60] did not count much in this narrative of Hindutva, whereas in the most popular formulation of Hindutva by V. D. Savarkar the ideological edifice of a 'common holy land' and 'common blood' has been established.[61] Both of these factors were crucial to exclude and include the 'other' religions in the framework a Hindu nation,[62] while denies any agency to the alternative visions of Hindutva being a category of self-articulation committed to spiritual-cultural insinuations. The racial overtone present in Savarkar's ideas were taken to the extreme by M. S. Golwalkar, a leader of the RSS.[63] Savarkar, being a freedom fighter and an ardent nationalist, strategically deployed the Hindu–Muslim question in the political terrain, while Golwalkar simply pushed the non-Hindus to the point of adopting the Hindu culture and language, keeping the Hindu religion at high esteem and living in surrender to the Hindu nation (Golwalkar 1939, 47–48). Golwalkar eventually became the mastermind of Hindu nationhood in India—he established one overriding pattern of political Hindutva by putting all its earlier traits into a puzzled outlandish zone. It happened to be a purposeful move to establish the supremacy of Hindu nationhood equal to nationalist regeneration. As a natural corollary to his propositions, Golwalkar trivialized the importance of 'democracy' as articulated by the Indian national movement and concluded, '…we have almost completely lost sight of our true Hindu Nationhood, in our wild goose chase after the phantasm [sic] of founding a "really" democratic "State" in the country' (Golwalkar 1939, 14).

If the rhetoric of a 'true Hindu nationhood' constituted the quintessential plea for nationalist reconstruction, then all that has been done as *seva* by the RSS must reflect such understandings. RSS's claim of being influenced by the Ramakrishna Mission should be viewed as ambiguous, since Golwalkar, in spite of having received initiation from Swami Akhandananda of the Ramakrishna order, did not get any official recognition from the Ramakrishna Mission. When considering Golwalkar's perceptions of spirituality and social activism, it becomes important to note that this man left all his official duties assigned to him by Hedgewar in the RSS just to pursue the life of an ascetic under the Ramakrishna Mission in the year 1936. His brief stay in Bengal and coming into contact with Swami Akhandananda reveal little of the actual relationship shared by the RSS and the Mission. However, after the death of Swami Akhandananda, Golwalkar returned to RSS and continued to live like a sadhu/guru,[64] with a strong humanitarian inclination towards social activism. Beckerlegge has pointed out that it was Hedgewar, not Golwalkar, who promoted the *seva* activities of the RSS from the very beginning, while Golwalkar only developed the practices of *seva* in specific circumstances that helped the strategic interests of the RSS. Charges of being involved in the assassination of Mahatma Gandhi forced the RSS to face an official ban, which tarnished its image to a great extent. Organized *seva* activities helped the RSS recover its reputation after the ban was lifted in 1949, and the changing pattern of *seva* came out as a 'strategy to rehabilitate the RSS and its affiliates in the eye of Indian politicians and people'.[65] Whatever its intentions were in initiating organized *seva* activities all over the country, the RSS nevertheless picked up frequent references from Swami Vivekananda[66] to provide a philosophical rationale to the spirit of *seva* as worshipping the living divine within men. However, for Golwalkar, the living God denoted not an individual man but the entire nation, that is, the Hindu nation. Vivekananda's ideas were tailored in the RSS vocabulary to fit into a predetermined narrative of *seva*, which turned out to be politically effective and ideologically tantamount to promoting Hindutva on a shared narrative.

In reality, the universal–spiritual essence of Hindutva was missing in the politically motivated notion of Hindutva by the RSS. Selective adoption of Vivekananda's ideas was evident in the RSS discourse of physical training programmes on character building, and also for man's attainment of education to revitalize the Hindu nation. But for a section of the RSS ideologues (Beckerlegge 2000, 54–55), RSS's search for Hindutva was driven not by any liberal–spiritual quest but to teach the internal and external 'enemies' a lesson, and to bring the poor and the oppressed people into the fold of a Hindu Rashtra. The political overtone of excluding the Muslims and Christians from the purview of the so-called Hindu Rashtra kept the observers fascinated about the changing facades of *seva*, which no more remained tethered to identity formation but became a paradigm for regulating the political representation of a Hindu *sangathan*. Key to this understanding is the difference between the variants of Hindutva, celebrated either as a universal–spiritual category of nationalist reconstruction or as a political–mechanical proposition to calibrate a future 'utopia' of a Hindu Rashtra.[67] Both these approaches claimed to be legitimate traditions of Hindu nationalism, which adopted theatrically separate but culturally conducive frameworks of operation; however, the former had often been denied any motivational spirit under reprehensive politics and remained dormant with respect to the latter. Having said that, it is important to look for the binaries of their relationship at a regional setting or to trace out the manners by which they transformed their traditions in the normative terrains of spiritual/political, regional/national or mainstream/local.

Explorations surrounding these approaches could best be understood in reference to the relationship shared by the BSS and the RSS–VHP in Bengal. Bengali Hindus did not ever become much exposed to the thoughts of Savarkar or Golwalkar and almost took a sceptical stand to the ideology of political Hindutva and Hindu right-wing politics (Dasgupta 2020, 2–7). Proposal of Hindutva on the basis of counting Hindu heads for election purposes did not ever become a useful category in Bengal and created enough tensions at both the non-political and political spaces of Hindu nationalism. The *seva* organizations like BSS might have come forward as the mouthpiece of Hindu solidarity in times of communal disputes, but BSS collected lots of accolades from each and every section of the society because of the secular–universal nature of its *seva* projects. Unlike the sadhus from the Ramakrishna Mission, Swami Pranavananda did not adopt a highly incredulous attitude towards politics[68]; his open discourses on the question of protecting Hindu-minority interests hardly showed any clandestine desire but extended his symbolic support to the Hindu Mahasabha in the decade before the partition. Despite this, when he welcomed Dr Syama Prasad Mookerjee as the president of BSS's annual Hindu conference in 1938, it created enough buzz in the political circles and helped the Hindu Mahasabha get some amount of popular legitimacy among the Hindu electorate. The association of the Mahasabha with the BSS in the 1940s earned the former greater reputation, while causing severe damage to the public image of the latter.[69]

The so-called Hindutva proponents in Bengal left no stone unturned to project the Mahasabha and later the RSS as a natural ally of the BSS. As mentioned earlier, in Bengal, the BSS pulled together a considerable amount of its non-Bengali support base from the Marwari trading communities, who contributed a lot to RSS–VHP's fundraising programmes in one way or the other. It is utterly surprising to note that in post-partition West Bengal, the BSS- and RSS–VHP-type organizations retained their distinctions purely at a cultural level; however, they shared their respective platforms when issues of mutual concern conflated one another. The RSS was not a popular political choice in West Bengal; not even the VHP generated a considerable amount of sensitivity in the political mainstream of Bengal, while the BSS continued to enjoy an autonomous existence as the flag-bearer of Hindu consciousness for long. The BSS expressed its strong dissatisfaction with the culture of political militancy promoted by the RSS–VHP and denied any association with these organizations. Evolving as a spiritually motivated *seva* organization since the 1920s, the BSS functioned mostly on selected aspects of Hindu identity formation, carefully discarding any direct political interest. If the taking of political interest indicated boosting the cause of Hindu numerical representation or paying heed to socio-economic propaganda, the BSS-type *seva* organizations certainly had nothing to offer. Had there been no such conditions or criteria to judge what makes a public organization politically active, Swami Pranavananda would definitely be called a conscious agent of Hindu politics in an alternative way. What makes this quite ironic is the fact that Swami Pranavananda's occasional interaction with the Mahasabha or capitalization of a moral, masculine Hindu militancy for self-protection brought him harsh criticisms from all corners.

The shadowy presence of the Mahasabha–RSS proponents inside the close-knit circle of the BSS showed the swami in a bad light, and all the *seva* projects of the BSS were made to look like an extension of RSS-type activities in disguise. In states outside of Bengal, the BSS worked in regular cooperation with the RSS–VHP nexus, in order to put forward its voice in the greater Hindu arena by completely jeopardizing its endeavours for the lower castes practised in the home state.[70] In the case of Bengal too, the RSS–VHP made several successful attempts of penetration into the BSS and continued to play hide-and-seek. Swami Pranavananda happily received Dr Syama Prasad Mookerjee as the most proficient leader of the Bengali Hindus mainly because of the latter's competency and leadership skills, reflected on both regional and national platforms. The Mahasabha leaders simply took it as the symbol of a social mandate received from a highly acclaimed sadhu who had been enjoying power and authority over cross-sections of the Hindu society. In later years, the RSS and VHP too claimed their intimacy with the BSS while organizing similar kinds of *seva* work, especially during natural calamities, and tried to orchestrate a kind of partnership with the BSS over specific issues.

The Hindutva movement of the BSS itself remained lackadaisical to various issues. It failed to incorporate the agrarian aspects of caste and never challenged the pattern of hierarchy existing in the system. The basic ambivalence of the BSS on *seva* as an instrument to meet certain sociopolitical goals under circumstantial compulsions indicated the inner conflicts of the colonial society. The metaphors of a Hindu *samaj* presented many contextual binaries over caste and class, and no autonomous collective space was perpetuated for the sake of a predetermined narrative.[71] The shift in the position of the BSS from idealism to reality, or its adoption of programmes similar to those of the RSS for creating a Hindu militia for Hindu self-defence, reflected the amount of suspicion and anxiety stemming mostly from growing political uncertainty under a tense communal situation. The BSS lost its appeal of being a solely spiritual *seva* organization in post-partition Bengal and strived to recover its image afterwards.

Having said that, it makes sense to pose the question: why did most of the sadhus working in the public domain always end up fetching some amount of 'pseudo-political' authority of their own, and how did they handle the subtle transition from being non-political to becoming political in the wider context of social accountability? Swami Pranavananda might have successfully translated spiritual attributes of selfless service or *niskama karma* in a nation building project, but all the while he missed strong middle-class support for his ideology. Bengali bhadralok chose to be indifferent to or irresponsible for the issues of Hindu identity formation or Hindu consolidation from the bottom, and they accordingly rejected the idea of a *samaj samannay* through mobilization of the lower castes. It took many efforts on the part of the Hindu Mahasabha to gain a foothold in Bengal, and only after Dr Mookerjee took charge of the Bengal branch did the Mahasabha type of politics gain some visibility in Bengali politics. Such ideas as *shuddhi*, removal of untouchability and restrictions on temple entry hardly had any takers in Bengal; it was merely because of the personal charisma or the very bhadralok background of Mookerjee that a few high-caste individuals got attracted to the Mahasabha politics, that too only in the decade before the partition.

Not going into the merits and demerits of the BSS, it is evident that Swami Pranavananda, being an ascetic or a sadhu, stood committed to the policy of non-involvement in active politics, but an array of his activities in the public domain, as well as his messages to his followers, reveal the patterns through which Hindu nationalist traditions survived and flourished independent of high politics in early 20th century Bengal. It was not like transforming political Hindutva into a cultural one, rather opening up of an alternative site of 'observing' Hindutva at the periphery of the society. Swami Pranavananda symbolized a kind of peripherization of Hindutva, whereby providing material aid or spiritual bliss to the suffering poor might have worked as a mobilization strategy for Hindu subject formation. Herein lies the crux of the explanation for why the politically neutral sadhus from *seva* organizations never disapproved of being provided political agency by the society at large, or why the Hindutva forces always found the latter beneficial for the success of their own brand of politics.

NOTES

1. Christophe Jaffrelot marked the rise of Hindu nationalism as a distinct ideology since the latter half of the 19th century in northern and north-western parts of India and recognized it as a form of political mobilization in the 1920s. Hindu nationalism has often been identified with communalism; scholars, like John Zavos, however, specified communalism as a historical condition, not an ideology. Hindu nationalism might have informed the condition of communalism but kept its existence separate from communal articulations. For a detailed discussion, see Christophe Jaffrelot, *The Hindu Nationalist Movement in India 1925 to the 1990s* (New Delhi: Viking-Penguin India, 1996); Christophe Jaffrelot, 'Hindu Nationalism: Strategic Syncretism in Ideology Building', *Economic and Political Weekly* 20, nos. 12–13 (March 1993): 517–524; John Zavos, 'Searching for Hindu Nationalism in Modern Indian History: Analysis of Some Early Ideological Developments', *Economic and Political Weekly* 34, no. 32 (7–13 August 1999): 2269–2276.
2. Christophe Jaffrelot, 'Hindu Nationalism as a Social Welfare Stratergy: Seva Bharati as an Educational Agency', in *The Sangh Parivar: A Reader*, ed. C. Jaffrelot (Oxford: OUP, 2006), 212.
3. C. A. Watt, *Serving the Nation: Cultures of Service, Association, and Citizenship in Colonial India* (Oxford: OUP, 2005); Jaffrelot, 'Hindu Nationalism'.
4. Mapping the shifting status of *seva* in the early 20th century seems to be challenging; however, it was evident that the Brahmanical ideal of *dana* was transformed into service for all, mostly though *seva* associations. The associational functioning of *seva* brought different actors and organizations into service, and these associations stared working at both the regional and national levels. The proliferation of the terms such as *samaj*, *sabha*, samiti

and society in the late 19th century indicated the shifting patterns of *seva* activities in different parts of India. Susan Baily, 'Hindu Modernisers and the "Public" Arena: Indigenous Critiques of Caste in Colonial India', in *Swami Vivekananda and the Modernisation of Hinduism*, ed. William Radice (Delhi: OUP, 1998), 92–137.

5. In Sanskrit, the noun 'guru' means a teacher in the sense of one who imparts transcendental knowledge or spiritual wisdom. The guru is one who dispels the darkness of ignorance. An iconic example is the dialogue between Krishna and his friend Arjuna in the Bhagavad Gita. A guru awakens dormant spiritual knowledge within the pupil. Gurus are respected people who are deemed to have what might be called saintly qualities. The true guru is characterized in the Upanishads in terms of five signs that become apparent in the disciple: knowledge flourishes, sorrow diminishes, joy wells up without reason, abundance dawns and all of a person's talents become manifest. (Philip Sheldrake, *Sprituality: A Guide for the Perplexed* [London: Bloomsbury Academic, 2014], 135–140) https://www.bloomsburycollections.com/book/spirituality-a-guide-for-the-perplexed/.
6. Gurus have been identified with several characteristics; however, according to Swami Vivekananda, 'a true guru should understand the spirit of the scriptures, have a pure character and be free from sin, and should be selfless, without desire for money and fame'. Sheldrake, *Spirituality: A Guide for the Perplexed*, 142.
7. Ketan Alder, *Arenas of Service and the Development of the Hindu Subject in India* (Unpublished PhD Thesis, University of Manchester, School of Arts, Languages and Culture, 2015), 24–27.
8. The claim of universality present in Hindu philanthropy comes from the thoughts of Vedantic Hinduism, sowing the seeds of a new syncretic culture, integrating the best from all other religions for the realization of the supreme Truth, 'moving towards one common universal goal'—nationalist reconstruction. The universalist presuppositions of Hinduism are evident in Aurobindo's ideas of 'syncretic universalism' and Bipin Chandra Pal's 'federation of cultures'. Peter Heehs, 'Bengali Religious Nationalism and Communalism', *International Journal of Hindu Studies* 1, no. 1 (April 1997): 129–130.
9. Carey Anthony Watt, in his study on the impact of philanthropic work in the early 1990s by Hindu organizations in North India, pointed out that the ideas of *sanyasa*, dharma, *seva* and other organic Hindu concepts conflated well the organized social service traditions mostly because of the fact that Indians, frustrated with colonial politics, sought to engage in public life through these organizations, and an associational culture had been proliferated by virtue of money circulation in this sector. See, Watt, *Serving the Nation*, 120.
10. Secularism, translated as *dharma-nirapeksata*, finds in roots in Europe. After the end of the Thirty Years' War in Europe in 1648, transfer of the properties of the Church to the princes denoted the process of secularization, while during the age of European Enlightenment, scientific, rationalist

and technological approaches pervaded the popular mindset, and Europe proposed a kind of superiority of the 'political' domain over the 'religious' sphere. This was the process that emphasized the relegation of religion to the private sphere and brought politics to the public sphere—a fundamental characteristic of secularism in the West. See, P. L. Berger, *The Social Reality of Religion* (London: Allen Lane, 1973), 113.

11. Postmodern European rationalist thinking often claimed universalism to be a kind of common standard imposed on the weak by the strong. Therefore, claiming one set of traditions universal makes way for homogenizing the differences through creating their dominance over others. Heehs, 'Bengali Religious Nationalism and Communalism', 130.
12. Hindu spirituality has been discussed from different perspectives. Because of the magnitude of the various expressions, it has been idolized as a meeting point of different traditions, rather than undergoing a single religious interpretation. Krishna Sivaraman, 'Introduction', in *Hindu Spirituality: Vedas Through Vedanta*, ed. Krishna Sivaraman (New Delhi: Motilal Benarasidas, 1995), xviii.
13. Explaining the nature of *moksha*, Dwijadas Dutta in a mindful piece elaborated, 'The attainment of Moksha depends upon certain preparations (sadhana)—among the most important of which is the performance of really good works without the desire of any outward rewards. It comes by a process of natural growth. In this respect Moksha differs from other schemes of Salvation; it does not come from without, as an extraneous reward for certain acts of merit, but grows endogenous, as it were, from the principle of our common humanity, acts of merit only favouring this growth. It is a case of becoming, not of getting something'. Dvijadas Datta, 'Moksha, or the Vedántic Release', *The Journal of the Royal Asiatic Society of Great Britain and Ireland,* New Series, 20, no. 4 (October 1888): 52.
14. According to Acharya Kripalani, one of the close associates of Gandhi, the 'Rama invoked by Gandhi with his dying breath was not the historical or the mythological Rama but rather the highest Self. So the Rama in Gandhi's thought is at one with the highest Self which in turn is identical with Truth. Given that no hard and fast line of demarcation is drawn between the Self and Truth here, it might be argued that this is consistent with Advait in teaching concerning the identity of Brahman-Atman, namely, that the Self within is at one with the substratum of the universe. For Gandhi, therefore, as for Sankara, to know the Self is to know Truth or Brahman and to identify with the Self is to identify with Truth'. *Truth is God*, (Ahmedabad, 1955), 12; *The Selected Works of Mahatma Gandhi* (VI Ahmedabad, 1968), 108, Quoted in Glyn Richards, 'Gandhi's Concept of Truth and the Advaita Tradition', *Religious Studies* 22, no. 1 (March 1986): 3–4.
15. The Gita places a high value on social stability. It sanctions the social order and allows the idea of duty to be regulated by the caste structure and different stages of life. 'Its doctrine of Niskama-Karma or disinterested action

can be understood only in the light of the ultimate end which is conceived as Moksa. Moksa means liberation of the empirical self from all bondage to the not-self—a total emancipation from the phenomenal world culminating in the realization of the self as pure Atman'. For an illuminating understanding of the philosophy of the Gita, see D. C. Mathur, 'The Concept of Action in the Bhagvad-Gita', *Philosophy and Phenomenological Research* 35, no. 1 (September 1974): 34–35. For a detailed discussion of Vivekananda and Gita, see K. Nagappa Gowda, *The Bhagawat Gita and the Nationalist Discourse* (New Delhi: OUP, 2011), 90–123.

16. *Sthitaprajna* is the ideal man in the Gita. 'The essential nature of such an ideal man is detachment, equipoise (samatva) and imperturbability while engaged in activity of the in tensest kind. The Gita believes that all action—good, bad, or indifferent—fetters the self because of the self's involvement in and desire for the fruits of action. If, therefore, the self is to attain the final goal of moksa and yet not withdraw from the field of action, it should firstly, perform all its 'duties (dharma) conscientiously in the light of its svabhava and svadharma; secondly action must be done in a spirit of nonattachment'. Mathur, 'The Concept of Action in the Bhagvad-Gita', 35.
17. Vivekananda held that the pursuit of *niskama karma* should be accessible to each and every person of the society. In his own understanding, 'Let every man and woman and child, without respect of caste or birth, weakness or strength, hear and learn that behind the strong and the weak, behind the high and the low, behind everyone, there is that Infinite Soul, asserting the infinite possibility and the infinite capacity of all to become great and good…' (*The Mission of the Vedanta,* Complete Works of Swami Vivekananda, Calcutta, Mayavati Advaita Ashrama, vol. iii, 1995, twenty first print, 193–197). Echoing this spirit of seeing the Supreme Soul everywhere, Vivekananda asserted, 'Serve the living god! God comes to you in the blind, in the halt, in the poor, in the weak, in the diabolical. What a glorious chance for you to worship' (*Krishna*, The Complete Works of Swami Vivekananda, Advaita Ashrama (A publication branch of Ramakrishna Math, Belur Math), Calcutta,1907–1997, vol. I, 441–442).
18. The link between the discursive practises of *seva* and Hindu nationalism has been illustrated to an extent by Ketan Alder in regard to the religious traditions of service contributing to the social construction of Hindu and national identities, a process that occurred, 'outside of the explicit nationalist political campaigns of the period and inside seemingly non-political associations such as religious reform and *seva* projects'. Alder, *Arenas of Service and the Development of the Hindu Subject in India*, 25.
19. Professor John Zavos described *sangathan* as a means of consolidating Hindu society, of unifying Hinduism, in response to the perceived unity of Indian Muslims. *Sangathan* was a deep-rooted idea in Hindu nationalism. This Sanskrit word has been translated as 'organisation, formation, constitution and composition of the Hindu society'. John Zavos, *Sangathan: The Pursuit*

of a Hindu Ideal in Colonial India: The Idea of Organisation in the Emergence of Hindu Nationalism 1870–1930 (PhD Thesis, University of Bristol, Department of Theology and Religious Studies, September 1997), 49–50. Also see, M. Chaturvedi and B. N. Tiwari, *A Practica.1 Hindi–English Dictionary* (Delhi: National Publishing House, 1970), 641.

20. The political implications of *seva* could be traced mostly to the Rashtriya Swayamsevak Sangh (RSS)-led *seva* projects with greater educational, economic and social initiatives. Such scholars as Christophe Jaffrelot, Nair and Bano discussed the strategic impotence of the RSS-led *seva* projects, pursuing its agenda of constricting a Hindu Rashtra by assimilating the marginal populations. Taking a slight diversion, Sumit Sarkar offered another framework to look into the Hindu nationalist *seva* projects as a tactical response to RSS's political isolation caused mostly because of the popularity of Nehruvian secularism and also to the waves of hatred and destruction created after Gandhi's assassination. Sumit Sarkar, 'Educating the Children of the Hindu Rashtra: Notes on RSS Schools', In *The Sangh Parivar: A Reader*, ed. C. Jaffrelot (Oxford: OUP, 2006), 198. Also see, Jaffrelot, 'Hindu Nationalism as a Social Welfare Strategy'; P. Nair and M. Bano, *Faith-based Organisations in South Asia: Historical Evolution, Current Status and Nature of Interaction with the State* (Working Paper 12, Birmingham School of Religions and Development, 2006).
21. Alder, *Arenas of Service and the Development of the Hindu Subject in India*, 50.
22. Hindu textual references to *dana* or donation are vast and wide-ranging. These texts refer to who is suitable to engage in *dana*, what the ideal *dana* should be and what the gains of *dana* are. Three primary categories of *dana* have been mentioned: *nitya-dana*, that which is given daily; *naimittika-dana*, that given at specified times; and *kāmya-dana*, that which is given with an aim to fulfil a desire. P. V. Kane, *History of the Dharmasastra*, Vol 2, Pt. 2 (Poona: Bhandarkar Oriental Research Institute, 1974), 841–847.
23. Western academic literature has shown tremendous enthusiasm in relating the idea of *seva* to the Advaita philosophy. Denigrating the ontology of Sankara's Advaita, which stressed on negating the world as *maya*, Western scholarship emphasized much the neo-Vedantins' or the neo-Advaitins' ideas of engaging with the world, searched for the Western and indigenous influences on the neo-Vedantins' ideal of *seva* and expanded the scopes of analysis on the philosophical propositions working behind the *seva* organizations in reference to modern Hinduism. For a detailed analysis of the question from different perspectives, see, Wilhelm Halbfass, *Philology and Confrontation: Paul Hacker on Traditional and Modern Vedanta* (Albany, NY: State University of New York Press, 1995); Wilhelm Halbfass, *Tradition and Reflection: Explorations in Indian Thought* (Albany, NY: State University of New York Press, 1991); Andrew J. Nicholson, *Unifying Hinduism: Philosophy and Identity in Indian Intellectual History* (New York: Columbia University Press, 2010); Gwilym Beckerlegge, 'The Rashtriya Swayamsevak Sangh's Tradition of Selfless Service', in *The Politics of Cultural Mobilization in India*, eds. John

Zavos, Andrew Wyatt, and Vernon Hewitt (New Delhi: Oxford Press, 2004), 105–135; Andrew O. Fort, *Jīvanmukti in Transformation: Embodied Liberation in Advaita and Neo-Vedanta* (Albany, NY: State University of New York Press, 1998); Carl T. Jackson, *Vedanta for the West: The Ramakrishna Movement in the United States* (Bloomington, IN: Indiana University Press, 1994).

24. Christian missionary activities were crucial to the development of the understanding of a modern Hindu identity engraved with meanings of service towards the vulnerable poor. 'Christianity' also became important to the reorganization of the Hindu community and social emancipation. The real implications of the Christian missionary service projects have been discussed by K. W. Jones, *Arya Dharm: Hindu Consciousness in 19th Century Punjab* (London: University of California Press, 1976); C. A. Watt, *Serving the Nation: Cultures of Service, Association, and Citizenship in Colonial India* (Oxford: OUP, 2005); John Zavos, 'Defending Hindu Tradition: Sanatana Dharma as a Symbol of Orthodoxy in Colonial India', *Religion* 31, no. 2 (2005): 109–123; Jaffrelot, 'Hindu Nationalism: Strategic Syncretism in Ideology Building', 517–524.

25. It is extremely difficult to define the term 'spirituality' in relation to religion. van der Veer describes it as 'wide-ranging nineteenth century transformation, a historical rupture'. The word 'spirituality' is derived from the Latin *spiritualitas*, which itself is a translation of the Greek noun *pneuma* meaning spirit. Spirituality is closely associated with religion 'but not exclusively contained by it'. Spirituality criticizes religion for the latter's being patriarchal and dogmatic, hierarchical and authoritative. It is religion that in fact distinguishes between the sacred and the secular, while spirituality as a holistic approach to life includes politics, the environment and sociocultural experiences, encompassing a universal world view. To use Peter Berger's phrase, spirituality may not have a sacred canopy, or any definite religious meaning; however, the unifying attributes of spirituality must be acknowledged.

 Brimadevi van Niekerk, 'Religion and Spirituality: What are the Fundamental Differences?', p. 10. *HTSTeologieseStudies/TheologicalStudies,/* Users/Intel/Downloads/Religion_and_spirituality_What_are_the_fundamental.pdf (accessed 22 February 2019); J. S. Jensen, *What is Religion*? (Durham: Acumen Publishing Ltd., 2014), 140–146; P. L. Berger, *The Sacred Canopy: Elements of a Sociology of Religion* (New York: Doubleday Garden City, 1969); U. King, *The Search For Spirituality: Our Global Quest for a Spiritual Life* (Norwich: Canterbury Press, 2009); van der Veer, Peter, 'Spirituality in Modern Society', *Social Research* 76, no. 4 (2009): 1097.

26. Partha Chatterjee and Sumit Sarkar repeatedly drew attention to the heterogeneous structure of 19th-century nationalism in Bengal with a systematic unfolding of nationalist thoughts and a high-class Hindu culture. This mode of discussion brings up the new narrative of reviewing the ideologies and movements that had been castigated traditionally as spiritual or religious.

The importance of these ideas in promoting a national consciousness in India received scant attention in the mainstream academia primarily because of their inclusion in the project of political Hindutva in later years. However, contemporary studies on the Hindutva movement have focused on the critical relationship shared by late-19th-century and early-20th-century spiritual/religious ideas with the development of a nationalist identity in India. Two books are relatively important in this context: Partha Chatterjee, *Nation and Its Fragments: Colonial and Postcolonial Histories* (Princeton, NJ: Princeton University Press, 1993); Sumit Sarkar, *Writing Social History* (New Delhi: Oxford University Press, 1997).

27. Details of its *seva* programmes are provided in the small pamphlets published by the *sangha* at regular intervals. See, *Activities of the Bharat Seva Asram Sangha (illustrated) ... in the year 1933-34-35.* Bhārata Sebāśrama Saṅgha (Calcutta, India), 1935 (British Library, Indian Office Library Records).
28. For biographic details on Swami Pranavananda, see, Swami Vedananda, *The Prophet of the Age: A Short Life Sketch of Acharya Swami Pranavanandaji Founder of Bharat Sevashram Sangha* (Calcutta: Swami Nirmalananda, [n.d.]). (British Library, India Office Library Records).
29. Swami Nirmalananda, *Śrīgurusaṅge, Śrīguruprasaṅge*—1915 (Kalikātā: Bhārata Sebāśrama Saṅgha, 1397 [1991]). (British Library, India Office Library Records).
30. To get an overall understanding of the gender approach of the Bharat Sevashram Sangha (BSS), see, Koushiki Dasgupta, 'Textualing Women as "Hindu": The Bharat Sevashram Sangha Perspective on Hindu Women in Twentieth Century', *The Indian Historical Review* 44, no. 2 (2017): 270–284.
31. Zavos, *Sangathan: The Pursuit of a Hindu Ideal in Colonial India*, 51.
32. Zavos, *Sangathan: The Pursuit of a Hindu Ideal in Colonial India*, 53.
33. Professor A. P. Sen has discussed in length why Hinduism does not claim a 'natural state of existence' unlike the other religions like Islam and Christianity, which assert their lineage to a doctrinal core not determined by any historical or cultural change. He has brought into notice the gap between Hinduism as an intellectual–textual tradition and Hinduism as experienced, lived and practised in everyday affairs. Amiya P. Sen, *Hinduism and the Problem of Self Actualisation in the Colonial Era: Critical Reflections* (South Asia Institute Papers, South Asia Institute, Heidelberg University, Issue 1, 2015). www.sai.uni-heidelberg.de (accessed 12 December 2019).
34. Commenting on the puzzling metamorphosis of the word, 'Hindu,' Robert Frykenberg mentioned, 'Unless by "Hindu" one means nothing more, nor less, than "Indian" (something native to, pertaining to, or found within the continent of India), there has never been any such a thing as a single "Hinduism" or any single "Hindu community" for all of India for that matter, can one find any such thing as a single "Hinduism" or "Hindu-unity" even for any one socio-cultural region of the continent. Furthermore, there er

been any one religion-nor even one system of religions-to which the term du" can accurately be applied. No one so-called religion, moreover, can lay claim to or be defined by the term'. Robert Frykenberg, 'The Emergence of Modern "Hinduism" as a Concept and as an Institution: A Reappraisal with Special Reference to South India', in *Hinduism Reconsidered*, eds. Sontheimer and Kulke (Delhi: Manohar, 1989), 29.

35. The all-pervasive nature of Savarkarism attracted attention from scholars. Chetan Bhatt, one of the early writers on the subject, acknowledged, 'Indeed, the key political ideas of the contemporary Hindutva movement were being articulated by Savarkar and the Hindu Mahasabha some eighty to ninety years ago in virtually identical languages.... The story of Savarkar's revolutionary nationalist and anti-colonial activities and his influence upon early twentieth-century Hindu nationalist movements provides insight into the impact of political Hinduism on several ideological currents within and outside the Indian freedom movement, and which extended well beyond the Gandhian movements that were to become prominent after the 1920s'. Chetan Bhatt, 'From Revolutionary Nationalism to Hindutva', *Hindu Nationalism: Origins, Ideologies and Modern Myths*, ed. Chetan Bhatt (London: Bloomsbury Academic, 2001), 77–78. Bloomsbury Collections.
36. Bhatt, 'From Revolutionary Nationalism to Hindutva', 79.
37. Savarkar, *Hindutva: Who is a Hindu*? 3.
38. For the teachings of Swami Pranavananda, see, Swami Vedananda, eds., *Sangha Geeta: Inspiring Teachings of Jagadguru Swami Pranavanandaji Maharaj* (London: Bharat Sevashram Sangha, Sangha, 2007) (Swami Nirliptananda on behalf of the BSS); Swami Vedananda, *Ideals of Indian Education and Culture. Acharya Swami Pranavananda Memorial Volume*. (2nd edition.) [By various authors.] (Calcutta, 1967). (British Library, India Office Library Records).
39. In the caste vocabulary, the word *jati* stands for an occupational unit in the society. In this case, the phrase 'Hindu jati' followed the collective construction of identity, even though vaguely defined. The collective nomenclature of *jati* follows the idea of Bankim Chandra Chattopadhyay, who used the term *jati* to refer to caste, race, nationality, religious community and linguistic community. See Sudipta Kaviraj, *The Unhappy Consciousness: Bankimchandra Chattopadhyay and the Formation of the Nationalist Discourse in India* (New York: Oxford University Press, 1995), 112–113.
40. The idea of ascetic masculinity contested the orientalist visions of an other-worldly, passive Hindu and emphasized a unique combination of manliness and celibacy essential for nation building in India. It challenged the colonial understanding of the wandering ascetic Hindu mendicancy producing indolent parasitic subjects linked to a lack of vigour, strength and consciousness. The 19th-century ideal of ascetic nationalist masculinity altered the colonial construction of Hindus being indifferent to their social responsibilities and

instead led them to conceive the new ascetic Hindu as someone who was self-controlled, disciplined, strong and dedicated to the service of the nation.

41. Kaviraj, *The Unhappy Consciousness*, 34, note 30; Zavos, *Sangathan: The Pursuit of a Hindu Ideal in Colonial India*.
42. Bandyopadhyay, *Caste, Protest and Identity in Colonial India*, 3–4.
43. Bandyopadhyay, *Caste, Protest and Identity in Colonial India*, 14
44. At an assembly of *sangha* monks at Bajitpur in 1923, the fundamental objectives of the *sangha* were declared. *Brahmachari* Binode took *sanyasa* in 1924, along with his *brahmachari* friends. From then onwards, he was called Swami Pranavananda—*acharya* and *gurumaharaj* in the popular parlance of the *sangha*. The title *acharya* entrusted him with the responsibility of a 'guru' or the supreme guiding/enlightening spirit behind the *sangha*. Strict disciplinary and customary principles were taken by the *sangha* to maintain its strength and cohesiveness among the workers. The *sangha* in fact emerged as a monolithic monastic organization where obedience to the leader or the guru became obligatory and essential for the disciples. In the rigid structure of the *sangha*, the guru was declared similar to the supreme God and the main *shakti* or pillar of the organization. For the principles and messages of the *sangha*, see, Swami Pranabananda, *The Sangha Geeta* (Calcutta: Bharat Sevashram Sangha, 1967). (It is a collection of the speeches, letters and advice by the *sangha* leader/guru.)
45. Jordens, *Swami Shradhananda: His Life and Causes*, 134.
46. Mukherjee, U. N., *Hinduism and the Coming Census: Christianity and Hinduism* (1911).
47. Swami Shraddhanand, the chief protagonist of the Sangathan movement, declared in a speech in Patna in 1925 that his encounter with U. N. Mukherji and reading of the *Dying Race* (1909) had motivated him to start the *sangathan*. *Amrita Bazar Patrika*, 17 June 1925.

    However, justifying the expansion of the *sangathan*, Swami Shraddhanand argued that 'a united Hindu community was essential for maintaining peaceful relations with Muslims. He tried to dispel the fears of the Muslims by saying that the Sangathan was not aimed against them. But Shuddhi and Sangathan were increasingly being viewed by many Hindus in Punjab as powerful symbols of the Hindu communitarian consciousness of this phase when it was acquiring chauvinistic communal overtones and Hindu identity was being projected as a nation'. K. L. Tuteja and O. P. Grewal, 'Emergence of Hindu Communal Ideology in Early Twentieth Century Punjab', *Social Scientist* 20, nos. 7/8 (July–August 1992): 19; J. T. F. Jordens, *Swami Shradhananda: His Life and Causes* (Delhi: Oxford University Press, 1981), 131–134. Also see the statement of Swami Shraddhananda, *The Tribune*, 23 May 1923.
48. The orientalists, privileging the antiquity and splendour of the classical past, also provided the basics of an Aryan-race theory which for long influenced the caste question in Hindu identity movements. Swami Dayananda

specifically propagated the superiority of the Vedic Aryans in contrast to Islam and Christianity and talked about purification rituals (*shuddhi*) to bring back those who had been converted to other religions. *Shuddhi* is a Sanskrit word that means purification. In religious terminology, it is now applied to: (a) conversion to Hinduism of persons belonging to foreign religions; (b) re-conversion of those who have recently or at a remote period adopted one of the foreign religions; and (c) reclamation, that is, rise in the status of the Depressed Classes. See, Dhanpati Pandey, *Builders of Modern India Swami Dayanand Saraswati* (Publication Divisions of Ministry of Information and Broadcasting, Government of India, 1985), 104.

49. Organized lower-caste movements came to be known in official parlance as 'Depressed Class' movements. See, Bandyopadhyay, *Caste, Protest and Identity in Colonial India*, pp. 14–84.
50. Hitesh Ranjan Sanyal in his influential work described pre-colonial society as not as rigid as to deny professional mobility between the castes and the sub-castes. It was not segregated or completely stiff, rather allowing various degrees of social dynamism for agricultural and commercial purposes. Hitesh Ranjan Sanyal, *Social Mobility in Bengal* (Calcutta: Papyrus, 1981), 18–19.
51. The term 'Depressed Classes' was not used to indicate any caste or creed but commonly used in British records between 1920 and 1937 to denote the people of several oppressed castes. It can be seen in the first volumes of the Bombay Gazetteer published in 1877. It has also been found in the official records between the years 1920 and 1935. It was freely used during round-table conferences and in all commission reports. The census superintendent attempted to create a separate category of 'Depressed Class' during the 1921 census, to include members of those castes that suffered from special disabilities, mainly the untouchables and socially isolated groups; many of these were tribal people admitted into the Hindu fold. For details on the census, see, K. W. Jones, 'Religious Identity and the Indian Census', in *The Census in British India: New Perspective*, ed. N. Gerald Barrier (New Delhi: Manohar, 1981), 73–101.
52. Sarkar, *Writing Social History*, 368–369.
53. The holistic spirit of Hindu Samaj Samannay was defined through a network of different *seva* programmes. In the Hindu Mahasammelan (greater Hindu conference) of Bajitpur (the main centre of the *sangha*) in 1934, a number of resolutions were taken to accelerate the mission. It was decided that: (a) in every district of India one Hindu Milan Mandir (temple of Hindu unity) would be established; (b) in the Hindu pilgrim centres certain reformist programmes would be introduced; (c) steps would be taken to receive the converted Hindus back into the Hindu fold through Vedic rituals; (d) anti-untouchability campaigns would be initiated at the grassroots level; and (e) advice and suggestions would be sought from the Hindu spiritual leaders in favour of the Hindu Samaj Samannay Movement (Swami Yuktananda 1414 BS, 51–54).

54. The Namasudras were an agricultural community concentrated mainly in Faridpur, Jessore, Khulna, Bakarganj, Dhaka and Tippera. They were also found in Pabna, Nadia and Rajshahi. *Census* (1921), 356. *District Gazetteer*, Faridpur, 47. In the latter half of the 19th century, some of them became prominent as peasant cultivators. The condition of those in the western part of Bengal was comparatively worse than that of their eastern counterparts. There were sharp regional variations in their status as 'untouchable'. See, Sekhar Bandyopadhyay, *Caste, Protest and Identity in Colonial India; The Namasudras of Bengal, 1872–1947* (London: Routledge, 1997), 6. Already around 1909, the possibilities of a united front by the Namasudras and the Muslims of Jessore became visible when they decided not to work as servants in the houses of high-caste Hindus. *Bengal District Gazetteers,* p. 50.
55. In the rural space, collective memories at many points connected the lower levels of the rural society with the high-caste society; especially, 'families of low origin', observed Professor Rajat Kanta Ray, 'were tied to families of higher status; and…most commonly these ties of dependence would continue from generation to generation' (Ray 2001, 138).
56. See, Swami Vedananda, 'Sangher Hindu Jati Gathan Andoloner Suchana, 1934, December', in Nirmalananda, *Śrīgurusaṅge, Śrīguruprasaṅge*, 410–441.
57. Chatterjee, *Nation and Its Fragments*, 5–6.
58. Aurobindo wrote, 'Hindu-Mahomedan unity cannot be affected by political adjustments or Congress flatteries. It must be sought deeper down, in the heart and in the mind, for where the causes of disunion are, there the remedies must be sought…. As a political question the Hindu-Mahomedan problem does not interest us at all, as a national problem it is of supreme importance'. Sri Aurobindo, *Sri Aurobindo Birth Centenary Library*, 30 Vols. (Pondicherry: Sri Aurobindo Ashram, 1970–72), Vol. 2, 24.
59. Unlike the superficial apprehensions of the Hindu Mahasabha against the 'enemy other', Swami Pranavananda emphasized maintaining good terms with the Muslims, since social harmony, he believed, was a matter of mutual understanding, not of mutual competition.
60. The Hindu Mahasabha of V. D. Savarkar provided one of the dominant versions of Hindutva in the 1920s, claiming that the Hindus share a 'common nation' (*rashtra*), 'common jati' (race) and a 'common civilization' (*sanskriti*). The first aspect, that is, common *rashtra* or common territory, identified a Hindu as one who regarded the entire subcontinent as his/her motherland/fatherland and holy land. In the words of Savarkar, '…some of us were Aryans and some Anaryans…some of us are Brahmins and some Namasudras or Panchamas; but Brahmanas or Chandalas—we are all Hindus and own a common blood…. We are not only a nation but a jati, a born brotherhood'. V. D. Savarkar, *Hindutva: Who is a Hindu*? (Bombay: Pandit Bakhle Publications Division, 1923), (1999 edition), 4–8.
61. Savarkar, *Hindutva: Who is a Hindu*?, 90–93.

62. According to Savarkar, there were three essential criteria for being a Hindu; these were: (a) paternal descent; (b) common blood or a racial bond called *jati*; and (c) a common civilization or *sanskriti*. This formulation left out the Muslims and Christians, as they were outsiders and did not count India—the land of their birth—as a holy land (Savarkar, *Hindutva: Who is a Hindu*?, 101, 113). Savarkar was obliged to bring in the holy land in his formulation of Hindutva, because he had to find a way to exclude Indian Muslims and Christians. Savarkar, *Hindutva: Who is a Hindu*?, 90, 110.
63. The RSS was established in 1925 by Hedgewar, a member of the Hindu Mahasabha, out of his concern about the Muslim influence inside the Indian National Congress. The RSS has been recognized as a cultural organization of the Hindu right-wing forces and has refrained from direct political involvement. The internal dissensions between the Hindu Mahasabha and the RSS, and especially between Savarkar and Golwalkar, formed the major ideological strands in Hindu nationalism. For details, see, Andersen and Damle, *Brotherhood in Saffron, The Rastriya Swayamsevak Sangh and Hindu Revivalism* (New Delhi: Westview Press, Vistaar Publications, 1987), 36–40. Also see, Gwilym Beckerlegge, 'Saffron and Seva: The Rastriya Swayamsevak Sangh's Appropriation of Swami Vivekananda', in *Hinduism in Public and Private: Reform, Hindutva, Gender and Sampraday*, ed. Anthony Copley (New Delhi: Oxford University Press, 2003), 40–41.
64. In the RSS order, only Golwalkar, a *sarsanghchalak* by designation, is called 'Guruji', and a guru–*sishya* model of training has been implemented within the RSS, with the *swayamsevaks* paying annual guru *dakshina* to their 'guru'. In almost all *sangh*-affiliated organizations, the word 'guru' is frequently used to address someone in a superior position, and such a tradition carries the spiritual legacy of an ancient Hindu nation. Anderson and Damle, *Brotherhood in Saffron*, 37, also, Beckerlegge, 'Saffron and Seva', 59.
65. Beckerlegge, 'Saffron and Seva', 48–49.
66. Beckerlegge pointed out that in Golwalkar's *Bunch of Thoughts*, his teachings are arranged around the proposition of 'Live Positive Dynamic Hinduism'—an idea similar to that of Vivekananda's 'Dynamic Religion'. Just like Vivekananda, Golwalkar emphasized the non-dualist aspect of service, duty as selfless spirit to the worship of man—the manifestation of divinity and service of humanity as equal to service of God. See Beckerlegge, 'Saffron and Seva', 53.
67. This point has been discussed detail in the introductory chapter of this book.
68. Secret reports were made by the Home Department on the 'suspicious' visits of the *sangha* workers in Pabna; however, the *sangha* peacefully kept their actions in control. Government of Bengal, *Fortnightly Report*, 1st half of August 1926.
69. Under the presidentship of Satkanpati Roy, a close associate of Chittaranjan Das, a Bengal Hindu Mahasammelan was organized on 2nd and 3rd Falgun,

1344 BS. Here, different resolutions were taken in favour of drawing the Hindus away from the influences of the Hindu Mahasabha. See, 4 Bangla 1344, Bajitpure Anusthita Bangiya Hindu Sammelan. 'Swami Nirmalananda, Jati Sanghathak Sri Sri Achrjeer Abadan Boisista', in *Sri Sri Pranabananda: Satarupe, Satamukhe,* ed. Swami Nirmalananda (Calcutta: B. S., 1395), 3–10.

70. The proximity of the BSS and the RSS–VHP (Vishva Hindu Parishad) could be explained in terms of a common Hindu brotherhood. Voix mentioned, 'both groups attend common conferences and Svastika, the RSS Bengali weekly publication, is available in all the BSS's ashrams and schools. However, in some cases, cordial relations lead to close collaborations between the RSS-VHP and BSS' (Voix 2011, 232).
71. See, Swami Vedananda, *Sangher Hindu Jati Gathan Andoloner Suchana*, 1934 AD, December, in Nirmalananda, *Śrīgurusaṅge, Śrīguruprasaṅge*, 410.

'Traditional' Sadhus in Hindutva Politics

Problem and Paradox

The appointment of a Hindu sadhu, Yogi Adityanath, to the post of chief minister of the state of Uttar Pradesh by the Bharatiya Janata Party (BJP) in 2017 brought into focus the age-old template of religion influencing politics, or vice versa. In the absence of a vast gamut of studies discussing the influence of the Hindutva movement on sadhus, it becomes an ambitious project to trace how the sadhus-turned-politicians stepped into the muddled world of party politics in independent India. The existing studies on the subject, however, remain highly selective of the narratives governing the nature of the relationship between the sadhus and the Hindutva forces at both organized and unorganized sectors of politics. For instance, journalist-cum-writer Dhirendra K. Jha's book[1] peeped into the secretive world of the Naga sadhus and focused on the shifting status of the RSS towards the sadhu community. Rajesh Pradhan's book[2] documented the role played by sadhus in Indian nationalist politics and mostly emphasized how the RSS–VHP liaison served in dragging the sadhus into the courtiers of Hindutva. These two popular works preyed on the problems and prospects of asceticism as part of the political drama created by the Hindutva organizations; they hardly took note of the enigma of Hindu politics when addressed by individual voice of dissents. Making a silent departure from the much-politicized zone of RSS–VHP-led Hindutva, these highly individualistic, strong-willed sadhus, especially those from the *sanatanist sampradayas*, registered their plucky presence at the edge of the Hindutva movement while keeping an utmost balanced approach towards the common issues of political concern. Undoubtedly, in the citadel of political Hindutva backed by a dedicated middle class, the *sanatanist* sadhus looking for their individual political agency turned out to be a beaming affair for a while, and all that was achieved in the long run a simple gulping down of all the trends and textures of Hinduism by one monolithic construction of militant Hindu nationalism. Reformist, liberal, traditionalist or *sanatanist*—all shades of Hindutva (when used in the sense of 'Hindu-ness' only) were forced to submit before one ethno-cultural monochromatic form of Hindutva which attempted to transform Hinduism into a 'one-church, one-book, one-gospel' entity, leaving little or no room for others. Discussions on the sadhus in politics also followed the same trajectory of looking at the subject through an RSS–VHP lens, even though the narrative itself evolved as self-critical and self-explanatory in all respects.

My primary interest in this chapter is to explore the spirit of 'individualism' reflected by the *sanatani* sadhus in organized politics, especially in the context of a regional party whose political implications remained indecisive for long. Focusing on a less explored but highly influential sadhu-turned-'politician' called Swami Karpatri Maharaj,[3] I explain how the dominant form of Hindutva had been challenged by this man and how the Akhil Bharatiya Ram Rajya Parishad (All India Council of Rama's Kingdom; RRP)—the party established by Swami Karpatri in 1948—introduced a new brand of politics within the larger framework of the Hindutva movement in post-independence India. I must not call the RRP a threat to the dominant form of Hindutva but rather a discourse that functioned as a site for discursive knowledge production through presenting the idea of 'Sanatana Dharma',[4] crucial to the construction of a pan-Hindu identity. The RRP had garnered the support of the *jagirdars*, zamindars and old feudal lords from the North Indian Hindi belt, especially from Uttar Pradesh, Madhya Pradesh and Rajasthan. In one of his published articles, Professor Hilal Ahmed claimed that the RRP took a prominent part in raising the 'Ayodhya Ram Janmabhoomi' issue for the first time in history but refrained from including the issue in its first election manifesto in 1952. The author called out the RRP for its tactical silence on the demolition of a local *mazar* near the Babri Masjid in 1949, followed by a 9-day, uninterrupted 'Akhand Path' of the 'Ramcharitmanas' around the site organized by Swami Karpatri and Baba Raghav Das,[5] leader of the Akhil Bhartiya Ramayan Mahasabha and a local Congress sympathizer from Faizabad.[6] Citing this incident as the symbol of Hindu religious outrage against the Islamic site, Ahmed moved to the most appalling part of the story with an evocative narration of events.

> This *Akhand Path* was followed by an organized and successful attempt to place idols of Lord Ram forcibly inside the Babri Masjid on the night of 22 December 1949 . A FIR on the incident mentioned around 60 people who trespassed and desecrated the mosque. The district administration took possession of the mosque on the same day. However, it did not remove the idols from the inner part of the mosque. A civil suit was filed in 1950 to seek the right to worship.[7]

A series of events[8] following this orchestrated incident helped Swami Karpatri grab the limelight all of a sudden, with the RRP soon running in its first election. The RRP might have had its own ideological perception of reviving the sacred kingdom of Lord Rama; however, it had nothing similar to the design of demolishing the Babri Masjid or building a Rama temple at Ayodhya. Germane to the perception of a mythical 'Ram Rajya' were the pragmatic needs to make it a reality in actual politics; however, Swami Karpatri did not get much help from his political friends to generate a nationwide propaganda on the subject. Dithered about the possibilities of making 'Ram Rajya' an employable issue in electoral politics, the Hindutva forces in general stepped away from the Ayodhya question but nevertheless joined hands with Swami Karpatri for immediate electoral gains.

It is astonishing to note that the Hindutva forces have maintained a sort of mischievous silence on Swami Karpatri's political career, in specific, and on the RRP, in general. Despite conveying a deep sense of regard for Swami Dayananda, Swami Vivekananda, Swami Pranavananda and even Gandhi, they sustained a kind of lackadaisical attitude towards the *sanatanist* sadhus like Swami Karpatri. The explanation for their coldness to Swami Karpatri was not just in a fundamental inertia to accept the brand of conservatism shared by Swami Karpatri but also in the problems of justifying a new narrative of Hindutva other than that owned by V. D. Savarkar. The anti-reformist impulse in Swami Karpatri's understanding of Hindutva seemed to less attractive to them; however, they hardly missed any opportunity to take hold of the *sanatanist* support base in favour of their political programmes. Despite having a strong obscurantist image among the common masses, the Hindutva organizations always claimed their capacity to initiate large-scale social reforms and very obviously took on a kind of surreptitious attitude towards all those ideas similar to orthodoxy or conservatism.

After independence, the survival of political Hindutva hinged largely on the extent of its reach and access to the masses and in turn depended on its reputation of being unprejudiced in its outlook and receptive in its approach. Had there not been any such approach adopted by the Hindutva organizations, their political journey in India could have ended early. However, making Hindutva a favourable choice for the common masses, including the Dalits, *adivasis* or other lower-caste groups had never been an effortless job, since Savarkar and other ideologues had always placed Hindutva as an 'elitist defence' of casteism.[9] The high-caste underpinnings of Hindutva found no reason in letting down the caste structure, imperative for keeping the noble bloodline intact. The *sangathan* model of Hindu consolidation also reflected the tensions of protecting upper-caste interests, since all those who were in charge of executing the task belonged to the upper castes, precisely Brahmins. All the first-generation Hindu nationalist leaders were Brahmins; even the RSS *swayamsevaks* were upper-caste urban youths.[10] The casteist bias of the Hindutva proponents arrested Hindutva's growth towards a purely reformist line and repeatedly manifested their *sanatanist* bias in one way or the other. However, building up an organizational network through employing a pro-people image required strong involvement in the public domain, and the Hindutva forces gradually moved towards social service activities, combined with youth-oriented militancy programmes for self-defence.

Those making politicized expressions of Hindutva might have had their own reservations against the *sanatanist* orthodoxy, but they did not make any sincere effort to muzzle it. Having said that, it is necessary to acknowledge the contributions made by the *sanatanists* to the Hindutva ideology in its early decades, so that one could trace the shades of thoughts, opinions or narratives present in the Hindutva discourse. Keeping aside the fact that most of these ideas lost their relevance early or failed to face the trial of political potency, one should take cognizance of the relationship shared by the *sanatanists* and the reformists in the development of Hindutva. It is polemical to note that in the last few decades, the *sanatanist* viewpoints regained some strength at the core of the Hindu politics and proved that counter-reformist tendencies had always remained entrenched in the inexorable Hindutva movement.

Approaches to Sanatana Dharma espoused by Swami Karpatri attempted to relocate traditions of orthodoxy in a modern democratic set-up, conflicted with the reformists and survived differently within the greater networks of Hindu nationalism. The *sanatanist* viewpoints were crucial to the understanding of the spirit of Hindu politics in the 20th century,[11] since the vague perceptions related to Sanatana Dharma or timeless religion kept coming back to the political milieu in the name of 'true' Hinduism. The word 'dharma' resonates with the meaning of a natural law or righteousness, while 'Sanatana Dharma' implies an amorphous homogeneous signifier of Hinduism bearing an eternal universal practice.[12] Most of the contemporary Hindu religious organizations claimed to offer the ideal version of Sanatana Dharma to their devotees irrespective of sectarian affiliations; some of them even denied Sanatana Dharma's association with the notions of orthodoxy.[13] Negating the so-called boundary between orthodoxy and modernity, they created greater possibilities for looking at the ideal from a much-nuanced perspective. Scholars have discussed how Sanatana Dharma evoked a good amount of sensibility in modern associational spaces, called *sabhas* or *samajs* since the late 19th century, especially in the formation of the modern Hindu self.[14] These discussions brought to the forefront the historical trajectory of Sanatana Dharma *sabhas* in the framework of Hindu nationalism in the early 20th century but skipped tracing the ideal of Sanatana Dharma inside the Hindutva discourse. Moreover, contemporary studies on the subject have missed outlining a conceptual framework that draws attention to the process by which the Indian National Congress continued to accommodate the *sanatanist* viewpoints in mainstream politics but went on nullifying the charges of stepping into the sloppy terrain of Hindu orthodoxy.

The shifting status of the Congress in terms of its views towards the *sanatanists* working inside the party indicated the problems of appropriating such ideals in a modern democratic structure; however, the ideal had never been run out of context either within or outside the party. Importantly, concurrent with the patterns of how Sanatana Dharma continued to remain active in the Congress sphere of influence, the Hindutva political forces developed their own model of interaction with *sanatanism* as a contested domain, which asserted its presence in the organizational networks of Hindu nationalism through discursive practices under its formative power. The belief that the world, negating the withdrawal syndrome present in the Hindu orthodox philosophical traditions, produced politically indolent subjects lost its essential grounds in the early 20th century when political actors drew inspiration from these traditions, and the traditions themselves received new meanings and perceptions in their understanding of new forms of governance, civil society and politics.

Perceptions leading to the *sanatanist* ideal of orthodoxy suggested ways of addressing the question of politics with regard to the guru-based sectarian communities. These developments included a critical analysis for unfolding the complicated relationship between the ascetic and the householder, or the ascetic's response to the society.[15] Sadhus, representing the monastic orders and asking for legitimacy to be counted as the natural leaders of Hindu society, often landed up in a debate on whether traditional ascetic orders and their associational attachments to a devotional public culture (Kasturi 2015, 6) could be useful in the making of a modern Hindu self! It is highly problematic to conclude that the guru-based sectarian communities committed to one or the other *sanatanist* philosophy lost their relevance in the new formulations of Hindutva which promoted politicized configurations of a Hindu community in the early decades of the 20th century. Importantly, maintaining monastic affiliations, or continuing with the *sampradayik* patterns of *guru-bhakti*, did not allow the *sanatanists* to influence the patterns of Hindu polities; rather, it created difficulties in their efforts to fit into the project of formation of a universal Hindu identity. In different North Indian pockets, the *sanatanists* deployed approaches to reformulate their understanding of a universal

Hinduism emphasizing the integrating elements of Sanatana Dharma. They made equal space for sectarian *sampradayas*, such as Shaivas, Vaishanavas and Shaktas, through a united set of practices and rituals, which in turn contributed to the development of a pan-Hindu community (Kasturi 2015, 10). Essentially, in the new associational spaces crafted by the *sanatanists*, the sectarian disputes never disappeared; rather, Shaivas doing over the Vaishnavas often caused serious fracas around the leadership question within the institutional power hierarchy through subordinating one sect to the other.[16]

Key to the understanding of the ambivalent relations shared by the Hindu nationalists and the *sanatanists* in the early 20th century was the debate on sectarian sadhus participating in the colonial public space and working for the Hindu identity formation. Serious objections were raised by a section of the non-ascetic leaders of the Bharat Dharma Mahamandala—the most important orthodox *sanatanist* organization of the 20th century—regarding sadhus taking part in the pan-Hindu identity formation, because they apprehended that the patterns of a guru–disciple relationship present at the core of sectarian beliefs could spoil the universal spirit of the Hindu nation building in India. Simultaneously, the lay leaders and followers of the Mahamandala challenged the idea of putting the Shaiva sectarian worldview at the heart of the *sanatanist* movement by superseding the Vaishnavas; they also contested the monastic practices of taking endowment grants from wealthy zamindars or rajas. The internal dissensions led to a formal spilt in the Mahamandala in 1902, followed by the emergence of dharma *sanghas* and Hindu *sabhas* in different parts of North India. Renamed as Shri Bharat Dharam Mahamandal, the original organization sustained the spirit of a *sanatanist* Hindu organization by placing sadhus and *pracharaks* at the front line and disseminated the knowledge of *sastric* literature based on the principles of *varnashram* dharma. The altercations between the *sanatanist* viewpoints, the issue of sadhus taking charge of organizing the Hindus, Brahmins regulating the life principles of the masses, sadhus emerging crucial to the revival of the Arya Hindu *jati*—all created enough discords and fractions with the *sanatanist* movement. The Mahamandal's own ventures of identifying the pitfalls within the sadhu order and identifying some of the sects as morally corrupted led to a kind of internal purification process, especially in the second decade of the 20th century. It fitted well with its objectives of portraying the 'true' sadhus as the natural leaders of the Hindu society. Sadhus entrusted with the duty of protecting the legacy of Sanatana Dharma could have built an intellectual tradition based on Hindu knowledge systems had there not been the natural-leader theory, which triggered great controversies in the Hindutva movement in subsequent years.

In a regular sense, surrendering to the will of a guru might have generated a sense of security among the disciples and offered the urban middle-class disciples an escape from the uncertainties of the modern world (*Warrier* 2003: 254–289). Interestingly, the guru tradition created around a North Indian devotional culture of vernacular Hindu practices appeared to be challenging to the Hindu nationalist organizations, mostly because of the fact that if not challenged early, the sectarian sadhu orders would likely endorse a narrow *guru-bhakta* model of social engineering. Based on its sectarian ideologies, it could hamper the fabric of a proposed Hindu Rashtra in India (Kasturi 2010, 107–139). Furthermore, unconditional allegiance to the guru claiming to be a 'natural leader' of the Hindu society could have been a threat to modern representative politics as well. Heartfelt commitment to a certain kind of ideology or giving in to the will of an individual might bring disastrous results for the success of democracy. Through capturing the imagination of large segments of the population, it could lead to authoritarian tendencies among the leadership and the *bhaktas* being manipulated to accept all the decisions of the guru/leader regardless of how flawed they were.

Controversies of a similar nature were reflected in the post-independence Hindu political discourse when the politically inclined sadhus from the old *sanatanist* sectarian schools, especially those who managed to survive on their individual merit either in close association with or independent of the Hindu nationalist organizations, stepped into the troubled zone of democratic politics. The notion of sadhus holding the status of 'natural leaders' of the Hindu society, along with the Brahmins having incontestable supremacy over the caste structure, fetched mixed responses from the Hindu electorate. However, the Hindutva forces in general took a rather flexible approach towards this tiny section of *sanatanists* operating jointly from the political and religious spheres. The surreptitious nature of the adjustment made between the *sanatanist* sadhus and the Hindu nationalists worked only in the case of some selected political issues of common interest; the partnership failed miserably on the electoral front, due to a general lack of consensus. Hindutva's switching over to the VHP in early 1960s apparently signified the ephemeral presence of the *sanatanist* ideal as an independent political force, at least for a limited period of time, even though it made a quick comeback from within the VHP, revealing shades of conflicts and disagreements in a decade or less.

In addition to how Swami Karpatri and the RRP emerged to be a *sanatanist* response to political Hindutva in post-independence politics, how the Indian National Congress addressed the question of Hindu traditionalism remains intriguing. After taking note of these dynamics of *sanatanism* as a distinctly normative process of Hindu identity formation, this chapter explores the critical question of locating orthodoxy in a democratic praxis while setting down the points of discomfort between *sanatanist* perceptions of Hindutva and the perceptions of political Hindutva.

THE MAN AND HIS MISSION

Swami Karpatri came under the limelight immediately after the partition for his active participation in the anti-cow slaughter[17] and anti-Hindu Code Bill movements. Prior to that, in 1940, he formed a united platform of various Hindu traditionalist organizations, or the *sanatanists*, dedicated to the cause of protecting the Hindu religion and culture. Born as Hari Narayana Ojha at Uttar Pradesh in 1907, Swami Karpatri was initiated as a Dasnami ascetic[18] at the age of 24 by one Swami Brahmananda from the monastic order of Shankaracharya. After attaining profound knowledge in grammar, philosophy and metaphysics, Swami Karpatri entered politics in his early 30s and started publishing the newspapers like *Sanmarga* and a periodical *Siddhanta*. *Sanmarga* was backed by the merchant Mulchand Chopra and edited by Vijayanand Tripathi and later became a daily newspaper published from Banaras and Calcutta. Having been mostly ignored by the English-language press, Swami Karpatri utilized these vernacular Hindi publications as the mouthpiece of the organization RRP, established in 1948. Being a sadhu of high scholastic repute, Swami Karpatri joining active politics and, picking up issues of moral and spiritual decadence, confronted the hitherto existing patterns of Hindu politics based mostly on consolidating a Hindu block against the so-called religious 'other'. The 'otherness' of the religious other remained central to the idea of a Hindu community consciousness, which in turn initiated approaches of *sangathan* and *shuddhi* in the early decades of the 20th century. Simultaneously, the Savarkarian ideal of Hindus being one ethno-religious– cultural entity (Varshney 1993, 227–261) equally remained effective at the psychosomatic level of the Hindu consciousness, which believed in making India a Hindu Rashtra.

Far from engaging with these ideas, Swami Karpatri established the RRP with an aim to restore the Ram Rajya (ideal kingdom of Lord Ram)—Ram Rajya should be kept a state where the values of justice, equality, idealism, renunciation and sacrifice would prevail. Swami Karpatri's ideal of Ram Rajya seemed to be a bit different from that of Gandhi, who had extolled Ram Rajya as a perfect democracy in which inequalities based on possession or non-possession, colour, race, creed or sex would vanish. In it, 'the land and state would belong to the people, justice would be prompt, perfect and cheap, and therefore, there would be freedom of worship, speech and the press—all this because of the reign of the self-imposed law of moral restraint'.[19] In contrast to Gandhi, Swami Karpatri unequivocally declared Ram Rajya to be a revival of the glorious reign of Ram to bring a fresh awareness and enlightenment to society.[20] The ideal society that he had contemplated was very much orthodox and Hindu in nature, since Swami Karpatri categorically opposed the legislations permitting untouchables to enter Hindu temples, resisted liberal social reform and championed the cause of the anti-cow slaughter movement all over the country. When asked about his opinion regarding the actual spiritual meaning of the term Ram Rajya by one of his contemporaries, named Paramhans Swami Aagmanandji, Swami Karpatri replied that he could not wait for the inward spiritual instructions to make

Ram Rajya a reality.[21] Swami Karpatri was questioned on the grounds that unless one attained a special spiritual bliss in one's heart, as described by the word *manas* (a calm and composed consciousness) by Tulsidas, one would not be able to bring the Ram Rajya anywhere on earth.[22] When the RRP appeared in the electoral arena with the first parliamentary elections of 1952, Swami Karpatri faced similar objections from his opponents. Not only were his intentions questioned, rather questions were raised whether he was 'ordained like Jagat Guru Sankaracharya to launch a movement for the establishment of *sanatana dharma*'.[23]

Swami Karpatri might have had the opportunity to invest in the metaphoric construction of the Sanatana Dharma for the purpose of appropriating the mythical state of a Ram Rajya. However, he rather highlighted the much bigger need to build public opinion on how religious beliefs and related social practices could best be addressed in the realm of politics. Given the idea that Indian religions, especially the 'Hindu religion', are committed to diverse sociocultural practices, which produced the discourses of Indian political imaginations, Swami Karpatri's *sanatani*/orthodox visions of looking into the issues of greater socio-religious concerns unleashed the existing dichotomies of Hindu politics, mostly overlooked and denied any importance so far.

TRAJECTORIES OF ORTHODOXY: RESPONSE AND REACTION

Engaging with politics had never been an unfamiliar choice for the sadhus or the religious leaders in colonial times. Despite being symbolized as the epitome of wisdom and spirituality in the orientalist construction of India, these outwardly holy men gathered much attention from the imperial writers, though mostly for the wrong reasons. A certain section of the imperial ideologues always remained critical of these 'holy men' because of their being physically weak, politically unconscious and socially indifferent.[24] Bankim Chandra Chattopadhyay's confrontation of the stereotype of the 'effeminate' Indian and Swami Vivekananda's teachings of moral manliness helped re-frame the identity of a passive ascetic as a vigorous nationalist ascetic.[25] Nevertheless, the fact that the ideal of renunciation often offered the 'holy man' an alternative source of power and authority, 'distinct from both priestly power and the coercive authority of the state',[26] did not get much attention in the imperial literature. There were historical examples of ascetics encouraging masses to resist socio-economic oppression; a few of them were even found taking mainstream politics seriously to impart the sense of ethics and morality to the system. The term 'mainstream politics' did not, however, relate to institutional politics in any sense. The latter appeared to be coincidental with the concept of formal power, which the principles of asceticism hardly allowed one to crave. Furthermore, under the colonial regime, 'power' became a subject of contemplation by a section of the educated Indians. The society that had always celebrated renunciation of power as the highest form of ethical virtue now became ambivalent about the thought of getting at least some amount of political power from the British government. The idea of assuming office under the government came with a feeling of abhorrence with the growing popularity of the national movement. Gandhi, for instance, emphasized the importance of non-governmental activities to bring sustainable change in the society. There were leaders who preferred to stay away from holding any official portfolio in their own political circles. In this regard, Gandhi was joined by many leaders, like M. S. Golwalkar and Jayaprakash Narayan, and even a *sanatanist* like Swami Karpatri. Despite having different sets of ideas in politics, they chose to remain outside the formal structure of power.

What makes the *sanatanist* ideal relevant to 20th-century Hindu politics is the legacy of the *sampradayas* or the orthodox sects that appeared to defend the Sanatana Dharma or the eternal religion. In the face of the growing popularity of the reformist organizations like the Brahmo Samaj and the Arya Samaj, the *sanatanists* provided Hindu scriptural defence over the issues of social reform and met with the challenges posed by the proselytizing activities of the Christian missionaries. These guru-based monastic *sampradayas* that played an important part in shaping up the ideas of Hindu orthodoxy in the early 20th century claimed to be the ideal representative of the Hindu society for long. Recognizing Sanatana Dharma as something like a cementing factor between each and every tradition of Hinduism, these *sampradayas* rejected any attempts to reform the society, which were considered akin to contaminating the purity of the rituals and practices. Needless to say, the sectarian, guru-based Vaishnavite or Shaivite *sampradayas* found the reformist spirit of Hindu nationalism far more precarious to their own survival. In the first two decades of the 20th century, many dharma *sabhas* and dharma *mahamandals* were established to project the visions of a Sanatana Dharma codified and sanctified by sacred texts and rituals.[27] Interestingly, the Hindu nationalist interactions with the *sanatanists* remained highly problematic to the growth of a homogeneous–hegemonic construction of Hinduism in the early 20th century. Institutionalized as part of the colonial associational networks since the late 19th century, Sanatana Dharma *sabhas* used to stand for a particular group of people, but in reality they claimed to represent the Hindu society as a whole—a pan-Indian Hindu tradition against the churlish attacks from the reformists.

In Punjab, the Sanatana Dharma Sabha was established by Pandit Din Dayalu Sharma only to protect a few practices and rituals against the reformist spirit of the Arya Samaj; however, on occasions, they shared some porous space of operations, with overlapping membership, issues and networks. The *sanatanist sabhas* and the reformist organizations did not ever work from a competitive platform, rather working together with a consensus on selected themes, like *shuddhi* or cow protection.[28] Nevertheless, differences between the reformists and the *sanatanists* triggered anxieties and tensions to a great extent. Considering the act of *shuddhi* highly alarming for the uninterrupted extension of the Aryan traditions, the Bharat Dharma Mahamandala, one of the leading *sanatanist* organizations, asked for the defence of the Varna system to protect the religion from all sorts of 'unsastric' acts from both within and outside.[29] While taking care of the exaggerations, John Zavos, one of the leading scholars of this field, has categorically pointed out that the *sanatanist* perception of a horizontal restructuring of the Hindu society (*shuddhi* perceived as a means of reclaiming or converting individuals from the 'foreign' religions of Christianity and Islam) conflicted with the reformist (Arya Samajist) ideal of vertical mobilization of the society by making *shuddhi* a medium of purification to encourage the lower castes/untouchables to enter into the Varna society.[30] When the Hindu *sangathanist* organizations like the

Hindu Mahasabha attempted to release a critique of untouchability, the *sanatanist sabhas* re-established their claims of being the actual defender of the Hindu society again.

Rejecting the vertical model of restructuring the Hindu society, the Mahasabha's leaders, in its 1923 session at Banaras, stood in favour of a horizontal mobilization through reclaiming the converted Hindus into the original fold.[31] The Mahasabha taking over the *sanatani* claims of Hindu unity, however, brought further patterns of conflict into focus. Far from continuing their earlier position of being projected as the self-proclaimed guardians or defenders of the Hindu society, the *sanatanists* now lost that privilege to the Hindu nationalist organizations.

The spiritual 'gurus', so far acknowledged as the 'natural leaders' of the Hindu society, expected to revive the ancient knowledge traditions of a timeless dharma (religion) for the larger interest of a 'spiritual' Hindu *jati*. The Hindu nationalists in turn promoted the idea of a Hindu Rashtra on the principles of territorial, cultural and religious integrity among the Hindus. Indeed, the *sanatanist* idea of Hindus being an aggregate of different sects appeared to be ambiguous for a politically motivated theory of Hindu nationalism in India; however, the most puzzling part of the story came out when the *sanatanists* looked for some avenues of adjustment with mainstream politics for their individual rights and existence. They might have continued as a symbol of orthodoxy within the broader networks of Hindu nationalism or re-articulated the ideological shades of traditionalism within the Congress; however, the *sanatanists* did not ever end up facing sheer dejection. It is difficult to come to a conclusion about why the *sanatanists* did not show the confidence to enter politics by virtue of their own individual propositions; however, the assumption that they had lost their individual agency or remained subservient to the Hindutva movement does not make any historical sense. The vernacular Hindi press, especially Gita Press (established in 1923), and the magazines like *Kalyan* continued nurturing the ideology of Sanatana Dharma through bringing out issues on cow protection, *shuddhi*, women's education, widow remarriage, *kalapani* and others. A number of intellectuals, activists and gurus with scholastic reputation contributed in publishing these hitherto unresolved issues with the common understanding that Sanatana Dharma should have a role in shaping the middle-class Hindu consciousness. Especially in northern India, the vernacular Hindi press became instrumental and gradually emerged as a medium of popularizing the inchoate ideology of Sanatana Dharma.[32] In fact, the coming together of Sanatana Dharma leaders and the reformists in 1923, at Banaras, shored up the conservative groups further, and the vernacular Hindi press helped in nourishing the viewpoints for a much larger audience.

The *sanatanists'* attempts of wielding influence over the Hindu society dragged them into the process of seeking recognition and approval from both the masses and the elites through constantly harping on the claims of not being reactionary or contemptuous to others. In spite of their having flaunted their doctrinal prejudices, the Mahamandala asserted that the *sampradayas* practising a different set of ideas or performing a different set of rituals would not have considered Sanatana Dharma to be a berserk exercise but displayed explicit tendencies to reach at a point of consensus on the basis of common objectives. *Sanatanism* could have set its own vocabularies of expropriating the truth and never pushed the question of Hindu unity into jeopardy. The question of Hindu unity, as projected by the Mahasabha type of *sangathan* propaganda, however, did not match fully with the standards set by the *sanatanists*, since the idea of putting all *sampradayik* and casteist affiliations into the common basket of a Hindu nation could not do justice to the sectarian knowledge systems preserved by the *sanatanists*. The latter might have reached a kind of situational settlement with the Hindu Mahasabha in 1923, but incorporating the sectarian visions into one obscurant philosophy of political Hindutva did not ever become a reality. Occasionally, they stood in favour of the Hindu Mahasabha and supported some of its programmes in the decade before the partition; for instance, M. M. Malaviya earnestly brought the *sanatanists* closer to the reformists, and even a Natha sadhu named Yogi Digvijay Nath[33] of Gorakhpur took charge of the Hindu Mahasabha in North India. However, the fundamental dichotomies between the *sanatanists* and the Hindu Mahasabha remained unchallenged.[34] The Mahasabha's ardent call for caste reformation or its *sangathan* propagandas were received with much suspicion and speculation by the North Indian feudal–conservative cluster, for whom playing with the Varna order was similar to hitting at the backbone of the Hindu society (Kasturi 2015, 52).

In search of an alternative to the reformist version of Hindu nation building, the *sanatanists* looked for other avenues to live with their own sectarian experiences, and in the 1940s, they showed palpable interest in active politics. Furthermore, new *sanatani* organizations gradually replaced the authority of the Mahamandala as the sole defender of Sanatana Dharma.[35] These new organizations carried on the monastic traditions but discarded the existing model of privatized *guru-bhakti* or *mohantahood* coming with huge financial gains; they rather shifted to a new liberal/public model of *guru-bhakti* suitable to the new political culture. The partition and independence drastically changed the existing understanding of Hindu unity, and these organizations aptly recognized the fact that the sanatanists would have deprived of its due historical agency, had there been isolation from the political process from their part. They faced an urgent need to reconfirm the political credibility of the sadhus as the most trusted allies in the nation building process, and new *sanatanist* organizations renamed as dharma *sanghas* or dharma *parishads* started taking pivotal places in the new political atlas of the country.[36] Significantly, all that was done arrived within the all-inclusive networks of the Hindutva movement, sometimes in close collaboration, and in a mode of adjustment at other times. Swami Karpatri, the founder of the Dharm Sangh and later the RRP, inherited the legacy of the *sanatanist* tradition in such an out-and-out manner that from the late 1940s, he unequivocally projected the sadhus and the Brahmins as the uncontested leaders of the Hindu society. Engaged in taking forward the Mahamandala's legacy of Hindu orthodoxy, Swami Karpatri initiated a new era in Hindu *sanatanist* polities; however, he met with severe ambiguities and uncertainties while fixing its relation with the Hindu Mahasabha or the RSS.[37]

The Mahasabha had never been an ideal choice for Swami Karpatri, and with the ban imposed on the RSS after its being accused of Gandhi's assassination in 1948, Swami Karpatri was left with no option but to accomplish his objectives independently. However, in his zeal to reclaim Ram Rajya in a democratic India, Swami Karpatri drove himself into a web of political negotiations with like-minded organizations during the first general elections. How would he take forward the spirit of *sanatanism* in a secular India? What were the points of conflict emerging between an old-world sectarian ideology and modern democracy? All these issues appeared tantamount to the fundamental problem of sanctioning historical agency to a 'traditional sadhu' operating from a completely different setting. In an era of Congress ascendency combined with the principles of Nehruvian secularism[38] in North India, a party like the RRP, sharing a conspicuous relationship with the Hindu Right, managed to get a sizeable amount of political visibility for a considerable period of time. Interestingly, local Congress leaders did not ever carry out a rant against the RRP or slam Swami Karpatri on the personal front. The inexplicable position taken by the Congress towards Hindu traditionalist waves, nevertheless, brought out the convolutions of Indian politics in general.

THE ENIGMA OF 'TRADITIONALISM' IN THE CONGRESS

Working on the trends of Indian nationalism since the 1920s, the scholars like Bruce Graham and Christophe Jaffrelot identified patterns of Hindu traditionalism which 'stressed the need to preserve Hindu religious beliefs and social practices and to foster the study of Hindi and Sanskrit languages and their literatures'.[39] Unlike the Hindu nationalist endeavours to endorse the model of Hindu *sangathan* for social transformation, the traditionalists were keen to perpetuate the Hindu social order. Engaging with the Congress or any other public organization fetched nothing despicable to their ideological commitments; rather, such men as M. M. Malaviya, Lajpat Rai, K. M. Munshi and others conceptualized the foundations of the nation on the edifice of the Hindu religion and culture. An amount of ideological overlaps often brought the traditionalists closer to Hindu nationalists, accompanied by an occasional purging of the differences between the Congress and the Hindu Mahasabha, at least at a political level.

The arguments placed by Richard Gorden[40] of the Mahasabha being an amorphous pressure group within the Congress seem problematic in regard to the former's relationship with the Congress, because after Savarkar took charge of the Mahasabha in 1939, the organization-turned-party carved out a separate niche for itself.[41] The Mahasabha might have endorsed a negotiating approach towards the British government in its wartime efforts in the early 1940s, and the Congress might have been aggressive in dealing with the Mahasabha for its own reasons; the common Mahasabha workers, however, could not resist from taking part in the Congress rallies in protest against the arrest of Congress leaders.[42] Amid the Quit India affair, the gradual liquidation of Savarkar's influence inside the Mahasabha indicated a further change in leadership patterns, combined with a rise of Congress sympathizers in the party. Syama Prasad Mookerjee's coming into the limelight as the new president of the Mahasabha in 1942[43] laid out his percipience of realistic politics through cuddling up to the pro-Congress elements within the Mahasabha, thus far ignored or dismissed by the Savarkarian factions. One could mark this policy as a tactical adjustment by Mookerjee to bring the Congress and the Mahasabha closer to a common platform for wielding influence over the British; however, it hardly brought the desired impact.[44] Nevertheless, Mookerjee's efforts of balancing the political camps did not go in vain, as the Congress traditionalists and local Congress leaders found in Mookerjee a fresh wave of pragmatism, which in turn resulted in a sense of admiration for Mookerjee in the Hindu nationalist circles around the country.[45] Whatever might be the shifting facades of Mahasabha politics in the 1940s accompanied by a change of political tactics by Mookerjee in the years before partition, his resignation from the Mahasabha in 1948[46] ruffled up the situation for a while. Subsequently, the formation of a new party called Bharatiya Jana Sangh by Mookerjee with the help of his old Mahasabha allies and his RSS friends brought down the clumsy transitions of Hindu politics within a couple of years. The Jana Sangh provided unanticipated opportunity to the RSS, which used the liberal–moderate platform of this new party for its own image rectification purpose. Unless the RSS had a political mouthpiece like the Jana Sangh, it would have been rather difficult for the Hindu Right to survive in the popular front with a commendable hold over a section of the electorate.

IN THE WHIRLPOOL OF ELECTORAL POLITICS

With the growth of the Bharatiya Jana Sangh, the power-peddling face of the Hindutva movement became obtrusive at different levels. The Jana Sangh successfully served up a networking package to the Hindu political forces and appeared to be a fresh approach to the hitherto grounded stereotypes of Hindutva. Mookerjee's wholehearted efforts to form a national democratic alliance with all the anti-Congress forces brought Swami Karpatri close to the Jana Sangh prior to the first general election. It was not the first instance when a *sanatani* sadhu got associated with direct politics; there were others like Mahant Digvijay Nath and a few Dasnami ascetics who came in contact with the Hindu Mahasabha. However, none of them invested on their individual existence, instead joining politics as Hindu Mahasabha activists. Swami Karpatri established the RRP by his own merit, continued to operate through his *sanatanist* networks and maintained a honourable distance from the Jana Sangh. While searching for the early connections between Dr Mookerjee and Swami Karpatri, the letter written to Mookerjee by Hanuman Prasad Poddor of Gita Press should be mentioned. In his letter dated 24 May 1951, Poddar requested Dr Mookerjee to work jointly with the Hindu Mahasabha, RSS and the newly formed RRP at least for the duration of the first election. He also advised Dr Mookerjee to 'sink their minor differences' for the welfare of Hindu culture.[47] Subsequently, Poddar also made an appeal to the leaders such as Swami Karpatri, M. S. Golwalkar and Dr N. B. Khare from the Hindu Mahasabha to meet at Calcutta or Delhi for a joint venture in the upcoming elections.[48] Poddar, being a person from a different field, took keen interest in bringing all the Hindu political forces onto a common platform and thought of hurling a challenge at the Congress in the elections. For the advocates of Hindutva like Poddar, the Congress was no longer just a political opponent but also a symbol of the Nehruvian secular–socialist order championing the interests of an anti-Hindu, pro-Western polity.

Importantly, Dr Mookerjee did not subscribe to the cluster of ideas promoted by the *sanatanist* circle from North India. Nor did he ever uphold the idea of pigeonholing Hindu nationalism as a casteist phenomenon. He had crafted his own liberal–flexible model of Hindutva differently from Savarkar or Golwalkar.[49] He might have entered into political collaborations with Golwalkar and his old Mahasabha friends, but he had every reason to defy the narratives of a Hindu Raj or a Ram Rajya. In fact, for an intellectual Bengali like Dr Mookerjee, the *sanatanist* outlook of Swami Karpatri did not appear that appealing, what Dr Mookerjee could have expected from a liberal politician at that point of time. He was susceptible to being identified as the mouthpiece of a limited constituency represented partly by the feudal elements and mostly by the high-caste Hindus with strong orthodox sentiments.

Then what brought the Jana Sangh and the RRP closer on the electoral front? Was it simply the anti-Congress spirit? It was the Jana Sangh's philosophy of *Bharatiya sanskriti* (Indian culture) and *Bharatiya maryada* (Indian dignity) and its call for 'one country, one nation and one culture' (precisely the message of Akhand Hindustan) which shaped notions of an uninterrupted glorious Indian past in continuity with the Hindu religion and culture. The rhetoric of Swami Karpatri's Ram Rajya, even if explained in terms of a less spiritual but more dogmatic formulation of the 'ideal' kingdom of Lord Rama, floated fine with the dynamism of *Bharatiyatva* coalesced with the message of *akhandatva* (territorial–cultural–racial compositeness of India). The slogan of 'Akhand Bharat' raised by both the Jana Sangh and the RRP added further reasons to form an alliance between a *sanatanist* sadhu and a liberal politician in a partitioned India. It seemed to be an awkward combination, considering their backgrounds, networks, support base and strategies of mobilization. Apparently, the god-man trajectory present in Swami Karpatri's life journey, the patterns of *guru-bhakti* reflected by his *sanatanist* tradition and his overall understanding of politics contrasted dramatically with the moderate–populist line of politics deployed by Mookerjee.

Additionally, the Jana Sangh's fostering of the ideology of Hindu *sangathan* in tune with the reformist spirit of Hindu nationalism turned down Swami Karpatri's visions of upholding the Varna order in Hindu society. The popular slogans thus far raised by his Dharm Sangh in *sanatani* religious congregations, like *dharma ki jai ho* ('may religion conquer') and *adharm ki nash ho* ('may irreligiosity be destroyed'), indicated the thrust areas that made up the rationale of a traditional pattern of politics in future India. It should not located as a setback to the proposed secular democratic fabric of new India, because this sort of traditional politics, tinged with orthodoxy, always enjoyed the support of a small segment of the upper-caste–upper-class Hindi-speaking communities, specifically those from Uttar Pradesh, Rajasthan and Madhya Pradesh.[50] I do not have the liberty here to delve into the details of how the Congress managed to grab support from the other segment of the same caste–class configuration; however, it is crucial to note that the sadhus from a monastic order having a strong political inclination always found a solid support base among the urban middle classes and the old feudal order. In Swami Karpatri's coming together with the Jana Sangh, one can trace the quintessential desire for clubbing Hindu majoritarian sentiments, which they assumed would be a threat to the Congress and the proposed narrative of secularism. Simultaneously, it would be an effort to rectify all the misdoings of the Congress and its allies in the past decades, especially the disaster of the partition that cut Bharat Mata into two pieces.

This political combination of the Jana Sangh, RSS, RRP and a section of the Hindu Mahasabha indicated the first generation of the rightist opposition formed against the Congress. RRP's coming into terms with the Jana Sangh seemed to be disputed, since Dr Mookerjee endorsed his party at a democratic parliamentary set-up and attempted to reach each and every section of the Hindu society. His initial attempts to subsume the streams of Hindu orthodoxy and Hindu nationalism into one political stream remained troublesome and incongruent for obvious reasons, while Swami Karpatri's involvement with politics did not ever seem unprecedented or exceptional. The Dasnami Dandi sadhus from the holy cities like Varanasi and Ayodhya had never been fully absorbed into the solitary world of devotion away from the public life but rather remained connected to political and trading networks, as reflected in the case of the Mahamandala, which wielded its influence over the world of politics through different Dasnami maths, *akharas*[51] and *sanatani* learning institutions in important cities of North India.[52] Swami Karpatri, coming from the guru–*sishya*–akhara type of *sanatani* background, would have contributed positively to the Hindu nationalist visions of a political alliance had there been a middle way of adjustment between the moderate approaches of the Jana Sangh and the strong conservative insights of the RRP. This could not happen mostly due to the rigid strands of thought shared by Swami Karpatri on several sensitive issues. Even a possible understanding between Swami Karpatri and Mahant Digvijay Nath, the head of the Gorakhpur *math* and leader of the Hindu Mahasabha, did not become a reality. Rather, short-time, issue-based negotiations between these actors came out to be an exposé of what amounted to the paradox of Hindu politics in the decades after independence.

The issues of mutual conviction, however, reflected the patterns of an age-old paranoia shared by the so-called defenders of Hinduism in India. The Hindu Code bill—a much-anticipated threat to the stability and integrity of the Hindu society—grasped most of their energy in the first place.[53] Rejecting the bill, Swami Karpatri called it a gross violation of Hindu scriptures and Dharmasastras and declared, 'Under the Constitution every citizen has been assured of his or her religious freedom, but, in the name of reforms direct interference is being shown in religious matters of the Hindus by adopting such measures as the Hindu Code Bill…'.[54] Swami Karpatri fetched considerable limelight while vehemently opposing the Hindu Code Bill that was proposed to provide a civil code in place of the Hindu personal laws. He made countless statements against B. R. Ambedkar's position of a law minister, commenting that an untouchable should have no agency in the matters of law—a subject so far restricted to the Brahmins. Referring to Swami Karpatri's unmistakable reactionary approach to the issue, Professor Ramachandra Guha mentioned,

> To the Law Minister's claim that the Shastras did not really favour polygamy, Swami Karpatri quoted Yagnavalkya: 'If the wife is a habitual drunkard, a confirmed invalid, a cunning, a barren or a spendthrift woman, if she is bitter-tongued, if she has got only daughters and no son, if she hates her husband, [then] the husband can marry a second wife even while the first is living'. The Swami supplied the precise citation for this injunction: the third verse of the third chapter of the third section of Yagnavalkya's Smriti on marriage. He did not however tell us whether the injunction also allowed the wife to take another husband if the existing one was a drunkard, bitter-tongued, a spendthrift, etc.[55]

Adding further momentum to the anti-Hindu Code Bill protest, the RSS and the RRP jointly organized rallies in Delhi using the slogans like 'Down with Hindu Code Bill' and 'May Pandit Nehru perish'. The Anti-Hindu Code Bill Committee conducted several meetings all over the country, where a large number of sadhus took part in defence of the Hindu legal system. In a statement issued by the temple authority on behalf of His Holiness Jagadguru Sri Sankaracharya Swamiji of Kanchi, it was declared,

> In the course of incessant travel from village to village both in North India and in South India for the last 30 years, His Holiness has been in touch with the feelings and ideas of the Hindu public, high and low, and His Holiness is convinced that the Hindu general public neither demand nor approve of any changes that deviate from the existing Hindu law.[56]

Most of the orthodox Hindu organizations shared the same amount of anxiety and fear of losing their Hindu identity in case the bill was legislated. Mahamahopadhyaya Pandit Vasudeva Shastri, the main disciple of His Holiness Srimad Jagadguru Madhwacharya, Uttaradi Math, Sholapur, sadhus and religious leaders from the Bharat Dharma Mahamandala of Banaras, the Sanatana Dharma Sabha, the All India Hindu Mahasabha—all expressed their deep concern against the proposed bill and apprehended that the bill would push the Hindu religion and society into grave danger. Swami Karpatri, the strongest critic of the lot, brusquely attacked Dr Ambedkar, suggesting that 'a former Untouchable had no business meddling in matters normally the preserve of the Brahmins'.[57] He vehemently opposed the bill, especially the provisions referring to divorce, inheritance, adoption and others. For Swami Karpatri, Guha pointed out,

> divorce was prohibited in Hindu tradition, while 'to allow adoption of a boy of any caste is to defy the Shastras and to defy property'...as is clearly laid down in the Dharmasastras, to forcibly defy the laws of God and Dharma very often means great harm to the Government and the country and both bitterly rue the obstinate folly.[58]

Significantly, Swami Karpatri and the other orthodox sadhus were not fighting the bill alone. The groups opposing the venture included the hardcore conservatives within the Congress party, the Hindu fundamentalists within the Congress party, a group of Muslim hardliners and a few female politicians.[59] The traditionalists within the Congress tried to incapacitate the attempts of Ambedkar at both the national and local levels and pushed Nehruvian ideals of a liberal/secular–democratic society into complete jeopardy. The entire Hindu Code Bill debate mirrored the contest between *sanatanist* India and new India—a recurrent theme for recognizing the multiple identities of the state. The Congress traditionalists, especially at the local level, made a peculiar case in regard to their position under the Nehruvian system. A special mention to this group is needed here.

After independence, the Hindu traditionalists, those who had continued to survive within the Congress with their individual propositions so far, found the secular line of programmes of Nehru a bit perplexing to their long-cherished ideology of a Hindu nation in India. Nehru's secularism appeared to be just an alternative, not the conclusion, to an intricate collection of possibilities in politics. However, in reality, it became the touchstone of post-independence nation building—pushing other possibilities to a distance. In a constant interplay of definitions of secularism, Congress traditionalists and Hindu nationalists redefined its contours by presenting the idea within the contours of Indian traditions. Secularism, in its theoretical sense, deals with the separation of religion from politics, but in everyday Indian politics, caste or community identities are being continued through the language of tradition, which itself makes religion an influential category of political mobilization. Portraying secularism as anti-Indian or anti-tradition fitted well with the Hindu-nationalist variants of revival of *Bharatiya maryada* or *Bharatiya sanskriti*, combined with a plea for Akhand Hindustan—a section of the local Congress leaders espoused a unique trend of politics assured of validating the 'noble' traditions of Hinduism.[60] These people frequently spoke in languages similar to the Hindutva leaders, and a section of the Uttar Pradesh Congress even showed solidarity with the anti-Hindu Code Bill campaign initiated by such Congress veterans as Vallabhbhai Patel, Rajendra Prasad, J. B. Kripalani and others at the centre (Som 1992:172).

Startlingly, a bunch of moderate and conservative leaders generated ideas and opinions that were in conformity with those of

Swami Karpatri. Despite dissonance over the eventual objectives, the *sanatanists*, traditionalists, Hindu nationalists and a few liberals vivified a range of cherished Hindu religious traditions in the name of Indianness. The conflation of Indian identity with Hinduism created much bewilderment around India's multi-religious fabric, while the critics alleged that Nehru and his allies had endeavoured to sabotage the Hindu religion and culture in the name of codifying the Hindu laws. Undoubtedly, it was a calibrated impression that boosted the outrage against Nehru to a different level. The Hindu nationalists called out Nehru for misleading the connotations of equality and pluralism in terms of providing equal opportunities to all the religions,[61] especially when there was no such 'imposition' like the Hindu Code Bill on other religions. The Muslims, for instance, were permitted to carry on with the special Sharia law while the Hindus faced tremendous pressure against continuing with their own personal codes. Apparently, the Hindutva forces could have reached a certain logic if they had maintained at least some amount of transparency in their own ideological propositions. However, the so-called fatherland/holy-land syndrome present in the official narrative of political Hindutva and their efforts to narrow down Indian identity to Hindu identity simply made them lose the plot.

Hindu traditionalists, by contrast, stressed more on reviving ancient Indian cultural practices, such as the use of traditional Ayurvedic medicine, use of Hindi over Urdu and maintenance of Hindu religious practices inherent to caste/community identities. Fazed by the challenges from within, Nehruvian visions of a secular–liberal India did not become a reality overnight. Unless the questions over caste, class, gender and religion were addressed, the idea of change could not figure as part of the nationalist ideology.[62] Therefore, the moment the Indian state claimed to have a hold over liberal–secular principles, it faced challenges from a traditional India—a complicated ideological position championed by the proponents of Hindutva. It is a matter of relative inquiry as to what extent Nehru and his friends managed to get success in setting up a dialogue with that ideological position, or alternatively masqueraded to justify a unique sense of 'Hindu secularism' for the sake of their own survival. Undoubtedly, after the landslide victory of the Congress in the first general elections of 1951–1952, the exponents of secular nationalism registered their instant success over how to trickle down the issues of religion in state affairs; however, their long-term victory depended largely on the approaches adopted by the opposition in the near future.

The Jana Sangh entered the parliament with three seats, while the Hindu Mahasabha ended up with four seats. Interestingly, RRP's winning of three Lok Sabha seats and several Vidhan Sabha seats created some effervescence inside the political circles. With three wining candidates from Rajasthan, Swami Karpatri recorded his political existence in the parliament[63] and managed to gain the support from the local rulers. The nature of the latter's support to the RRP was conditioned by different factors; especially, their political equation with the Congress often suggested the character of feudal involvement with democratic politics in Rajasthan. Getting bungled up with the Congress leaders, the Maharaja of Jodhpur supported the RRP and the Congress had to face a major setback in the assembly polls at the Jodhpur division. It performed badly in the Lok Sabha elections in the Jodhpur division, while in Bundi and Bikaner it faced the same disaster. The RRP leader Thakur Madan Singh got the support of the Rajpur *jagirdars* of Jodhpur and Jaipur and successfully fanned their anti-Congress sentiments. The RRP got 27.72 per cent of the vote share in the Legislative Assembly with 24 seats and continued to keep its hold in the Rajasthan legislature for the consecutive elections, though with a declining rate in total vote share.[64]

Now, due to the deep-rooted feudal structure and caste-based factionalism, it was almost impossible to develop a competitive party structure in Rajasthan. Almost all the parties suffered from group factionalism,[65] and this left a smear on the political fate of the RRP against the Congress in the state. Swami Karpatri's party wielded some influence in the Uttar Pradesh and Madhya Pradesh assemblies and managed to win a couple of seats in the following elections. There was nothing impressive in RRP's election manifesto. It assured the electorate a return to the golden days of Lord Rama 'when every citizen "was contented, happy, gifted with learning, and religious minded. ... All were truthful. None was close-fisted; none was rude; none lacked prudence; and above all, none was atheist. All followed the path of religion'.[66] Myron Weiner reported that in the 48-page manifesto of the party, specific policy issues did not get any reference, the barter system was preferred over the use of legal tender, the traditional Ayurvedic system of medicine was supported, confiscation of land without compensation was opposed (very much in tune with the feudal interests) and, above all, a ban on cow slaughter was proposed. Recapitulating the utopian regime of Lord Rama, the manifesto stated,

> the days of slavery were not our days. We were under foreign domination. We should write off those days from our Calendar. So far as our fresh activities are concerned, we should bridge over the gulf of the foreign domination and thus link our glorious past with the budding present.[67]

The manifesto scored high in espousing moral–ethical passions full of Sanskrit quotations, rejected the constitution as a blunt imitation of the Western style of governance and, unlike that of the Jana Sangh and the RSS, clamoured for a constitution based on dharma. Very obviously, the party received scant attention from the national media, and the left–liberal elites turned a deaf ear to the programmes of Swami Karpatri, even though 'over 2 million voters (including 14.2% of the voters in Madhya Bharat and 9.4% in Rajasthan) gave it their support in the 1952 general elections.'[68]

Now, in the case of the Hindu nationalist parties, poor performance in the electoral domain should not be counted as the definite parameter of the strength of its ideological substance in India. The Congress itself included conservative and traditionalist forces that were averse to play a decisive role in policy implementation. The RRP was very much new to the electoral game, restricted in its outlook and orthodox in its approach. Despite that, it survived for some years in the greasy terrain of Hindi-belt politics, fighting against the giants. Its initial victory in certain pockets of North India was certainly propped up on the ideological ancestry of the cult of Rama transcending the attributes of an ideal king, as well as a divine figure, much like God-Kings 'who walk on the earth in the form of men'. Rama's transformation from a religious–cultural cult figure to a political symbol drove a wedge between the private and the public and presented the power of popular imaginations in extolling the divine king as the messiah or *avatara* fighting against the evil. This evil also embodied the imageries of a religious 'other', or the non-Hindus, at different occasions.[69]

The sectarian perception of Sanatana Dharma landed Swami Karpatri in the psychosomatic world of living traditions of texts, popular beliefs, myths and legends to make his own political logic trustworthy. In his framework of Hindutva, the high-caste Hindus were presented as the defenders of the traditions, the upholders of one standardized notion of collective memory over others. A Shaiva Dasnami sadhu by origin, Swami Karpatri used the myth of a Ram Rajya in the form of a political package where the art of remembrance and reconstruction appeared to be convenient and beneficial. Far from engaging with the dynamics of mass politics, he took greater interest in enunciating the long-lost dharmic traditions of the country with an intention to establish an alternative model of Western democracy. This alternative model of a Ram Rajya was sharply drawn in contrast to the Nehruvian secular type of governance and eventually opposed the hyper-nationalist, ethno-religious narratives of a Hindu Rashtra proposed by his Hindutva counterparts.

Swami Karpatri's long-cherished idea of a Varna society as part of the Ram Rajya project encapsulated a hierarchical social order where everybody would keep to the limits of authoritative scriptures. Unlike Gandhi, Swami Karpatri did not fall for the undeniable potential for transforming the authoritative spirit of the Ram Rajya into a popular democracy, rather staying true to the mooring of a *sanatanist* narrative of Varna-based hierarchy where popular moot points, like *harijan* upliftment or temple entry, remained quiescent to maintain peace and stability in the society.[70] RRP's manifesto could have been dismissed as a 'handbook for Indian reactionaries and obscurantists', but it must be remembered that Swami Karpatri got a constituency of his own and that the RSS, the Hindu Mahasabha and the Jana Sangh too rallied together with Swami Karpatri on such issues as banning of cow slaughter, promotion of Sanskrit and revival of Ayurvedic medicine. The reasons for their discomfort with Swami Karpatri, however, conflated with his stance on *harijan* upliftment or entry of the untouchables into temples. The Jana Sangh stood in support of these demands, while

Swami Karpatri completely rejected any such demands as the symbol of a protest against *sanatana dharma* and Ram Rajya. Does this mean that proponents of Hindutva other than the RRP were far more liberal and tolerant? The *sangathanist*/horizontal model of Hindu solidarity proposed by these parties embroiled the society in utter bewilderment, mostly because it tried to route the fear and frustration of the lower castes into one united propaganda movement against the so-called enemy other—an abstract figure of a Muslim, Christian, sometimes the state, or even the West.

The utopian trope of Hindu-ness caged in the formulations of *Bharatiyatva* incongruously fixed the lower castes in the mirror image of potential fighters combating the so-called enemy for their own survival. Since the *sangathan* model had hardly anything to offer to the lower castes to ameliorate their socio-economic discrepancies, the Hindutva forces deployed different strategies to win over the unemployed/low-income lower-caste electorate without estranging their urban middle-class–upper caste support base. The social service programmes of the RSS, the issue-based moderate politics of the Jana Sangh, the pro-Hindu hyper-nationalist politics of the Hindu Mahasabha and the ethno-cultural politics of the VHP—all suggested at least some patterns to address the lower-caste Hindu electorate. Exceptionally, it was Swami Karpatri who, despite sharing the same platform with these organizations, designed his individual understanding of the Hindu society on 'pure' *sanatani*/orthodox lines, snubbing all tendencies to fit into real-world politics. A loner in the mythical hyperbolic world of virtue politics, Swami Karpatri made a strong case for a muddled ideology that loses ground halfway. This was quite common with sadhus treading into the ambitious zone of electoral business where the gap between the real and the virtual, or idea and practice, often turns out to be a complicated affair. Unlike the camouflaging montage of the popular images used to create the organizational variables of political Hindutva, Swami Karpatri choose to remain committed to sectarian politics, lacking non-ideological support at large.

Growing out of the dense network of *sanatani* orthodox associations of North India, counting almost 600, with similar objectives by the early decades of the 20th century,[71] Swami Karpatri invoked the 'Ramcharitmanas' as the sole authoritative text bearing the essence of the Puranas, Smriti and the Vedas. In his perception, the Vedas were manifest in the form of Ramayana, which was manifest in the form of 'Ramcharitmanas'.[72] Unlike in the case of the Vedas, specifically taught to the twice-born males, the *sanatanist* proponents of the *Ramcharitmanas* portrayed a kind of paternalist flavour in projecting the text as accessible to all, irrespective to caste, class and gender. Furthermore, it sermonized reverences for cows and Brahmins, presented a synthesis of Shaivism and Vaishnavism, maintained social equilibrium and stood for a unique sense of nationalism, presenting the nuances of the sacred geography of an all-powerful model state.

This paternalist perpetuation of the popularity of the *Ramcharitmanas* might have brought the *sanatanists* some amount of social legitimacy, but it hardly denoted any political success at large. The success of the Ram Rajya depended on the useful transformation of Rama's divine authoritarianism into democratic populism under the cosmic network of righteousness, justice and truth. It required both ideological and non-ideological support to introduce the transcendental into an orderly structure. In an era of competitive demography, it seemed almost impossible. Had Swami Karpatri been a little flexible in his ideas, he would have managed to stay in politics for long. What was seen in later years was however a paradoxical slithering of the Hindutva forces from liberalism to orthodoxy and from orthodoxy to fundamentalism. It is ironic that those Hindutva forces that accused Swami Karpatri of obstinacy and pig-headedness periodically unpacked the old rhetoric of *sanatanist* sentiment and returned to the same ideological milieu settled by the *sanatani* sadhus long ago. They continued referring to cow slaughter, uniform civil code, promotion of Hindi and revival of the traditional mode of learning, strictly maintained upper-caste bias in the distribution of party portfolios, supported landlordism and protested against untouchables entering sacred temples, and the RSS even fostered the model of absolute devotion or a guru–*sishya* type of hierarchy. Eventually, they survived through every charge and allegation of promoting orthodoxy in a democratic set-up. Philip Lutgendorf called it the 'power of euphemism' employed by the Hindu rightist parties when addressing sensitive issues that could have landed them in sheer embarrassment.[73] He called Swami Karpatri a big failure in the sense that he 'never mastered the language of euphemism favoured by the English educated intellectuals'.[74]

Swami Karpatri might have become a liability for the Hindutva movement when every possibility of a merger between the RRP and any of the rightist parties ceased to exist in the early 1960s. Prevented from delivering a harangue in public, Swami Karpatri published the controversial book *Rashtriya Swayamsevak Sangh aur Hindu Dharma* in 1970 and accused Savarkar and Golwalkar of yielding to European nationalism and fascism. Pointing to the initiative of Professor Harihar Nath Tripathi of Kashi Hindu University, who first attracted Swami Karpatri's attention to Golwalkar's book *Vichar Navneet* (Bunch of Thoughts), Sri Virbhadra Mishra, the publisher of this book (Vedshastranusandhan Kendra, Varanasi) described this piece of writing as similar to a critique of Golwalkar's Hindu Rashtravad. In this book, the cultural graphic of oneness promoted by the RSS was compared to Hitler's fascism and Golwalkar's ideal of Hindu Rashtravad as anti-*sastric* and even anti-Hindu. Swami Karpatri strongly condemned RSS's all-round efforts to stigmatize the Christians and Muslims as threats to the Hindu society. Infact, nowhere in the proposed *Ramraj* narrative of Swami Karpatri, the 'enemy other' syndrome remained evocative ever, and the Swami preferred to maintain silence on the issue. Written in Hindi and circulated to a limited extent, most of Swami Karpatri's political publications, like *Adhunik Rajneeti Aur Ramrajya Parishad* (1974), did not reach the English-language readers, barring those published by Gita Press, like *Marxwad Aur Ramrajya* (2014). Some of his spiritual writings later got translated or discussed at a wider level by his European followers like Alain Daniélou or Jean-Louis Gabin (Daniélou 1987).

Having started his career as a Vedantin scholar, this *sanatani* sadhu, popular as Dharma Samrat, craved a separate niche in Indian politics. In addition to his orthodox sectarian engagement with the Sanatana Dharma movement in North India, Swami Karpatri augmented a unique brand of traditional ascetic politics within the courtiers of political Hindutva. The RSS–VHP inheritance of drawing upon the network of sadhus and their monastic orders symbolized the long-drawn dialects of traditional asceticism within the Hindutva movement. Swami Karpatri's patterns of involvement with the Hindutva movement indicated a balanced relationship between these two mutually corresponding ideas; it hardly mirrored sadhus as the spontaneous agents of the movement. Acquiring the same legacy of equitable distance, the RSS in later years launched the VHP in 1964—a separate outfit for the sadhus outside of politics to circumvent the compulsions of a secular government in power. Undoubtedly, it was a smart move, because the VHP offered the RSS a unique scope to run large-scale canvasses among a large section of the Hindu population. Interestingly, Swami Karpatri provided a platform for politically motivated sadhus in search for greater political legitimacy after independence, he maintained a dignified distance from the RSS and the Jana Sangh as long as the RRP remained alive in active politics.

The rhetoric of Hindu victimhood, or the very conspiracy theories[75] promoted by the Hindutva brigade, did not bother Swami Karpatri even a little, rather everything what the sanatanist sadhus had imagined a revival of the utopian space of Dharmarajya. While the Hindutva forces alluded to an end of Hindu doctrinal systems of knowledge and declared the supremacy of the Vedas over other texts and interpretations, the *sanatąni* sadhus ushered in the studies of non-Vedic texts, and according to Swami Karpatri, 'Ramcharitmanas' evoked the highest values of human excellence. It was the ideal of Ram Rajya, not the 'Vedic golden age', which outlined the actual legacy of Hinduism, and Hindu identity, then, is one that submits not to the structure of an ethno-cultural nationalism but to a system run by the divine dispensation of Lord Rama—the ideal form of governance. One can see here the distinction between Ram Rajya and Hindu Raj—a model welfare state and an ethno-cultural state; the former had no interest in running down the religious 'others' or 'distancing and defining the Hindu self from the Islamic non-self',[76] whereas the latter worked to define the Hindu identity/self in opposition to the Islamic non-self.[77]

In view of the utopian name of Ram Rajya, the RSS–Jana Sangh leaders remained a bit sceptical about the prospects of the RRP in a democratic–secular structure. Since Swami Karpatri and the other *sanatanist* sadhus did not fall in line with political Hindutva, they were pushed to the margins, or even ignored if required. The RRP contested elections till 1967 in selected pockets of North India; however, it lost its electoral presence in a couple of years. The assumption that the party eventually merged with the Jana Sangh lacks authenticity, because until recently, the party was nominating candidates against the BJP in the general elections. For instance, the party named Shri Bhagwan Vedantacharya as its candidate against BJP's Narendra Modi at the Varanasi constituency in the 2019 Lok Sabha elections. The leading daily *Times of India* noted that the Shankaracharya of Jyotish Peeth and Dwarka Sharda Peetham Swami Swaroopanand Swaraswati's disciple Avimukteshwaranand Saraswati announced the candidature of Bhagwan Vedantacharya, who is the convenor of the Akhil Bharatiya Sant Parishad (ABSP). The RRP held Modi responsible for the demolition of the Kashi Viswanath corridor project in its manifesto.[78]

The current equation between the *sanatani* sadhus and the ruling BJP should be explained in terms of the complex relationship shared by the VHP and the Hindu *sanatani sampradayas* from 1980s. Other than this, it is really intriguing to see how the Hindutva brigade toyed with the symbolic space of Ram Rajya as the citadel of a Hindu state for electoral gains. Despite showing strong inhibitions to the ideal of Ram Rajya when it was promoted by Swami Karpatri, the Hindutva leaders eventually snapped up the divine-kingdom theory, claiming their legacy on Lord Rama. The entire Ram Janmabhoomi episode and the nationwide sloganeering of 'Jai Shri Ram' might have contributed to the Hindutva profit-making politics; they brought to the fore the all-embracing power of political Hindutva as a collective formulation of every thought and perception that claimed to be Hindu in approach. The spirit of individualism introduced by the *sanatanists* like Swami Karpatri lost its agency in the whirlpool of convictions and prejudices that form the basis of a Hindu Rashtra in India.

NOTES

1. Jha, Dhirendra K. *Ascetic Games: Sadhus, Akharas and the Making of the Hindu Vote* (New Delhi: Westland Publications Private Limited, 2019).

2. Pradhan, Rajesh. *When the Saints Go marching in': The Curious Ambivalence of Religious Sadhus in Recent Politics in India* (New Delhi: Orient BlackSwan, 2014).
3. For a short biography of Swami Karpatri, see, Bansidhar Tripathi, *Sadhus of India* (Bombay: Popular Prakashan, 1978), 224–225.
4. The term Sanatana Dharma (eternal religion) could be translated in a number of ways. Halbfass called it the 'self-representation of Hinduism which grew out of its encounter with the West'. Wilhelm Halbfass, *India and Europe: An Essay in Philosophical Understanding* (Delhi: Motilal Banarsidass, 1990), 344. The plethora of positions shared by Sanatana Dharma denote Hinduism to be a monolithic construction in which different sectarian traditions have been developed. For details, see, John Zavos, 'Defending Hindu Tradition: Sanatana Dharma as a Symbol of Orthodoxy in Colonial India', *Religion* 31, no. 2 (2001): 109–110.
5. Sadhu-turned-politician Baba Raghav Das used to be a conspicuous character. He fought elections as a Congress candidate but received complete support from the Hindu Mahasabha in the 1948 by-election to the Faizabad assembly against socialist leader Acharya Narendra Deva. He had been a regular contributor to Gita Press. Akshaya Mukul and Aksheya Mukul, *Gita Press and the Making of Hindu India* (Delhi: Harper Collins India, 2015), 184–185.
6. Christophe Jaffrelot, *Hindu Nationalist Movement and Indian Politics: 1925–1990s* (Delhi: Penguin, 1999), 94.
7 Hilal Ahmed, *Muslim Political Discourse in Postcolonial India: Monuments, Memory, Contestation* (Oxon: Routledge, 2014), 213.
8. A small except from Ahmed's article would be enough to trace the relevance of the incident in a nuanced manner: 'Both Jawaharlal Nehru and Sardar Patel criticised this incident and asked the chief minister of Uttar Pradesh, G.B. Pant, to protect the status of the mosque. Although Pant did not support the Hindu Rightists' version of the conflict, he remained reluctant to follow the advice of Patel. Nehru was deeply worried about the situation, especially at a time the country was going for the first Lok Sabha election. In a letter written to K.G. Mashruwala on 5 March 1950, Nehru said 'Baba Raghav Das gave his approval to it…District Officer…took no step…Pant condemned the act… but refrained taking definite action…. I have been greatly distressed about it'. The Uttar Pradesh government did not disappoint Nehru. It controlled the situation firmly in the coming months. The status quo was maintained at the site of the dispute; and at the same time, the main leaders and supporters of the temple agitation, including the local secretary of Hindu Mahasabha, Gopal Singh Visharad, were arrested'.

   For details, see, Hilal Ahmed, *How a Hindu Party Wanted Ram Mandir But Didn't Raise it in India's First Election Under Nehru*, 22 August 2019, https://theprint.in/opinion (accessed 10 February 2020. Also see, A. G. Noorani, *The Muslims of India: A Documentary Record* (Delhi: Oxford University Press,

2003), 242; Jaffrelot, *Hindu Nationalist Movement and Indian Politics*; Ahmed, *Muslim Political Discourse in Postcolonial India*, 213; Noorani, *The Muslims of India*, 242.

9. Using the ideas of the much-controversial 'Purusha Sukta', Golwalkar described the Hindu people as parts of a *Virat Purusha* (Divine Man/first incarnation of the Hindu God Brahma) in which 'the Brahmin is the head… and Shudras the feet'. Commenting on Golwalkar, K. R. Malkani, another noted Hindutva theoretician, mentioned that Golwalkar in fact 'saw no reason why Hindu law should break its links with *Manusmriti* [the laws of Manu]'. See, Madhav Shadashiv Golwalkar, *We or Our Nationhood Defined* (Nagpur: Bharat Publications, 1939), 36; K. R. Malkani, *The RSS Story* (New Delhi: Impex India, 1980), 73, as quoted in Subhash Gatade, 'The Ideological and Institutional Incorporation of Dalits Into Hindutva Maelstrom', *South Asia Citizens Wire*, 27 January 2009 (accessed 2 February 2009).
10. To get a detailed impression, see, Walter K. Anderson and Shridhar D. Damle, *The Brotherhood in Saffron: The Rashtriya Swayamsevak Sangh and Hindu Revivalism* (New Delhi: Vistar Publications, 1987); Walter K. Anderson and Shridhar D. Damle, 'RSS: Ideology, Organization, and Training', in *The Sangh Parivar: A Reader*, ed. Christophe Jaffrelot (New Delhi: Oxford University Press, 2005), 23–55; Paola Bacchetta, 'Hindu Nationalist Women as Ideologues', in *The Sangh Parivar: A Reader*, ed. Christophe Jaffrelot (New Delhi: Oxford University Press, 2005), 108–147.
11. It would not be irrelevant here to mention the point of view shared by Mahatma Gandhi on Sanatana Dharma. Defining himself as a *sanatani* Hindu, M. K. Gandhi declared, 'my own veneration for other faiths is the same as that for my own faith' and 'because I am a Sanatani Hindu, I claim to be a Christian, a Buddhist and a Muslim' (quoted in, Vishwanath Prasad Varma, *The Political Philosophy of Mahatma Gandhi and Sarvodaya* [Agra: Lakshmi Narain Agarwal, 1972], 63). Gandhi tried to sluice out the Sanatana Dharma off all its orthodoxy, and taking pride in the egalitarian, plural spirit of the Sanatana Dharma, he explained his own religious faith based on eternal law, free from all communal prejudices. Ashis Nandy pointed out, 'Traditional Hinduism, or rather Sanatan Dharma, was the source of his religious tolerance'. Ashis Nandy, 'The Politics of Secularism and the Recovery of Religious Toleration', in *Secularism and Its Critics*, ed. Rajeev Bhargava (New Delhi: Oxford University Press, 2010), 321–34.
12. Zavos, 'Defending Hindu Tradition', 109.
13. Tracing the history of the *sanatani* organizations would reveal their evolution from the late 19th century. The Sanatan Dharma Rakshini Sabha (Association for Defence of the Eternal Religion) was formed in Calcutta in 1873, and the Hindu Dharm Prakashik Sabha (Society for the Promulgation of the Hindu Faith) formed in Ludhiana, Punjab, more or less at the same time. Sanatana Dharma societies in Haridwar and Delhi came into existence around 1895,

and the Bharat Dharma Mahamandala was established in Mathura in 1902. Different minor organizations also appeared in the public domain by the first decade of the 20th century. J. N. Farquhar, *Modern Religious Movements in India* (New York: Macmillan Company, 1915); reprint ed., Delhi, Munshiram Manoharlal, 1967, p. 318.

14. Projected commonly as defending the old, orthodox narratives against the waves of religious reforms in the 19th century, Sanatana Dharma *sabhas* seemed to be antithetical to modernity; however, new studies, like that of Vasudha Dalmia, presented an alternative to the existing narratives. Dalmia noted, 'the spokesmen [of the *sabhas*] in the very name of orthodoxy, of tradition itself, were in fact accommodating and articulating wide-reaching changes', and so, 'it would be a mistake to imagine that these institutions came into being only to conserve inherited practice. As always one of their vital functions was also to sanction change however minimal it might have appeared at first sight'. Contrary to showing Sanatana Dharma as a reactionary approach, the alternative narratives helped validate its strength in producing a pan-Hindu identity based on the model of pan-Hindu traditions. V. Dalmia, *The Nationalization of Hindu Traditions: Bharatendu Harischandra and Nineteenth Century Banaras* (New Delhi: Oxford University Press, 2010), 2.
15. These sectarian communities or *sampradayas* manifested the importance of institutional affiliation in the life of the ascetics who had been incorporated in the orthodox traditions maintained through the relationship between the guru and the disciples. These sects were different from caste, and unlike a Christian sect did not stand in relation to a church. Louis Dumont, in one of his influential theories on Indian religions, conceived the presence of the ascetic first in relation to the caste system and second in relation to the dichotomies present between the ascetics and the householders/Brahmins. The relation itself looks hypothetical, because the sectarian traditions 'have reclassified social relations in the transient world so as to derecognise or neutralize the house/houseless distinction and to prevent the Brahman as Brahman from mediating the opposition of ascetic/non-ascetic'. Richard Burghart, 'Renunciation in the Religious Traditions of South Asia', *Man* (New Series), 18, no. 4 (December 1983): 640–641. Also see, Louis Dumont, *Homo Hierarchicus* (Paris: Gillimard, 1966).
16. By the early 20th century, Sanatana Dharma *sabhas* were emerging in different parts of North India around an orthodox network of guru–*sishyas* and devotees. In Banaras, the Bharat Dharma Mahamandala was formed by Din Dayalu Sharma for the expansion and propagation of Sanatana Dharma. It was noted that after 1902, when Swami Gnanananda, a Shaiva sadhu from the Dasnami order, took charge of the Mahamandala, the Shaiva sectarian outlook became dominant in the devotional culture of North India. It led to the growing influence of the Shaiva Brahmanical thoughts on the Mahamandala. For details, see, Dalmia, *The Nationalisation of Hindu Traditions*, 82–110;

M. Kasturi, 'Asceticising Monastic Families'. Ascetic Genealogies, Property Feuds and Anglo-Hindu Law in Late Colonial India', *Modern Asian Studies* 43, no. 5 (2009): 1039–1083.

17. Cow protection and cow slaughter has been a pertinent issue in Indian politics. Freitag described the cow as a sacred symbol that attracted a sizeable amount of public attention during the first public campaign in 19th-century India to the Hindu reaction against the Allahabad High Court's ruling, in 1888, that the cow could not be qualified as a protected 'sacred object' under law. The cow protection issue evolved as a religious sentiment for the Hindus against the beef-eating Muslims and Christians, and many *gaurakshini sabhas* came out mostly in northern and north-western parts of India since the late 19th century as part of the *sanatani* programmes. On this issue, a pan-Hindu identity movement gathered momentum, gradually leading to violent outbursts by the cow-protectionist individuals and organizations in the 20th century. For a detailed discussion on the cow protection issue, see, Sandria B. Freitag, 'Sacred Symbol as Mobilizing Ideology: The North Indian Search for a "Hindu" Community', *Comparative Studies in Society and History* 22, no. 4 (1980): 597–625; Anand A. Yang, 'Sacred Symbol and Sacred Space in Rural India: Community Mobilization in the "Anti-Cow Killing" Riot of 1893', *Comparative Studies in Society and History* 22, no. 4 (1980): 576–596; and Peter van der Veer, *Religious Nationalism: Hindus and Muslims in India* (Berkeley: University of California Press, 1994); Anthony Parel, 'The Political Symbolism of the Cow in India', *Journal of Commonwealth Political Studies* 7, no. 3 (1969): 179–203; Francis Robinson, *Separatism Among Indian Muslims: The Politics of the United Provinces' Muslims, 1860–1923* (London: Cambridge University Press, 1974); Gyanendra Pandey, 'Rallying Around the Cow: Sectarian Strife in the Bhojpur Region, c. 1888–1917', in *Subaltern Studies: Writings on South Asian History and Society*, Vol. 2, ed. Ranajit Guha (Delhi/New York: Oxford University Press, 1983), 60–129; Cassie Adcock and Radhika Govindarajan, 'Bovine Politics in South Asia: Rethinking Religion, Law and Ethics', *South Asia: Journal of South Asian Studies* 42, no. 6 (2019): 1095–1107.
18. D. G. White, *The Alchemical Body, Siddha Traditions in Medieval India* (Chicago, IL: Chicago University Press, 1996); D. G. White, *Sinister Yogis* (Chicago, IL: Chicago University Press, 2009).
19. Anand T. Hingorani, ed., *M. K. Gandhi—Towards Lasting Peace* (Bombay: Bharatiya Vidya Bhavan, 1966), 219–220. For a detailed discussion of Gandhi's concept of statehood see, Bhikhu Parekh, *Gandhi's Political Philosophy: A Critical Examination* (New Delhi: Ajanta Publications, 1995).
20. Swami Karpatri's visions on the Varna order sharply differed from those of Gandhi. Talking at a meeting of untouchables in 1925, Gandhi proposed, '…I would therefore appeal to Hindus of the higher castes present here that, if they call themselves Sanatan Dharmi, if they love the cow, they should not hate members of the untouchable classes'. Gandhi, *Collected Works of*

Mahatma Gandhi (New Delhi: Publications Division, Government of India, 1958–1984), 28, 179.

21. Swami Adgadanand, *Jeevanadarsh Evam Atmanubhuti: Ideals of Life & Self-Realisation* (Mumbai: Shri Paramhans Swami Adgadanand Ji, Ashram Trust), 145–146.
22. Ibid.
23. Ibid.
24. Missionary scholar John Nicol Farquhar held the view that unlike Christianity, Hinduism did not have the strength to push men and women into selfless service to the nation, since the Hindu philosophy promotes inaction, and that Hinduism springs from renunciation (John Nicol Farquhar, The *Crown of Hinduism* [London: OUP, 1913], 294). Famous imperialist scholar James Mill asserted that the Hindu sanyasi is debarred from all moral duties (James Mill, *The History of British India*, Vol. 1 [New York: Chelsea, 1968], 294), while John Campbell deemed Hindu monasticism as a 'gloomy religious abnegation' and opposed to any form of patriotism (John Campbell Oman, *The Mystics, Ascetics and Saints of India* [London: Fisher Unwin, 1905], 15). All these assumptions indicated the lack of masculinity and marital spirit among the Indians; however, the East India Company encountered a different experience in the 17th century when a group of warrior ascetics and Muslim fakirs fought against the British. Contrary to the dominant Western understanding of passive asceticism, these warrior ascetics were branded as criminals or dacoits in colonial records. In the same manner, the British found it very difficult to locate the warrior, trader and rebel monks in the general perceptions of asceticism, while the rise in the number of 'political sannyasis' during the Swadeshi movement also appeared to be a threat for the government. See, Indira Chowdhury, *Frail Hero and Virile History: Gender and the Politics of Culture in Colonial Bengal* (Delhi: OUP, 1998), 155.
25. Sudipta Kaviraj, *The Unhappy Consciousness: Bankimchandra Chattopadhyay and the Formation of the Nationalist Discourse in India* (New York: Oxford University Press, 1995), 72–106.
26. Romila Thaper, *Cultural Transaction in Early Idea, Tradition and Patronage. History and Beyond* (New Delhi: OUP, 2002), 13.
27. The official publication of the Bharat Dharma Mahamandala informed that Pandit Din Dayalu Sharma tried to bring together all the dharma *sabhas* scattered around Calcutta and Peshawar and visited these places quite often. The *mahamandala* came into existence for this reason only. *Sri Mahamandal ki Balyavastha* (Bañaras: Shri Bharat Dharma Mahamandal Head Office, 1910), 43.
28. Kenneth Jones, *Arya Dharm: Hindu Consciousness in 19th-Century Punjab* (Berkeley, CA: University of California Press, 1976), 26, 111, 189–193.
29. In regard to protecting the religion from undesired influences, the *mahamandala* paradoxically mentioned, 'By the grace of God the people are united

under one chhatrapati rule of the British in which we have got facilities like the railways and telegraph and post offices. Our welfare is taken care of by the government. But, as the rulers are from another country and they belong to another religion we need to work for our religious development ourselves.... God has sent the most liberal people (Jati) of the world to rule over us and be the saviour of this country. Therefore, considering that it is the order of God it is the duty of every Hindu to leave external development in the hands of the British Government and work for religious, educational, industrial and agro-commercial developments.... First of all we need to develop our religion, education and society and for that we need a national organisation. We should not worry about politics and concentrate on these areas for our progress'. *Sri Mahamandal ki Balyavastha*, (Bañaras: Shri Bharat Dharma Mahamandal Head Office, 1910), 2, 7.

30. Zavos, 'Defending Hindu Tradition', 118.
31. In the Mahasabha resolution of 1923, it was determined that the policy of including the untouchables in the *shuddhi* programme would be 'against scripture and the tradition to give the untouchables yajyopavit [i.e., investiture with the sacred thread], to teach the Vedas and to interdine with them' (Zavos, 'Defending Hindu Tradition', 119).
32. Gita Press was established in Kolkata in 1923 by Jaydayal Goyandka and a group of fellow Marwari businessmen. Aimed at publishing Hindi translations of sacred Hindu works, especially cheap and well-produced editions of the Bhagavad Gita, Ramayana and Mahabharata, Gita Press appeared to be one of the largest religious presses in the world. It was Hanuman Prasad Poddar who helped in making Gita Press a platform for the *sanatanists* and the monthly magazine *Kalyan* the mouthpiece of Sanatana Dharma. Centred on the city of Gorakhpur in the then United Province (currently in Uttar Pradesh), Gita Press consolidated the Hindi–Hindu undercurrents of Hindu nationalism in India and continued to serve the cause of Sanatana Dharma—the unchanging, timeless tradition of Hindu dharma. For details, see, Mukul and Mukul, *Gita Press and the Making of Hindu India*; Shashank Chaturvedi, David N. Gellner, and Sanjay Kumar Pandey, 'Politics in Gorakhpur Since the 1920s: The Making of a Safe 'Hindu' Constituency', *Contemporary South Asia* 27, no. 1 (2019): 43–44.
33. Digvijay Nath was born in 1884 and was Mahant from 1934 until his death in 1969. In 1967, he won the Gorakhpur seat, standing officially as an independent (Avaidyanath had already won the MLA [Member of Legislative Assembly] seat in 1962 for the Hindu Mahasabha). Digvijay Nath was initially a member of the Congress and was arrested for encouraging the violence that led to the Chauri Chaura killings in 1922. In 1937, he joined the Hindu Mahasabha. For details, see, Chaturvedi, Gellner, and Pandey, 'Politics in Gorakhpur Since the 1920s', 44; S. I. Wilkinson, *Votes and Violence: Electoral Competition and Ethnic Riots in India* (Cambridge: Cambridge University Press, 2009).

34. 'An All India Sanatana Dharma Conference', *Suryodaya, Special Trilingual Quarterly Edition* (March 1941), 72–73.
35. Almost all the Hindu reform movements loved to call their understanding of Hinduism as an interpretation of Sanatana Dharma; however, they did not consider themselves *sanatanists*. Talking about the *sanatanist*–reformist contradictions, Diana Dimitrova correctly metioned, 'it would be appropriate to distinguish between Sanåtana Dharma in the narrow sense, that is, sanåtanist dharma, and Sanåtana Dharma in the broad sense, that is, the eternal true religion, claimed equally by sanåtani Hindus, the Theosophical Society, Årya Samåjists, Gandhi, and adherents of many other reform traditions and movements of modern Hinduism, in other words, by most Hindus as a designation for their systems of belief' (see Kenneth Jones, *Arya Dharm: Hindu Consciousness in 19th-Century Punjab* [Berkeley: University of California Press, 1976] 26, 111, 189–193). Diana Dimitrova, 'The Development of Sanatana Dharma in the Twentieth century: A Radhasoami Guru's Perspective', *International Journal of Hindu Studies* 11 (2007): 89–98, p. 91.
36. Three religious *peeths*—Jagannath Puri, Dwaraka Puri and Shringeri—actively participated in the promotion of Sanatana Dharma. Reportedly, there were 240 dharma *sabhas* and some *gaurakshini sabhas* all over the country. *Sri Mahamandal ki Balyavastha*, 33.
37. Philip Lutgendorf, *The Life of a Text: Performing the Ramcaritmanas of Tulsidas* (Berkeley: University of California Press, 1991), 384–391.
38. Nehruvian secularism has remained a controversial space in Indian democratic affairs so far. Commenting on its character, Sabyasachi Bhattacharya mentioned, 'Nehru belied that it was absurd to claim that we are a secular state, we have done something amazingly, we have only done something which every country does except a few misguided and backward countries in the world. The air was to ensure justice to the individual or the group in minority'. Sabyasachi Bhattacharya, 'Secularism and the State', *Frontline*, 5 February 2016, p. 66. For a detailed discussion see, Thomas Pantham, 'Indian Secularism and Its Critics: Some Reflections', *The Review of Politics* 59, no. 3 (5 August 2009): 523–540, https://doi.org/10.1017/S0034670500027704
39. Elaborating his points, Graham mentioned, 'while a Hindu traditionalist might devote much of his public life to cultural associations and institutions dedicated to the promotion of Hinduism, he might well support the Congress as the expression of a purely political nationalism with clearly defined representative and constitutional objectives', while Hindu nationalists urged 'not only to conserve Hinduism but to develop the latent power of the Hindu community and thus to promote the Hindu *sangathan*, the organization of the Hindus…'. Further, Graham identified V. D. Savarkar's ideology as manifested in *Essentials of Hindutva*, published in 1924, a case of Hindu nationalist ideology which did not have any commitment to Hindu traditionalism but was 'xenophobic' in its outlook. See, B. D. Graham, 'The

Congress and Hindu Nationalism', in *The Indian National Congress: Centenary Hindsights*, ed. D. A. Low (New Delhi: Oxford University Press, 1988), 174; Christophe Jaffrelot, *The Hindu Nationalist Movement and Indian Politics* (New Delhi: Penguin Books, 1996).

40. Richard Gordon mentioned, 'In its first phase, before 1922, the Hindu Mahasabha was not an all India organisation in any real sense, either in the extent of its organisation or in the scope of its activities. It was, at most, an inter- provincial organisation linking Hindu movements in the U.P. and the Punjab. As its conferences were held in conjunction with the annual Congress, it attracted casual platform support from other provinces'. R. Gordon, 'The Hindu Mahasabha and the Indian National Congress, 1915 to 1926', *Modern Asian Studies* 9, no. 2 (1975): 145–203.
41. In the perception of Savarkar, developed as the political rival of the Congress, the Hindu Mahasabha 'is not in the main a Hindu-Dharma Sabha but is pre-eminently a Hindu Rashtra Sabha and is a pan-Hindu organisation shaping the destiny of the Hindu Nation in all its social, political and cultural aspects…'. Significantly, Savarkar's definition of Hindu included any person who considered the land of Bharatvarsha as his motherland and holy land. If this formula of a holy land is omitted, it included people of every religion, even the Muslims who show allegiance to their motherland India. Savarkar's presidential speech at the 19th session of the All India Hindu Mahasabha in Ahmedabad, 1937. Samagra Savarkar Wangmaya, Vol. VI: Hindu Rashtra Darshan (Poona, 1964), 229.
42. For a nuanced discussion on Mahasabha's wartime efforts, see Nandini Gondhalekar and Sanjoy Bhattacharya, 'The All India Hindu Mahasabha and the End of British Rule in India, 1939–1947', *Social Scientist* 27, no. 7/8 (July–August 1999): 48–74.
43. On his resignation, Savarkar expressed in a letter to L. B. Bhopatkar that he wanted that Dr Syama Prasad Mookerjee to succeed him. It was utterly surprising, because Savarkar and Mookerjee had never been in good terms earlier. Gondhalekar and Bhattacharya, 'The All India Hindu Mahasabha', 57.
44. Bhatt observed that the Congress's claim to represent all Indians was rejected by the Hindu Mahasabha, which demanded to be recognized by the British as the sole legitimate body representing the whole Hindu population of India. V. D. Savarkar, 'Resolutions of the Hindu Mahasabha Working Committee 19.11.1939', 164–165; quoted in Bhatt, op. cit., 102. Chetan Bhatt, 'From Revolutionary Nationalism to Hindutva', *Hindu Nationalism: Origins, Ideologies and Modern Myths*, edited by Chetan Bhatt (London: Bloomsbury Academic, 2001), Bloomsbury Collections.
45. Gondhalekar and Bhattacharya, 'The All India Hindu Mahasabha', 59–60.
46. Mookerjee believed that the Mahasabha should accept all faiths and open its door for all people, including the Muslims, in the changed political circumstances after independence. In order to keep the Mahasabha free from being tagged as a communal organization, it should incorporate Muslims

in its ranks and files, at least for the time being. The other factions inside the Mahasabha, however, opposed him on the grounds that the Mahasabha would cease to exist as an organization committed to safeguard the Hindu interest. A Hindu origination whose raison d'être had so far been based on keeping the Hindu identity and interest intact against the so-called Muslim political nuisance now found it really bizarre to adopt an open-door policy overnight. When the Working Committee determined that the membership of the Hindu Mahasabha would be limited to Hindus only, Dr Mookerjee tendered his resignation on 23 November 1948. For a detailed discussion, see, Prashanto Kumar Chatterjee, *Dr. Syama Prasad Mookerjee and Indian Politics: An Account of an Outstanding Political Leader* (New Delhi: Cambridge University Press, 2012), 275–276. Joya Chatterjee, *The Spoils of Partition: Bengal and India, 1947–1967* (New Delhi: Cambridge University Press, 2007), 266–267.

47. Hanumanprasad Poddar to Dr Mookerjee, 24 May 1951, S. P. Mookerjee Papers, Installment II-IV, Subject File No. 168, p.15. (New Delhi: NMML).
48. Ibid.
49. For a detailed analysis on Syama Prasad Mookerjee, see, Koushiki Dasgupta, *Electoral Politics and Hindu Nationalism in India: The Bharatiya Jana Sangh, 1951–1971* (London: Routledge, 2020), Chapter I.
50. It has been estimated that upper-caste convictions were very much powerful in the North, especially in the state of Uttar Pradesh. Achin Vanik has pointed out, 'General, dominance at the centre has required dominance in the northern states, whose order of importance i first in Uttar Pradesh, then Bihar, followed by Madhya Pradesh and Rajasthan'. Achin Vanik, 'Communalization of the Indian Polity', in *India's Political Parties*, eds. Peter Ronald deSouza and E. Sridharan (New Delhi: SAGE Publications, 2006), 174.
51. 'Akhāṛā means "wrestling arena," from which akhāṛiyā derives, meaning "master fighter," "skilled manoevrer," or "strategist." The recruitment of nāgās into organized fighting units appears to have occurred around the time of Akbar's reign, although it is unlikely to have been in response to attacks by Sufis. Nearly all of the recorded conflicts between bands of ascetics have been between factions of Hindus, in most instances between Vaisṇava Rāmānandī vairāgīs/bairāgī and Śaiva Daśanāmī saṃnyāsīs (also known as gosāīṃs) at melās (festivals) over bathing priorities for particular akhāṛās. The Rāmānandīs and the Daśanāmīs are the largest of the 60 or so extant sādhu sects in India and Nepal, and also those with the greatest number of nāgās. The evidence indicates that organized nāgā military activity originally flourished under state During the latter half of the 16th century and the early part of the 17th century, a number of bands of fighting ascetics formed into akhāṛās with sectarian names and identities. These armies were of mercenaries who often largely disbanded during cessations of conflict and during harvest times, when many of the men would return home to attend to agricultural duties. The formation of mercenary nāgā armies

occurred largely in parallel with the constitution of a formal and distinct identity for many of the currently recognizable sects of sādhus, including the Rāmānandīs and Daśanāmīs' (https://brill.com/fileasset/downloads_products/35696_warrior_ascetics.pdf). For a detailed overview of the literature on the fighting ascetics of the *akharas*, see, J. S. Alter, *The Wrestler's Body: Identity and Ideology in North India* (Oxford: Oxford University Press, 1992); M. Clark, *The Daśanāmī Saṃnyāsīs: The Integration of Ascetic Lineages into an Order* (Leiden: Brill, 2006); J. M. Ghosh, *Sannyasi and Fakir Raiders in Bengal* (Calcutta: Bengal Secretariat Book Depot, 1930). G. S. Ghurye, Indian Sadhus (Bombay, 1953, 2 1964); R. L. Gross, *The Sadhus of India: A Study of Hindu Asceticism* (Jaipur: Rawat Publications, 1992); S. L. Hausner, *Wandering with Sadhus: Ascetics in the Hindu Himalayas* (Bloomington: Indiana University Press, 2007); D. N. Lorenzen, 'Warrior Ascetics in Indian History', *Journal of the American Oriental Society* 98, no. 1 (1978): 61–75; W. G. Orr, *Armed Religious Ascetics in North India* (Manchester, 1940); W. R. Pinch, *Warrior Ascetics and Indian Empires* (Cambridge: Cambridge University Press, 2006); J. N. Farquhar, 'The Organisation of the Sannyasis of the Vedanta', *The Journal of the Royal Asiatic Society of Great Britain and Ireland* (1925): 479–486.

52. From 1780 to 1940, Dasnami monasteries and akharas proliferated in Varanasi. Since the late 19th century, Dasnami maths emerged vibrant, and Shaiva sadhus formed 48 per cent of the population. The Dandi monastic institutions patronized the Sanskrit, Vedantic and Tantric ways of learning. Swami Karpatri belonged to this legacy of the Dandi Dasnami ascetic order from Varanasi. Kasturi, 'Asceticising Monastic Families', 19–40; For a detailed analysis see, W. Pinch, *Peasants and Monks in British India* (Berkeley: University of California Press, 1994).
53. The Hindu Code Bill was an attempt to codify the Hindu personal laws and to provide a civil code in place of the body of Hindu personal law. The bill was introduced by Dr B. R. Ambedkar in the Constituent Assembly on 11 April 1947 and covered: (a) the right to property; (b) order of succession to property; and (c) maintenance, marriage, divorce adoption, minority and guardianship. Reba Som, 'Jawaharlal Nehru and the Hindu Code: A Victory of Symbol Over Substance?' *Modern Asian Studies* 28, no. 1 (February 1994): 165–194.
54. John A. Banningan, 'The Hindu Code Bill', *Far Eastern Survey* 21, no. 17 (3 December 1952): 173–176 [Published by Institute of Pacific Relations].
55. Ramchandra Guha, 'Reforming The Hindus', *Hindu*, 18 July 2014.
56. Report of the Hindu Law Committee (Madras: Government Press), 414.
57. For a detailed discussion, see, Ramchandra Guha, India After Gandhi, quoted 'Uniform Civil Code: How RSS and Hindu Swamis Fought Tooth and Nail the Hindu Code Bill', by L. S. Herdenia, *The Milli Gazette*, 27 August 2017, http://www.milligazette.com/ (accessed 12 September 2019).
58. Ibid.
59. Som, 'Jawaharlal Nehru and the Hindu Code', 172.

60. William Gould, while talking of the expression of secularism in North India, referred to specific instances when local congress leaders virtually opposed the Hindu Code Bill. 'The UP Assembly debates about the Prohibition of Unequal Marriages Bill in 1954 mirrored the conservatism surrounding the Hindu Code Bill. Congress party member Badri Prasad Kacker, for example, opposed the principle that age differences of couples could not exceed 25 years by suggesting that the Shastras had opposed marriages of equal age' (*The Pioneer*, Lucknow, 23 September 1954), quoted in William Gould, 'Contesting Secularism in Colonial and Postcolonial North India Between the 1930 and 1950s', *Contemporary South Asia* 14, no. 4 (2005): 489.
61. For a better understanding of Nehruvian secularism, see, Sarvepalli Gopal, (ed.), *Jawaharlal Nehru: An Anthology* (New Delhi: Oxford University Press, 1980), 330; Christophe Jaffrelot, 'Composite Culture Is Not Multiculturalism: A Study of the Indian Constituent Assembly Debates', in *India and the Politics of Developing Countries: Essays in Memory of Myron Weiner*, ed. Ashutosh Varshney (New Delhi: SAGE Publications, 2004), 126–149.
62. Gould, 'Contesting Secularism in Colonial and Postcolonial North India'.
63. Hari Ram Nathany from Bhilwara, Raj Chandra Sen from Kota-Bundi and Nand Lal Sharma from Sikar won the election from Ram Rajya Parishad's (RRP) ticket. 'First Lok Sabha, Party wise details—Ram Rajya Parishad', https://loksabha.nic.in/members/partyardetail (accessed 18 September 2019).
64. To get a brighter picture of Rajasthani politics, see Kusum Bhargava, 'Rajasthan Politics and Princely Rulers: An Analysis of Electoral Processes', *The Indian Journal of Political Science* 33, no. 4 (October–December 1972): 413–430; The Statistical Report on the General Election, 1951 to the Legislative Assembly of Rajasthan, Election Commission of India, New Delhi, https://eci.gov.in/files/file/3378-rajasthan-1951 (accessed 18 September 2019).
65. Professor Ramachandra Guha recalled an interesting anecdote from the experiences shared by Shri Kamalnayan Bajaj, the Congress candidate from Sikar, Rajasthan. The latter lost the election to the RRP candidature and made out the personal rivalry between the local Congress leaders as one of the primary reasons for his defeat. He also pointed out that 'misleading and false propaganda carried on' by the RRP, whose leaders 'openly said that a vote given to the Congress would be tantamount to slaughtering a thousand cows and that a vote to the Ram Raj [Parishad] would bring them Punya of looking after a thousand cows...money was freely distributed particularly amongst Brahmins so that they may vote for the Ram Raj. Sweets were also distributed amongst the children for crying Ram Raj slogans. Ram Raj workers had offered money even to Harijans but at some places the latter spurned the offer and said that their votes would go to the Congress.... At many booths, Ram Raj workers with lathis and naked swords in their hands went round openly telling the people to precede to the booths only if they

wanted to vote for the Ram Raj, otherwise they asked them to go back. … Ram Raj workers threatened the poor and ignorant voters to make it impossible for them to live their normal life. In spite of this, however, the general feeling that Congress was likely to eventually come to power prevailed and this was to some extent responsible for the Congress securing some votes even in areas dominated by the Jagirdars'. Ramchandra Guha, 'Elections in 1951–1952, Not Much Difference', Columns, *Hindustan Times*, 20 April 2019, https://www.hindustantimes.com/columns/elections.html (accessed 23 November 2019).

66. RRP also promised to give untouchables 'high posts' in the management of the sanitation departments and leather and hides trade—traditional occupations for out-caste Hindus. The Election Manifesto of the All-India Ramarajya-Parishad (Delhi: Nigamabodha Ghat, 1951), 3. Quoted in Weiner, *Party Politics in India*, 174.
67. Myron Weiner, *Party Politics in India: The Development of a Multi-Party System* (Princeton, NJ: Princeton University Press, 1957), 174–175.
68. Weiner, *Party Politics in India*, 175.
69. Anne Vergati, in her paper, has shown the importance of myths in the construction of the Rama cult and how the same set of myths have been used by former rulers and present politicians for their respective interests. Anne Vergati, 'The Construction of Tradition: The Cult of the God Rama in Rajasthan, North India', *History and Anthropology* 15, no. 3 (2004): 263–271.
70. Tripathi, *Sadhus of India*, 225.
71. Farquhar, *Modern Religious Movements in India*, 318.
72. It is to be noted here that the *sanatanists* might have emphasized the 'Veda' as their ultimate authority, but as quoted by Philip Lutgendorf, 'they tended to use this term loosely to refer to all revered scriptures'. According to Swami Karpatri, 'That same *Ramayana* has been made manifest by Goswami Tulsidas-ji in the form of the *Ramcaritmanas* . In practical terms, the meaning of the Veda *is* the meaning of the *Manas*' (Lutgendorf, *The Life of a Text*, 367).
73. Lutgendorf, *The Life of a Text*, 388.
74. Ibid.
75. Jyotirmaya Sharma, in his thoughtful analysis of Hindutva, illustrated the so-called Islamophobic position adopted by Hindutva thinkers. The premise of this Hindutva vision put into practice the victimhood theory by dividing the world neatly between a set of friends and foes. Sharma mentioned, 'Enemies of the faith could come in numerous guises and disguises; Westernization, pan-Islamism, Buddhism, folk and tribal gods and goddess, missionaries, conversation, lifestyles, heterodox ideas, spiritual interpretations, modern Indian languages, net sects, creative literature, poetry, sexual mores. The list could be endless'. Sharma's listing of possible theatres for Hindutva seems to be attractive for a flexible model of investigation, as the amount of enmity or hatred displayed by each of these entities is different and mutually conflicting.

Jyotirmaya Sharma, *Hindutva: Exploring the Idea of Hindu Nationalism* (New Delhi: Penguin India, 2015), 15.

76. Sharma, *Hindutva: Exploring the Idea of Hindu Nationalism*, 162.
77. Ibid.
78. The RRP candidature was cancelled later by the election commission at Varanasi. The RRP leaders blamed Narendra Modi for such 'mischief' and declared him unfit to fulfil the expectations of Varanasi. *Times of India*, 23 April 2019, https://timesofindia.indiatimes.com/city/varanasi/ramrajya-parishad (accessed 3 August 2019).

(Re)Making of Hindutva

The Sadhus in the Vishva Hindu Parishad

> History is witness to the fact that whenever such a crisis has come on the country sadhus such as Vishwamitra, Bhardwaj, Valmiki, Agastya etc in Sri Rama's time through their organised efforts protected the identity of the nation. Similarly, during Sri Krishna's time Vyasa, Jamini, Maitreye, Asti etc brought about a colossal change through their efforts. During Shivaji's time great saints like Samarth Ramdas protected dharma. Today, society expects a similar intervention from mahapurusha like you who are bearers of the rishi parampara—legacies and tradition of sages.[1]

These alluring justifications supporting the 'intervention' of the sadhus in the sociopolitical affairs of the country came from the Dharma Sansad conference organized by the VHP in 1989. The VHP, or the World Hindu Council, was established in 1966 to protect and strengthen the Hindu dharma and hold Dharma Sansads, or Hindu religious parliaments, at regular intervals to address specific issues across the Hindu religion and culture.[2] The Dharma Sansads were largely constituted by sadhus and Hindu religious figures from main philosophical traditions and reflected the importance of the sadhus in consolidating the Hindutva agenda over politics. The VHP calibrated the most effective version of ascetic politics to accomplish its own objectives and political interests. The sadhus, in due course of time, found this platform highly volatile and often impulsive to make any real impact on the core of the Hindu society. The VHP expected the sadhus to provide a Hindu perspective on sociopolitical matters so that the popular appeal of Hindu asceticism could be used to revitalize Hinduism in an age of scientific–technological developments. It nurtured its own explanations of why it had invested much on the sadhus to organize, protect and revitalize the Hindu religion and culture. The sadhus in general showed a kind of indolence in coming out with a monolithic narrative, suggesting the real implications of their involvement with the VHP. The sadhu–VHP nexus left a grey area in between—especially in situations where the sadhus rendered the message of Hindutva by perpetuating the social hierarchy and legitimizing the power of the divine above being denounced by the common masses. In regard to the sadhus from different monastic orders, the VHP could hardly make a somewhat more promising conclusion that primarily benefitted the project of Hindutva in both political and intellectual terms. This chapter attempts to identify those issues and situations that stalled the equation between the VHP and its ascetic support base with the passing phase of Hindutva politics and delves into the prospects of Hindu civilization by exploring the sadhus as a cohesive category with great social acceptance. The studies so far undertaken on the VHP[3] have remained deeply grounded in the Ayodhya movement since the mid-1980s, giving little space to the contested confluence between asceticism and Hindutva from within the territory of a Hindu ecclesiastical structure. This chapter delves into the approaches central to the involvement of the sadhus with the VHP in India and abroad, citing the Ayodhya affair mainly as a reference point. The understanding of sadhus as influential agents of Hindutva politics thrived on multiple factors, including the arrival of newer social relationships in the wake of new industrial developments after independence. The VHP evolved as the perfect metaphoric solution to those existential tensions that pushed the established social hierarchies to a point of jeopardy after the secular–modern democratic structure emerged after 1947. Eventually, the affluent middle-class people—rich professionals, petty industrialists and rich peasants—fearing a class challenge from the so-called unprivileged masses, found VHP-like of organizations effective for maintaining the status quo (Puniyani 2005, 25).

The initial history of the VHP stayed in obscurity for a long time. The background of its early participants reveals an interesting combination of intellectual conglomeration supported by some ex-maharajas,[4] members from the vernacular literati, religious gurus and traditional ascetics. There were some ex-Congress men and independent personalities without any connection with the RSS or any other political association. Apart from some erstwhile rajas and zamindars, such figures as K. M. Munshi, Sant Tukdoji, the Dalai Lama of the Tibetan Buddhists, Sushil Muni of the Jains, Master Tara Singh of the Sikhs, Shivram Shankar Apte of the RSS, Brahmachari Dattamurti Maharaj, Sir C. P. Ramaswami Iyer, Bhai Hanuman Prasad Poddar, Swami Chinmayananda, the Shankaracharyas of Dwarka, Sringeri, Kamakoti, Jyotir and Govardhan centres and Guru Golwalkar of the RSS joined the VHP in its initial phase. Despite its open adherence to the RSS, the early VHP reflected a perfect blend of vernacular intellectualism and *sanatani* asceticism, which added to the understandings of a thought process that reproduced an order of domination. It was not like a textualized thought process of elites but connected to the world of the commoners, feeding into a wider conceptual refinement of traditions, practices and knowledge. The first World Hindu Conference of 1966 was chaired by the retired Chief Justice of West Bengal High Court Shri Ramaprasad Mookerjee, the brother of the self-righteous Dr Syama Prasad Mookerjee. Various sub-creeds of the Hindu society joined together, along with government dignitaries, eminent foreign delegates and pandits of different Vedic branches. His Excellency President of India Dr Sarvepalli Radhakrishnan also sent his greetings for the success of this historic *sammelan*. Shri Rudra Raj Pandey, Vice Chancellor of Tribhuvan University, Nepal, read out the greetings from the King of Nepal who looked forward to the achievement of the VHP conference in a way that

> ...if the unity of all the Pundits, Yogis and great intellectuals gathered here in this Hindu Sammelan is able to guide in a modern way for the scientific investigations of all the matters for uplifting the peoples standard of living on the basis of our ideals and models. This Dharma has come down to us absolutely unaffected, in spite of the greatest upheavals in the world; because of high thinking, liberalism and the spirit of "Satyam, Shivam, Sundaram (truth, wellbeing, and beauty) are throbbing in us.[5]

Almost all the dignitaries present at the first VHP *sammelan* at Prayag emphasized theories of a grave predicament encountered by the Hindu society at that point of time and frequently used the phrases like 'anxious historic moment' and 'critical juncture in the annals of Hindu dharma'; they concluded that 'the danger of war looming large over humanity could be averted only if we adopt the ideals of Hindu Dharma', because 'only Hindu Dharma can give us strength for establishing international peace and status for motherhood, while safeguarding the diversity of the ideals'. The VHP delegates unanimously asked for a common code of conduct for the Hindus, 'with a view to bringing harmony between our traditional ideals and present-day needs', and asked for the establishment of 'educational and social service projects on a widest possible scale…so that the message of our Dharma can actively reach to the down-trodden, poor, wretched, innocent, gullible common Hindus'.[6] The main sprit of the *sammelan* remained argumentative about why the Hindu society was on the wane despite the presence of *jagadgurus*, saints and *dharmagurus* well versed in the 'Dharma-marma' (most confidential essence of dharma). The VHP dignitaries thought of changing the utopian reality, since they all believed themselves to be occupied with truth only. The truth that only 'Hindu Dharma is capable of bestowing necessary inspiration and strength on the people' returned repeatedly to its own uniqueness in which both the chaos and the carnival, the old and the new, the temporal and the spiritual could coexist. The fallacy of secularism often fell flat before the connotations of coexistence when confronted with the modern propositions that the secular discourse of modernity in India could survive with the religious discourse that was not secular. In reality, the VHP produced the aura of coexistence at least in its initial years, when top-ranking academicians, intellectuals and traditional scholars shared the same platform as *sanatani* sadhus and *dharmacharyas* to save the Hindu religion and society from further disintegration and predicaments.

The founders of the VHP could have had their own thoughts on the cotemporary political crises. The actual feeling of anxiety over the fate of the greater Hindu society epitomized their concern for the lack of spiritual/ethical training and education for the masses—what they considered essential for character building and nation building at large. That is why Swami Vishwesha Tirtha, one of the speakers at the conference, spoke of the need for a 'Central Vidyalaya to train up the teachers for the propagation of Hindu Dharma', and all the delegates unequivocally clamoured for the promotion of 'Sanskrit bhasha'—a carrier of *Bharatiya sanskriti* inside and outside the country.[7] The modus operandi of the Nehru government did not ensure any such programmes and objectives; rather, it stretched the gap between the

Oxbridge-trained secular, English-speaking generation and the rest of the population. The concern of the VHP, especially the sadhus, over the future of Hindu society indicated the continuing influence of religious leaders in matters of public affairs, especially on the education system. They had their own response to the politics of India and reclaimed the authority of *sanatani sanskriti* in the name of *Bharatiya sanskriti*; however, it is difficult to determine what this *sanatani sanskriti* stands for. The critics of Hindutva opened alternative readings of the *sanatani sanskriti* which often involved debates around such issues as the Hindu Code Bill, campaign against untouchability and banning of cow slaughter but attracted new-age Indians in large numbers, particularly a substantial section of the Hindu diaspora in the United States. The universal perspective adopted by the VHP received its primary motivation from the VHP intellectuals and scholars, including a section of the sadhus, such as Swami Chinmayananda, Swami Dayananda and Swami Satyamitranand, and others who had initiated overseas missionary movements to propagate the idea of a global Hindu council. The *sanatani* Shankaracharyas were keener on combatting the 'conversions to Christianity and Islam in India'; modern gurus like Chinmayananda made maximum efforts for the Hinduization of the Indian diaspora in the United States.[8] Importantly, the VHP worked as an amalgam of various streams of thought with specific primary objectives. The *sanatani* sadhus and modern gurus both contributed in the growth and development of the organization in their own ways. It is to be noted again that the sadhus, as leaders of a particular Hindu sect, could have enjoyed their freedom to create their own rationale for Hinduism; they did not hold an office in the VHP and mostly represented it either in the Council of the Learned or in the Board of Trustees.[9]

Astonishingly, the VHP thinkers and intellectuals never occupied a significant position at the centre stage of the modern Indian knowledge world. The *sanatani* sadhus, *dharmacharyas* and even the non-ascetic members of the VHP were pushed to the category of ideologues who turned to the past in its immediate form and lived the present within the wholeness of the past. VHP's immediate connection with the RSS might have painted the former as a xenophobic Hindu organization working for the Hindutva agenda in its own capacity. Contrary to the popular perception, VHP's RSS connection did not attract much controversy in its early phase, mainly because the VHP leaders tactfully avoided any issue that could generate speculations and misgivings on the character and objectives of the VHP as an independent body. The non-RSS members of the VHP, however, did not ever show any such reservation; they systematically maintained,

> the entire functioning of the VHP—decision making and implementing—is in the hands of the RSS members who are in the VHP as organisational secretaries. The Governing Council and the Board of Trustees of the VHP are more or less ratifying bodies. They ratify the proposals of the RSS sangathan mantries.[10]

Unlike the Bharatiya Jana Sangh, the VHP might not have gone through the dilemma of going with the RSS; it perhaps faced the challenge of negative publicity from the broader debate on how the RSS–VHP nexus had spoiled the democratic fabric of India. The VHP leadership, on several occasions, clarified how the ideas of the VHP or the RSS had been misconstrued and vilified, but all their arguments seemed unconvincing up to a certain point. Guru Golwalkar, when he founded the VHP, thought of accommodating Buddhists, Jains, Sikhs and tribes as part of the Hindu fraternity and included many promising faces from different parts of the country. No one can question the spirit of munificence present in the early attempts of Golwalkar, mostly because he was not obsessed with establishing that Hinduism was the best religion, or did not show any such symptoms in the initial years; however, he failed to fit into the image of a reputed public figure. His critics lashed out at him for speaking in the same vein as a militant activist and portrayed him as a protean fascist. He was a sadhu, an ideological disciple of Swami Vivekananda and a reformer; but he was also the same man who frankly admired the Nazis for working hard to maintain racial and cultural purity,[11] appreciated their efforts and considered emulating them through Hindutva. Such a situation was not in favour of the VHP, and the organization had to employ multiple strategies to gain at least some amount of popular legitimacy in the long run.

Paradoxically, Golwalkar's primary image of a sadhu attracted a handful of ascetics into the VHP fold. Until his death in 1973, the VHP worked mainly in the tribal areas and especially in matters of religious conversion. The sadhus could have contributed to the VHP in a meaningful way. They could motivate the youths in leading a life of a celibate for the greater cause of the nation. Furthermore, the *akhara* culture—the martial tradition of ascetic masculinity—infused a sense of self-restraint and self-regulation among the young aspirants of the RSS, and the RSS *shakhas* developed in the model of an *akhara* throughout the country.[12] Golwalkar, being a radical sadhu, worked from below and organized a vast network of dedicated activists and *pracharaks* who were structured after celibate sadhus. Neither of them led the life of a householder, and the moment a *pracharak* started his spiritual journey, he would become a sanyasi; Swami Chinmayananda, the sadhu founder of the VHP, held that there was no clear difference between a *pracharak* and a sanyasi other than in their attires. There were many workers in the RSS and VHP who lived the life of a sanyasi but later joined active politics. The line of demarcation between religiosity and politics or asceticism and politics was emaciated and made transparent, because the RSS–VHP workers believed in politicizing religion, not in bringing religion into politics. That is why the RSS–VHP *pracharaks* often took recourse to *sanyasa*—just to intrude into the sadhu *samaj* organized around the *sanatani sampradayas*. The image making tactics of Golwalkar proved to be highly beneficial in the case of the VHP activists who worked relentlessly among the tribal people and Dalits—those who converted to Christianity, especially in the Northeast and other parts of India.

Hindutva's engagement with the ascetics had never been an abrupt affair. As discussed earlier, the Hindutva proponents didn't ever look less-enthusiastic in face of those excited politicians who intended to translate their political agenda on religious grounds. After Independence, the coordination between Hindutva and asceticism flourished on similar socio-economic conditions, and the camaraderie of the sadhus with the VHP–RSS revealed the nature of situational compulsions that impelled the Hindutva forces to rely on the sadhus embodying the real spirit of a 'Hindu' India. It is difficult to make vivid assumptions on what made the RSS conscious of the Hindu society being threatened in the early 1960s when already the notions of 'dying Hindu' and 'religious other' had been offering the master narrative to the 'Hinduism in danger' theory since the early decades of the 20th century. It is arguable that the RSS perhaps realized the limitations against openly playing the religious card from its restricted periphery and accordingly launched a separate organization to promote and protect the cause of the Hindu religion and culture exclusively at a global scale.[13] Now, how should we locate the rise of the Hindutva forces, especially an ethno-cultural organization like VHP, in the so-called secular setting of the post-independence political culture in India? In my view, the expansion of the VHP ideology was not viewed as a difficulty or challenge for Indian secularism at least in the decades spanning Indian independence, because secularism held different meanings to different political actors,[14] and it had no clashing interests with VHP's plea to defend the Hindu religion and culture at the initial stage. Far from invoking the stereotypes of the secular state being marked by struggles between Hindu nationalism, Muslim separatism and secularism or by Hindu nationalism acting as the antithesis to Western secularism, it is desirable to see the spirit of post-independence secularism as a state-driven elitist ideology that strived to enter the popular domain for a long period of time. Since secularism mostly worked in relation to the state-driven policies and institutions, it fitted badly with the vast territory of mass politics, while the Hindu nationalist ideology slowly grew rampant in the popular territory.

In fact, the unpredictability attached to the spirit of secularism in the decades after Independence created some unique sets of relationships with the Hindutva movement and the VHP. It calibrated a new kind of revisionist history, if not a competitive history to the ideologies of a modern state or to say the ideology of secularism in post independent India.[15] VHP's gradual emergence must be tracked as part of the unfolding of self-critical trajectories of Hindu politics hitherto denied any global agency of their own. 'Globalism' and 'revisionism'—these two aspects former the fundamentals of the VHP, at least until the 1980s, followed by VHP's radical leanings towards militancy and mass politicization later. To quote Manchanda, 'The political vacuum produced by the collapse of the Nehruvian vision, the frustration over the failure of the modernity project, the Mandal challenge, globalization, global Islamic resurgence, etc.' helped proliferate the militant–politicized version of Hindutva in the highly complex sociopolitical environment in the 1980s.[16] Adding to these dimensions, VHP's global appeal got affected by the great deal of negative reports in the national and international media after the Babri Masjid demolition episode, even though its earlier propositions to privilege Hindu organic solidarity through eccentric propagation of some religious traditions had led to its strategy of creating a political space teeming with nationalist–devotional symbolism that could have persuaded Hindus with different sectarian affiliations.[17] Throughout VHP's journey of being and becoming an agent of the Hindutva movement, the sadhus provided their support to the organization through making Hindu dharma an assertion of Hindu pride on local, national and global terrains. This notion of 'Hindu pride' helped put together the essentials of an anti-orientalist proposition that challenged the configurations of otherworldly Hindu sadhus and passive Indians through systematically reformulating them as self-conscious Hindus and socially sensitive sadhus who could claim a sizeable amount of 'authority' over the political space, if necessary. What constituted that authority? How did this authority differ from the popular perceptions of a political authority in secular India? Did the authority of the sadhus make the so-called political space of Hindutva a seemingly intelligible category? Did it clash with the so-called secular culture or get itself assimilated into the secular public sphere? These are the questions that need special attention while talking of the VHP as a 'unifying framework for the diverse elements of organized Hinduism' (ancient sectarian traditions).[18] I will return to these points later in my discussion. Before that, it is necessary to locate the VHP on the political spectrum of India's transition to modernity after independence, since the VHP appeared to be a reactionary organization standing in between the boundaries of modernity and tradition in a secular India.

It is extremely problematic to note that in the 1960s, when 'nearly every Western country saw a decline in church membership and attendance, and a drop in the number of clergy and other religious professionals',[19] while in India, sadhus and prominent religious figures got a new lease of life in politics. Hugh McLeod, one of the leading historians of Christianity, portrayed 1960s as the history of emancipation from the ancient regime with its social hierarchies, and greater representation of the previously subordinate social groups.[20] Part of the story was written with the secularization process in Europe, with, to use Max Weber's phrase, 'the disenchantment of the world' questioning divine presence in each sector of society and the influence of supernatural/magical forces over human life towards the end of the 17th century. Secularization as a cultural process of rationalization and modernity challenged religious institutions; however, religion did not get wiped out from society. Secularization rather reformulated religion in the context of tradition, and in different modern industrial societies, religion as redefined tradition continued to survive. Subsequently, what Europe witnessed in the name of providing legitimacy to the state in lieu of the church as part of the secularization process was a gradual wielding of state power over a newly found entity called nation—endorsement of the nation state model where commonalities of citizens as a 'nation' gradually infused the binaries of 'common we' and 'uncommon they'.[21] These internal dynamics of 'we' and 'they' soon resulted in the numerical fallacy of ethno-religious identification, leading to minority backlash against religious majoritarianism, and eventually the ideology of secularism appeared to be a self-critical means to withdraw religion from the nation state fiasco. Nonetheless, keeping politics and state immune from the abhorrent tendencies of religion, or denouncing the political profile of religion, did not indicate the death of religion or trouncing of religion by the state at all.

In India, such developments were missing, since nationalism in the country did not grow around any nation state commonality model[22] and no European-style ethno-religious politics ever became capable of challenging the pluralist spirit of anti-colonial nationalism in the pre-independence time. The Hindu–Muslim conflicts or communal riots in the pre-independence era might have disturbed the nationalist status quo a couple of times, but these incidents hardly provided justification to follow the European model of separating religion from state affairs. Celebration of plurality and equal treatment of all religions established the edifice of secularism in India, and what we call the process of secularization, in European parlance, started much later in India. Therefore, the spirit of Nehruvian secularism, if not as a political doctrine then as a psychosocial culture of individual freedom and autonomy, had been cathartic for the suffocating experiences of a long history of colonial subjugation and politically orchestrated communal contestations, especially in the decade before the partition and independence. The problem was, fostering a psychosocial culture of individualism was one thing, and challenging the existing social hierarchies was another. Unless the spirit of secularism had led to rants against the institutions of oppressions in society, the freedom of expression or choice would not have been a reality. To make secularism an instrument of war against oppression and injustice, it was crucial to employ the process of secularization first, that is, to question all that was 'unscientific' and 'irrational' or simply superficial but influencing the social structure in the name of religious traditions or cultural practices. In this regard, readings of Gandhi and Tagore could be of immense importance in realizing why modernity in India should not be judged on its face value; rather, its power to infuse rationality and reasoning into the inner structure of traditions and practices should be taken into cognizance. For Tagore it was the 'autonomy of judgement'[23] that symbolized modernity as an intelligible category of assertion that decided in what way a particular tradition or social institution should be treated. In respect of the modern scientific developments in India, the Indian scientists decided to forge a kind of 'selective assimilation'[24] of Western science with Indian knowledge on science and 'tried to construct their own brand of modernity, particularly through selective incorporation (or re-invention) of Hindu ideas and traditions, through a mix of elements'.[25] Thus, in considering the progress of a modern, rational and scientific culture in India, it is important to think about modernity as an assorted category that in all of its proposed perspectives on society embraced traditions and practices with succinct reflexivity. Thus, secularism, like other faculties of modernity, should have grown as a self-conscious process of reasoning, disavowing irrational traditions and practices, and through choices of 'selective incorporation' of some of the traditions, if required. Paradoxically, secularism, despite its pretence of valuing modern decisions over the traditional understanding of social relations, ran through severe ambiguities at both the ideological and political levels.

Primarily, secularism, with all its misrepresentations of *dharma-nirapekshata*,[26] evolved in India as a state-driven ideology, if not a codified norm, prior to the commencement of the process of secularization, which could have made at least a feasible alliance of reasoning with the traditional socio-religious networks. Nehru might have thought of seeking solutions to socio-economic problems by 'making full use of the secular principles but seemed a little disturbed when talking about the misinterpretations of the term at various contexts'.[27] Nehru himself offered possibilities of misreading his speeches at various occasions. Atal Bihari Vajpayee, the Jana Sangh leader and an ardent proponent of soft Hindutva, smartly picked up excerpts from the speeches of Nehru ether intentionally or by default to propose a potential integrity of thoughts on common issues of concern.

> Delivering the convocation address at the Aligarh University in 1948, Nehruji had said that he was proud of India, not only because of its glorious heritage, but also because of its extraordinary capacity to add something to it. '...what do you feel about the past. Do you feel that you too are a part of it and India's past belongs as much to you or you push it aside to go forward without realising or feeling the thrill that comes with the realization that we are the inheritors and trustees of a great heritage...'. You are a Muslim and I am a Hindu. We may have different religious faith or we may even not have any religious faith, but our cultural heritage remains the same. It is as such yours as mine.[28]

Now, it is utterly ambiguous what Nehru meant by 'cultural heritage' as a shared domain of uninterrupted legacy of the past; he might have explained the subject differently from his Hindu nationalist opponents. However, there were instances of early Congress secularists unravelling their choice of a tradition-bound modernizing agenda by the state while speaking in favour of a secular culture followed by scientific–technological developments in future India. For instance, Sampurnanand, one of the prominent leaders of the Congress from Uttar Pradesh and a leading figure of the Congress Socialist Party of the 1930s, explicitly mentioned, 'secularism in the only sense in which it needs to be strictly enforced has been known to India from the very beginning. Indian culture does not know of religious wars'.[29] The political culture in the Congress in the 1950s mostly represented such mutually convincing approaches to modernity and traditions and even mobilized religious traditions and cultural practices for the convenience of the ideology and programmes of the modern state.[30] The political climate in North India in the decades after independence unlocked greater possibilities for the Hindutva forces, because the state literally had no defence or argument for a strict separation of traditions from state affairs, or religious traditions and practices from the modernist propositions of the so-called secular state.[31] Furthermore, the predominance of the caste–community–ethnicity question in the electoral domain meant the least possible chance of keeping religion out of politics, and the RSS–VHP nexus tactfully worked on the fragile ground of secularism by swiftly penetrating into the complicated fabric of identity politics in North India. It is to be noted that the rise and growth of the VHP in the initial years should be viewed as the single largest organized movement concentrated mostly in the North Indian states, especially in the Hindi-speaking belt. VHP's gradual proliferation in other states was facilitated mostly by political exigencies, unfolding new contexts and dimensions. Within a few decades after independence, the state-sponsored development patterns initiated agricultural and industrial transformations and created moderately well-off classes comprising an alliance of wealthy farmers, bourgeoisie, intelligentsia and rising capitalists.

For long, these people managed to stay close to the higher stratum of power, while the urban petty shopkeepers, small businessmen, low-income professionals and others stayed at a disadvantaged position, mostly because of their lack of education, wealth and limited participation in resource formation. These people highly aspired for political power and spread fast across different small towns in North India. The Brahmin–Bania–rich peasant nexus formed the new urban middle classes that emerged as the principle buyers of the Hindi–Hindu identity in north India.

> These people were marked by intense internal competition, and steady pressure of new opportunity structure, ever expanding horizons of upward mobility and a compulsive consumption that keeps transcending its own limits. The very pressure of growth is disturbingly destabilizing, the brave new world of global opportunities created anomie and existential uncertainties.[32]

The Hindutva masters preyed upon the susceptibility and uncertainties of a population with real flesh and blood by fanning religious emotions and political agenda together with the demands of banning cow slaughter, promoting Hindi and making certain communities apologetic for their (un)authorized existence in Indian society. The sudden emotional outbursts through chanting 'Jai Mata Di' or organizing Vaishno Devi yatras, infusing the birth of a new Goddess called Santoshi Ma, named after a Hindi movie—all symbolized the proliferation of a majoritarian Hindu culture with legitimate popular appeal. The legitimacy gained in the course of the cultural-identity formation indicated a subtle opposition by the indigenous–traditional of the universal–Western. The continuing Hinduization of the popular cultural terrain since the 1960s was not reason for implicating a secular-versus-communal fight but posed a challenge to the entire value system and set of institutions that came under a package called 'Nehruvianism' in India. The language of resistance became overwhelmingly dominant in the Hindi-speaking belt of North India, even though it often seemed to look vulnerable and defenceless when at the disposal of the English-speaking elites and their agents. The English-language media and the Delhi-bound intelligentsia showed little or no interest towards this Hindi-speaking belt of North India—referred to scornfully as *go-boloy*, or cow belt, for a long period of time. Mostly because of the poor education and literacy rate in this region, the states in the Ganga–Yamuna river plain were seen as not worthy of being approved by the so-called English-speaking intelligentsia for a long period of time, and a new section of 'vernacular elites appeared after most universities in this region sanctioned Hindi as a medium of communication in later decades'. These people played a crucial part in promoting a culturally exclusive, eventually upper-caste rhetoric of Hindu nationalism, leading to the opening of an intellectual discourse between 'indigenous' India and 'exotic' India—a rivalry of thoughts between two echelons of the society.[33] Growing disillusion over the Congress government, especially after the demise of Nehru and change in public-policymaking decisions, pushed the indigenous actors to a level of much-awaited autonomy within the cultural fabric of the society. The powerful bourgeoisie so far working behind the scenes with the government to secure its interests and power over the rural landed groups 'got replaced by the latter and it eroded the Congress-centred stability of the party system for the next several decades'. The shifting patterns of power in the regional sector, as well as the realities of the rural bourgeoisie, soon revealed the new language of politics, an essence of pristine 'authentic rusticity of a harmonious pristine "Bharat" pitted against the menacing might of urban and industrial India'.[34] The political fate of the Hindutva organizations depended largely on the extent of incorporation of these new indigenous actors into the network of a united pan-Hindu identity movement and investment on the traditional pristine self of the nation deeply rooted in the historical dynamics of a traditional authoritative structure. The VHP, in the true sense, should symbolize this 'traditional pristine self' of the nation, the RSS thought while bringing the sadhus onto this platform. The VHP consolidated its position mostly in the Hindi-speaking belt of northern India, followed by a dozen states and union territories within a decade or more.

VHP's rise in Indian politics as part of the Hindutva movement has been discussed on the basis of some specific arguments. First, if we talk of the VHP in terms of identity politics in a multicultural modern society, it is important to note how the organization endorsed sadhus contributing to such politics as agents of a 'pre-modern' sacred order. It is important in the sense that identity politics in India came out as transformative projects of modernity which helped replace the pre-existing birth-based hierarchies through an urge for dignity, equality and recognition of the differences between the groups. Recognition of community attributes as superior or inferior to others or claiming of authenticity of group/community traditions underscored the veracity of identity movements in a modern world. The Hindutva movement in India as a meta-structure of identity politics claimed superiority and authority over other sets of community identities but sought to undermine the call for equality inherent in its own structure. Its lack of response to the micro-elements of family rights, women's rights, ethnic rights or caste rights suggested the succinct inertia of majoritarian politics that undermined the real issues of an identity movement through keeping the vulnerable members of its own community in sheer hopelessness.[35] Did these people respond to the common enemy theory of the VHP marking Christianity, Islam and communism as having an 'evil eye' over the Hindu world as expected? If yes, then it call for an inquiry into what made them believe in VHP's ideology when larger sections of the marginal poor practically had no valid reason to support the elitist ideology of Hindu nationalism or global Hindu consolidation. Furthermore, did the sadhus play any crucial role in mobilizing the lower-caste Hindus, especially when the latter's grievances had been channelized through caste-specific organizations and these people in general remained far less susceptible to being vertically incorporated into a common Hindu identity? The RSS found its support base mostly among the Brahmins, Banias, landed aristocrats and a section of the petty bourgeoisie.

Most of the sadhus who were attached with the VHP in its early days were men of scholastic repute holding power positions within the monastic orders or proved their worth by being revered as influential individuals by a certain section of the caste Hindu society. Swami Chinmayananda, a reputed scholar of Vedanta and the founder of the Chinmaya Mission,[36] took elementary steps to establish the VHP along with Guru Golwalkar and Shivram Shankar Apte, mostly to make the Hindus conscious of their 'proud place in the comity of nations', impart them the knowledge of the sacred sastras and to 'rouse the individual and national consciousness in the glory and splendour of our heritage'.[37] Swami Chinmayananda expressed his deepest concern over the declining state of knowledge and values among the Hindu diaspora abroad and vowed to convert these 'Hindus to Hinduism' so that these people could reconnect with their motherland in a more holistic manner. Chinmayananda, being a close associate of the RSS leadership, shared an identical concern over the gradual fragmentation of Hindu orthodox sects over ideological predilections and found it necessary to organize these sects on a common platform to sort out some points of disagreements as early as 1963. The inaugural meeting of the VHP was attended by prominent RSS leaders and figures, like Guru Golwalkar and Swami Shankarananda Saraswati from Yoganandeshwara Sarawathi mutt. The second conference of the VHP (1964),[38] however, registered much more success than the inaugural one, mostly because of the amount of support and acceptance it received from the sadhus and gurus, especially from the Shankaracharyas of Sringeri, Puri, Dwarka and Kamakoti. The VHP had already decided to form an advisory council comprising the Shankaracharyas, representatives from all the orthodox sects, saints from a non-monastic background, reputed thinkers and ideologues from different Hindu philosophical schools. Furthermore, the VHP strictly ruled out the possibility of any office-bearer from any political party enjoying any position in its executive structure. VHP's initial objective to constitute a common Hindu organization outflanking the sectarian differences did not go down well with the sects upholding the fundamental tenets of the Hindu religion and culture which disapproved of the existence of any standardized organization determining one common path of action for all Hindus. As a natural corollary to this situation, one can trace the varied shades of opinions and outlooks coming from both the ascetic and non-ascetic leaders inside the VHP. While Swami Chinmayananda continued to operate with a blatantly scholastic overtone of knowledge dissemination in India and abroad, the Shankaracharyas from Dwarka and Puri essentially carried on with the age-old *sanatanist* agendas like banning cow laughter and promoting the use of Sanskrit, *shuddhi* and others. The presence of the Shankaracharyas in the VHP conference was likely to bring the Brahmanical *sanatanists* close to the VHP; however, in reality, the internal conflicts between the Shankaracharyas created 'obstacles for VHP's integrationist project'.

Interestingly, in the Hindu *sammelan* of 1966 at Allahabad, the sadhus among the delegates proposed to take a serious note of Christian missionary activities in the tribal regions, in tune with the RSS; the orthodox sadhus in particular painted a kind of militant image to protect the essentials of Hindu dharma from all sorts of challenges.[39] The disputes over power and position inside the monastic orders, however, forced them to be a little incredulous and sceptical of their newly acquired positions, and some of these individuals flocked to the VHP to get their individual interests fulfilled.[40] By 1966, the Shankaracharyas from the Dwarka Sharada Peetham and Govardhan Peeth in Puri, as well as the ex-Shankaracharya 'Mahamandaleshwar' Satyamitranand Giri, extended their support to the VHP, and as pointed out by Chetan Bhatt, 'Satyamitranand Giri helped in furthering the aims of the VHP, especially outside India, and in developing an early and distinctly territorial form of devotionalism—a "geopiety" that sacralize symbolic devotion to the land'.[41] The Shankaracharyas, carrying the legacy of Adi Shankara,[42] had never been entrusted with any religious authority as such. They did not represent any sacred religious power within the Hindu society or religion; however, they symbolized the hegemonic presence of an authority over the sectarian traditions of Hinduism. Adi Shankara (born in the year 788 AD), the most reputed philosopher and religious leader of the Hindu Sanatana Dharma, is known to have established the Dasnami *sampradayas* of the Hindu monastic tradition and integrated the monks of these sects under four *maths*, with the headquarters at Dwarka in the West, Jagannath Puri in the East, Sringeri in the South and Badrikashram in the North. One of Shankara's four main disciples was put in charge of these *maths*; however, a section of them did not restrict themselves to only the specific teachings of Shankara, and some sects even worked in their independent capacity outside the control of the Shankara *maths*.

With the reappearance of the Shankara tradition in the VHP, indigenous intellectualism reclaimed its authority in the academic discussions, and therefore the discourse it produced remained responsive to critical analysis. The leftist critique of the Shankara tradition kindled the so-called debate over idealism and materialism—'a battle started long back in ancient philosophical discourse and ended in the defeat of the materialists before the hegemonic presence of the idealists'. The victor and the vanquished in our country were not two abstract philosophies but two social classes—the dominant and oppressed castes—with the former using the two philosophies as weapons in their arsenal. The victory of Shankara and his philosophy therefore was the 'victory of the Brahmin and other dominant castes, the defeat of the rest of Indian society', mentioned E. M. S. Namboodiripad, General Secretary of the CPI(M) (Communist Party of India–Marxist), in his seminal essay on Adi Shankara (Namboodripad 1989, 3–12). The concern that VHP would re-infuse Brahmanism and casteism through the Adi Shankara tradition out of a desire to supersede the influence of the leftist political influence had drawn rather little critical attention, although it represented the concentration of culpable forces around the political mainstream. Initially, these *sanatani* sadhus were accommodated within the VHP, with an acute understanding of the latter of making profitable alliances with like-minded forces. Later, these sadhus developed their successive group interests around a segmented social structure. The Shankaracharyas did not stand as trustworthy allies for the VHP socially when the Ram Mandir controversy got too shabby to handle in a judicious manner, and they went on their own trip in opposition to the VHP on various occasions.[43]

Part of the reason why the VHP played to the desires for a Hindu resurgence by Hindu monastic orders were their own tactical innovations to get into the domain of Hindu asceticism for the purpose of political profit-making. The answer to why the sadhus were drawn towards the VHP has shades of a complicated story involving business, power and politics—and a combination of uncertainty and allure offered by the project of political Hindutva since the 1980s. Prior to that, sadhus from the Shaiva and Vaishnava orders fetched little from the VHP, except for working with the RSS *pracharaks* to formulate common policy orientations to Hindu religious, social and political affairs; the real implications of the sadhus forming the 'margdarshak mandali' (guiding body) within the VHP earned public attention only in the 1980s. Despite getting a new lease of life through recruiting dharma *pracharaks* from the RSS and promoting its own group of sadhus initiated by the Shaiva *akharas* of Haridwar, the VHP received greater impetus only after the BJP was officially formed in 1984. Looking from another angle, BJP's victory on the electoral front would not have been possible unless it managed to mobilize the sadhus affiliated to the VHP, and the sadhus in turn employed much of their energy in those issues and movements that hardly dragged them into a clash with their own ascetic persona. Notwithstanding the fact that the VHP brought the sadhus only to use them as a backup force to the cause of Hindutva, the sadhus lent their support to the BJP-sponsored Ram Janmabhoomi movement and eventually emerged as the torchbearers of a Hindu Rashtra in India. Interestingly, the sadhus in reality hardly resolved their essential dilemma over getting into the world of politics and declared that all their actions were performed to protect the Hindu religion and culture in new India. The involvement of the sadhus with the VHP also implied the uplift of the status of Hindu religious figures, especially the old monastic sects, to a new power position, which undoubtedly benefitted the Hindutva movement but ruined the status quo maintained in the ascetic world so far.

The sadhus engaged with the VHP either as *pracharaks* or as *margdarshaks* might have assumed their exclusive role to be that of a guiding force behind Hindu politics in future India, but they failed to acknowledge the truth that a large section of the Hindu society did not ever appreciate or recognize their working for a political party or clamouring for some politicized agenda from a common platform. The VHP brand of politics turned out to be a highly disturbing zone for the sadhus in the long run; however, at the initial phase, the patterns of their involvement with the VHP registered major shifts in Indian politics and impacted profoundly BJP's performances in the parliamentary elections. The dense network of the *maths*, akharas and ashrams in northern India appeared crucial to BJP's electoral game since the 1980s, while the hazards of infusing politics into the Hindu monastic world soon ignited a storm of reactions across layers of the Hindu society. The politicization of Hindu ritualistic practices, celebration of Hindu gods and goddesses at public rallies and bringing of *akhara*-based sadhus to political gatherings disrupted the hitherto reticent world of Hindu monastic asceticism and led to questions being raised over Hinduism's claim of fostering a devotional, otherworldly spiritual experience. VHP's initiatives to undo the wrongs of the past through the Ram Janmabhoomi movement even besmirched the 'non-confrontational' image of Hinduism. With the turn of 1980s, Indian politics lay open to a new set of experiments infusing real flesh and blood into the ideology of Hindutva that had thus far survived on the 'ideological fodder of "ban cow slaughter," "Indianise Muslims," "abolish Article 370" and others'.[44]

Despite showing differences in their opinions and approaches to the ideology of Hindutva, the sadhus univocally agreed on bearing in mind the secularist onslaught on the Hindu religion and culture and the responsibilities imparted to them to revive the essential tenets of Hinduism in the public domain. How did the sadhus treat the project of Hindutva as part of their own interests remained decisive to dole out the range of their influence both as otherworldly ascetics and as power-clingy individuals? Maintaining a proper balance between these two categories seemed to be a difficult task for those sadhus who looked desperate to get a hold of the opportunities arising out of the Hindutva project since the 1960s. Now, these opportunities could be classified into two aspects. Political Hindutva, if viewed as the most essential incentive to the project of a Hindu Rashtra, put forward interesting prospects for monastic Hindu orders in terms of financial gains and other material benefits, while Hindutva as an alternative to Nehruvian secularism tapped into the aspirations of the sadhus looking for some amount of legitimacy from the political mainstream. This second proposition seemed to be a little perplexing, since the sadhus did not ever show any real intention to work for a certain organization with strong political inclinations. Undoubtedly, a new source of threat—the communists[45] and an entire group of leftist liberals—appeared to be equally precarious for the survival of the Hindu religion and culture like the 'religious others'. The Hindu monastic sadhus found Hindutva attentive to and innovative in bringing them back their position through constructing an exclusively Hindu vote bank. Collective Hindu interests and monastic sectarian interests merged with one another in the ascetic visions of Hindu politics, and the sadhus worked in parallel with the VHP in generating a consistent support base to meet the objectives for the near future.

The shifting patterns of the Hindutva movement since the 1980s re-articulated the existing understandings of the subject with new organizational and contextual rhetorical expressions. It appeared to be flexible and accommodative, encompassing a wide range of expressions within and outside the territorial boundaries of the nation. The ideological and material effects of an extraterritorial nationalism became evident in the Hindutva movement since the Sangh Parivar's ascendency in the late 1980s; the Hindu diaspora in specific started feeding the ideal of 'one nation, one culture and one people' through funding the Hindutva projects in India and abroad. The social–political milieu that persuaded the strategic deployment of Hindutva among the diasporic Indians emerged as a 'kind of newly valorized currency in a globalized environment which could have offered a sense of protection to one age-old identity in a newly uncertain environment while in many ways advancing the entry of transnational business interests' (Rajagopal 2001, 468–469). All the Sangh Parivar affiliates, the VHP in particular, legitimized their presence especially in the United Kingdom and United States through different *seva* activities, such as publishing literature on the Hindu way of life, arranging seminars and lectures and providing family counselling to immigrant Hindus. For long, the Hindus operated in the spiritual world of the West and developed a sustained influence over the spiritual seekers in the West; however, the VHP for the first time launched the ideal of 'Viswa Hindutva' systematically through the global council of Hindus, and groups of modern spiritual gurus associated themselves with the development. It was decided that the relation of the VHP branches outside India with the VHP in India be such that 'the VHP central office, New Delhi and its Board of Trustees is the Supreme Body having jurisdiction over the entire organization of the world'.[46] The modern gurus or sadhus who supported the cause of the VHP on a global platform built a transnational Hindu identity beyond the traditional spatial limits of a nation. It is difficult to conclude that these sadhus functioned as VHP agents in a diasporic setting. There were many prominent faces among them, including Maharishi Mahesh Yogi, Swami Dayananda, Swami Chinmayananda and others, and they undoubtedly accelerated the Hinduizing process among the Indian diaspora. For instance, the VHP in America received the blessings of Swami Dayananda—the founder of the Arsha Vidya Gurukulam, an institution to disseminate knowledge of the Vedas in a *gurukula* style. Swami Dayananda was not a VHP activist but continued to guide the VHP in America over the years. Paying their utmost respect to Swamiji, the VHP in America issued a public statement after his *mahasamadhi* at Rishikesh in 2015:

> It was Swamiji who directed us in late 90s to hold Dharma Sansad in USA to assemble all Saints and Gurus of Western hemisphere; it was with Swamiji's blessings that we embarked upon Hindu Mandir Executives' Conference (HMEC) initiative in 2006, which has become a great success. Very few people know that when Vishwa Hindu Parishad (VHP) was established in Bharat on 29 August 1964 at Sandipani Ashram of late Swami Chinmayananda Ji in Mumbai, it was Swami Dayananda Saraswati, then his disciple, who wrote VHP's draft constitution...he had expressed desire to meet Prime Minister Narendra Modi...before giving up his body. ... and as God would have wished, on September 11th, Modiji made a trip to Rishikesh and met Pujya Swamiji. Swamiji blessed Modiji, which is for the good of the nation.[47]

There were sadhus and preachers close to Golwalkar who fought for the cause of the VHP throughout their lives. For instance, Vishwesha

Tirtha, popularly known as Pejawar Swamiji,[48] a spiritual guru, head of the Sri Pejavara Adhokshaja Matha and one of the early associates of Guru Golwalkar in Udupi, organized massive re-conversion campaigns among the Dalits and other backward castes in remote corners of Karnataka when these so-called lower-caste people abandoned Hinduism as part of the movements initiated by E. V. Ramaswamy Naicker and Dr B. R. Ambedkar. Unlike the Hindutva activists, Vishwesha Tirtha did not attack Ambedkar or Naicker but tried his best to popularize re-conversion (known as Ghar Wapsi in today's parlance) campaigns throughout the region. He was the former president of the Sri Pejavara Adhokshaja Matha, one of the Ashta Mathas belonging to the Dvaita School of philosophy, originally established by Sri Madhvacharya. He was instrumental in organizing the first VHP conference in 1969, attended by 65,000 people and graced by Guru Golwalkar as the chief guest with the help of his friend, the Maharaja of Mysore, Jayachamarajendra Wadiyar Bahadur. The second Dharma Sansad of the VHP too turned into a success only through the initiatives of Swami Vishwesha Tirtha in November 1985. In its inaugural session, the keynote address was delivered by Swami Chinmayananda Maharaj, and more than 851 saints and Dharmacharyas hailing from across the country participated in this Sansad.[49]

Swami Vishwesha Tirtha was one of the leading figures who spearheaded the Ram Janmabhoomi movement in the 1990s, worked for the banning of cow slaughter and offered Vaishnava *diksha* (initiation) to the Dalits to keep them tied to the Hindu fold. He had been a source of inspiration for the VHP and the Sangh Parivar, and both L. K. Advani and Uma Bharti took his blessings on various occasions.[50] He offered his blessing to Prime Minister Narendra Modi after he got elected to office for the first time in 2014, even though the VHP in general was frequently at odds with the ruling BJP and forced the latter to take some steps that could have put the political fate of the party in trouble.

The sadhus of India were involved in the highest political drama of the country when in 1992 the Babri Masjid was demolished in Ayodhya. The series of events that led to BJP's proximity with the VHP sadhus in the 1980s culminated in the demolition of the Babri Masjid in Ayodhya and subsequent developments around the temple building project in the sacred site. Many sadhus joined hands with the BJP–RSS nexus to build a temple of Lord Rama at his birth site from their individual capacities, if not as a collective force; the VHP too demanded the 'annulment of the laws concerning government control of mutts [Hindu religious sanctuaries] and temples',[51] but the inner tensions between the BJP and the VHP continued for long. There were sadhus who wanted to be the sole defender of the Hindu cause out of their moral responsibility to recreate the real histories of the nation when the BJP picked up the Ram Janmabhoomi issue for electoral gains. The pro-RSS sadhus, including Swami Chinmayananda, Uma Bharti, Sadhvi Rithambara, Swami Ramchandra Das Paramhans, Swami Nritya Gopal Das, Mahant Adityanath, Acharya Dharmendra and Swami Vamdev Maharaj, aligned with the VHP and the Ram Janmabhoomi Nyas, or Ram Janmabhoomi trust[52]; Shankaracharya Swaroopanand Saraswati, Mahant Gyan Das, the Shankaracharyas of Puri and Kanchi, Swami Ramnareshacharya and a few others joined the opposition. Either camp had its own understanding of the Ram Janmabhoomi issue, and the latter camp did not want the VHP to settle the matter simply, as it was an integral part of the Hindutva discourse. Shankaracharya Swaroopanand Saraswati of Dwarka had been close to the Congress and did not like the idea of the VHP hijacking the Ram Janmabhoomi movement solely in favour of the BJP. Despite supporting the issues of banning of cow slaughter and lifting of Article 370, Swaroopanand Saraswati kept opposing the RSS–BJP–VHP trio for its alleged invoking of political aspirations in the garb of Hindutva.

The mutually conflicting groups of sadhus exchanged heated debates on the Ram temple issue, created chaos and confusions in the Dharma Sansads in the late 1980s and showed open resistance to the VHP in January 2019 in Allahabad during the Kumbh Mela congregation. The two-day Dharma Sansad of the VHP in Prayag turned into a high-voltage political drama when a boycott call was raised against the Dharma Sansad by the ABAP—a collective body of the 13 sadhu akharas, including a few established by the Shankaracharyas.[53] The ABAP was backed by Swaroopanand Saraswati and others who claimed that the VHP-led sadhu conference, as well as the temple construction strategy, would be used just to generate a pro-BJP tide ahead of the Lok Sabha elections due in a few months. The BJP, especially Uttar

Pradesh Chief Minister Yogi Adityanath, was charged of converting the Ardh Kumbh into a gala show through changing its name; BJP's efforts did not go down well with most of the sadhus, who took it to be a display of political power and an iniquitous move to make BJP's electoral campaigns look like a divine dispensation. 'The RSS and the VHP are using the temple issue to promote their politics...they are not interested in building a temple at Ayodhya. That's why we decided to boycott their Dharma Sansad. The VHP works for BJP, and sadhus should stay away from politics', declared ABAP president Swami Narendra Giri, while Devanand Saraswati, a prominent member of VHP's Kendriya Margdarshak Mandal (central governing body) and one of the secretaries of Juna Akhara, commented, 'This is extremely unfortunate. The Akhara Parishad is not even a registered body and its role is limited to promoting harmony among *akharas* and to organize Kumbh Melas. It should avoid taking decisions that may have political implications'.[54]

It was really astonishing that the ABAP did not take such a stance earlier, despite taking part in the Dharma Sansads for several decades, and that they did not realize earlier that the construction of the temple should be undertaken by the Dharmacharyas only and not by politically motivated groups. Nevertheless, the split within the *sadhu samaj* did not cause much harm to the VHP. Meanwhile, the Congress celebrated the success of the ABAP in letting down the so-called Hindutva agenda of the BJP–VHP elements. It took it as an early sign of RSS's failure in mobilizing the sadhus, as well as the Hindu vote bank for electoral gains, because for the first time in its history, the ABAP had taken the wind out of VHP's sails and spoiled any further possibility of the VHP emerging as the sole mouthpiece of the sadhus in the near future. ABAP's open challenge to the VHP–BJP might have caused the VHP some amount of discomfort, because all its endeavours to monopolize the Hindu vote through the temple construction strategy turned pointless. Having being sidetracked by the move of the ABAP, the VHP looked for other avenues to carry on with its agenda, because in no way had the RSS–VHP influence over the sadhus in general declined. The slogans like *Jo Ram ki baat karega, wohi desh par raj karega* (those who speak about Rama will continue to rule the country) had already motivated the majority of the sadhus to make India a Hindu

Rashtra, and both VHP sadhus and non-VHP sadhus parroted the same words used by the Sangh Parivar. *The Caravan* (Delhi Press Magazine) reported in 2019,

> The RSS organised in its Nagpur headquarters a three day conference of the select members of the RSS affiliated sadhus. Over fifty sanyasis including mahamandaleswars who had formerly been RSS pracharaks attended the meeting, and nearly thirty five such religious leaders could not turn up because of personal reasons...the meeting continued for three days and discussed the ways in which the sanyasis could play a role in uniting the Hindus and bringing tribals close to the Sangh Parivar. The entire central office bearers of the RSS including sarsanghchalak Mohan Bhagwat remained present for the whole of the meeting. (*The Caravan*, April 2019, 76–86)

The way the RSS quickly recovered the image of the VHP signified its all-pervasive presence in the sadhu circuit; it provided its own men to the *akharas* to get them recruited in the monastic orders. However, the RSS–VHP forces faced a real battle when the sadhus were brought into electoral fights and their traditional type of authority clashed with the crescendos of state power. The sadhus did not always show unassailable commitment to the political parties or their allied organizations, rather often displaying their own individual interests to uphold a certain political cause. Peter van der Veer discussed this point in reference to the Ram Mandir movement in Ayodhya, stating that the heads of some specific religious institutions stood at a safe distance from the issue just to maintain the status, reputation and individual existence of their own institutions.[55] Had there been no organization like the RSS or the VHP, the sadhus from different monastic orders or the rest of the community would have ended up fighting each other, since they had differing individual viewpoints on political affairs, and they differed even with the BJP on various occasions. In general, the sadhus mainly differed with the political parties not on ideological points but due to the utter cunningness of some of the leaders who could go to any extent to solicit votes. Time after time, the sadhus expressed their dislike for the innate wickedness of power politics, including the growing corruption and criminal influence inside the party structure. Furthermore, they had enough reasons to be ashamed of the sectarian approaches espoused by the political parties, especially when the parties appealed to voters in the name of caste or class. Interestingly, the sadhus often indulged in communal propagandas during electoral campaigns, although they preferred to stay away from mucking their opponents around.

Unfortunately, neither the VHP sadhus nor the others ever performed effectively in keeping a check over the interplay of various identities in electoral politics, especially when most of the political parties attempted to settle their political score over the caste question at the time of elections. The issue was far bigger than the factional conflicts inside the VHP or in the Dharma Sansads. It did not involve ego battles between two groups of sadhus but was an issue of social interest—an age-old stigma that could cause the dismantling of the Hindu social order if not addressed in a sagacious manner. The sadhus who ran for elections tried hard to play on the religious sentiments only, sometimes even addressing voters as a homogeneous category on their individual capacity, but the political climate of the country did not permit them to go on their own trip. The sadhus had to remain loyal to the RSS–VHP-type platforms, because only these organizations had the strength and authority to provide them a separate political environment of their own.

The RSS–VHP–BJP leaders made complete use of the sadhus who fought elections on their individual charisma, as in the case of Swami Avaidyanath who won from the Gorakhpur constituency continuously for four times since 1989, first as a Hindu Mahasabha candidate and in 1991 and 1996 as a BJP candidate. His successor Yogi Adityanath won from the same seat five times and became the chief minister of Uttar Pradesh in 2017. The individual charisma and appeal of these sadhus earned them power and influence in that region; especially, the prominence of the Gorakhnath temple played a crucial part in their respective political journeys.[56] Despite having his own individual authority over Gorakhpur politics, Avaidyanath continued to nurture good working relations with the RSS–VHP forces in that region. The RSS had its own political base in Gorakhpur, established by Varanasi Kalyan Chhatravas of the school Saraswati Shishu Mandir inside the Gorakhnath Math premises.[57] After his demise, all political parties extended their homage to this sadhu for his relentless service for the welfare of society without discrimination on the basis of caste or creed.

It may seem puzzling, but one could claim that while some of the political rhetoric of the sadhus might be communal or issue-based, a large number of voters supported them for their contributions through social welfare services. However, the use of a term like 'social welfare' tends to privilege one connotation over the other. Very often, the VHP sadhus were charged with instigating communal hatred and disrupting social harmony and peace in the name of promoting social welfare. There are enough media reports to show that the VHP sadhus were targeted mainly by the opponents and sometimes by the local state machinery for conducting 'social service' programmes in the SC/ST (Schedules Castes/Scheduled Tribes) and tribal areas. A number of police cases were registered against VHP sadhus for allegedly attacking poor villagers in different tribal regions across the country for converting to Christianity; it must be remembered that the VHP was established in direct response to the alleged threat of conversion to Islam or Christianity. Popular through different names, such as *shuddhi* (purification), Ghar Vapsi (homecoming) or just *parivartan* (turning back), the re-conversion issue remained in both the long-term and short-term agendas of the RSS–VHP nexus. The Sangh Parivar affiliates like the Dharma Raksha Samiti (Committee for the Preservation of Dharma), Hindu Jagran Manch (Forum for Hindu Awakening), Dharma Jagran Vibhag (Department of Dharma Awareness) and Bajrang Dal (Army of Hanuman) got extensive media publicity for their re-conversion programmes; several VHP workers and sadhus even received warnings from the law and order authority for allegedly spreading communal propagandas in the name of re-conversion ceremonies.

In the states where an anti-BJP government was in power, several such incidents were reported widely in the media—a process that unleashed further speculations and conflicts in the public domain. Often, the controversies arising out of such incidents defamed the BJP to such an extent that these sadhus became a liability for the party. Swami Aseemanand, Sadhvi Rithambara, Shankaracharya Jayendra Saraswati, Uma Bharti and Sadhvi Pragya Singh Thakur were some of the controversial sadhus who brought bad fame for the BJP and the VHP, either for their involvement in contentious affairs or for objectionable statements. Swami Aseemanand, accused in major terror blasts between 2004 and 2008, served as a close aide of the RSS–VHP duo and

> worked all his life converting tribals of the Andaman islands and the Dangs in Gujarat to Hinduism. Aseemanand's belief in violent Hindutva remained unwavering throughout his life. It included the period of his incarceration where he showed great courage in standing up and articulating his beliefs.[58]

Swami Aseemanand was arrested by the Central Bureau of Investigation, and reportedly, he recorded a confession admitting to the crime; however, the VHP completely condemned the 'Congress-led government's "attempt to malign image of Hindu leaders by terming them as terrorists" and argued that it was the greatest lie that Swami Aseemanand had confessed to the blasts'. Whatever may the facts be in this case, the VHP bashed its opponents and especially indicted a section of the media for spreading blatant lies. It also took note of the frequent use of the terms like 'saffron terror' or 'Hindu terrorism' by its opposition just to malign the RSS and VHP for malicious intentions. If the Swami Aseemanand case created a huge uproar inside the Sangh Parivar circle, the Shankaracharya Jayendra Saraswati case made the RSS–VHP leaders furious against the Tamil Nadu government for playing with Hindu sentiments. Jayendra Saraswati was arrested in 2004 after being accused in a murder case; however, in 2013, he was acquitted by the court. He was the pontiff of the Kanchi Kamakoti Peetham and one of the closest allies of the VHP, got involved in the Ayodhya issue during Prime Minister Atal Bihari Vajpayee's term and tried to settle the process as a mediator. He might have had a strained relationship with the BJP and the VHP in relation to the Ayodhya affair. VHP leader Praveen Togadia described his arrest as an onslaught on Hindus, and BJP and RSS spokesmen questioned the 'haste' with which a senior monk of a highly respected Hindu *math* had been arrested. The entire Sangh Parivar condemned the arrest of the Shankaracharya and alleged that it was the result of a political vendetta against the Hindutva forces.[59]

The Shankaracharya incident ignited uncontrolled outrage inside the national political circle, while the killing of Vedanta Kesari Swami Lakshmananda Saraswati, a member of the Kendriya

Margdarshak Mandali of the VHP, led to Orissa being set ablaze in 2008. Dedicating his life for the welfare of the *adivasis* of Kandhamal, Swami Lakshmananda emerged as the Sangh Parivar's chief patron in this region and hugely contributed to the re-conversion movement among the tribal people.[60] He became a controversial figure in the region, often being targeted for his virulent anti-conversion movements among the tribal people. The killing of this sadhu messed up the political situation in Orissa, especially after the claims made by the state government that Naxalite elements were involved in the attack, as quoted by *Indian Express*. Ajai Sahni of the Institute of Conflict Management added, 'Naxals may not have anything to gain but they could have realised that the reconversion drive of Lakshamananda was hitting at their base of mass mobilisation'. The VHP and the other members of the saffron brigade 'poured scorn on the claims of the government'. *Swarajya* reported, 'The Maoists might have pulled the trigger on the 84 years old sanyasi, but the several intelligence inputs suggest that the heinous crime was committed at the behest of Christian missionaries' (*Swarajya*, 25 August 2016). Poverty-stricken Orissa had encountered threats of the religious zealots for long. The RSS–VHP and its youth wing Bajrang Dal came into prominence after the 1960s[61] and developed an inclination for the regional language, culture and especially the cult of Jagannath.[62] The Vanvasi Kalyan Ashram (VKK), one of the affiliates of the Sangh Parivar, too built its base among the rural tribal people. These organizations were blamed for imposing the message of Hindutva on the poor tribal people in the name of doing social service or helping them be free from the influence of Christian missionaries (*Organiser*, 23 April 2003). Lakshmananda Saraswati happened to be one of the first VHP sadhus in the region who came from Madhya Pradesh mainly on the request of the RSS. Earlier, he was attached with the Goraksha movement and came into close contact with M. S. Golwalkar, who remained as an influence on Lakshmananda forever. The brutal killing of this man came out as part of an exposé on the problems and issues of religious conversion in India and its related impact on the oppressed communities.

The VHP lost its credibility as a non-political body mostly due to the activities of the Bajrang Dal—the militant youth wing of the VHP, which earned a bad name through Hindu–Muslim riots or in matters of anti-Christian rampages in the regions where tribal people and Dalits were high in concentration. The VHP might have discarded the aggressive behaviour of the Bajrang Dal on various occasions; it usually remained tongue-tied when this militant proponent of Hindutva catered to the needs of electoral politics with slogans like 'seva-suraksha-sanskriti' or started movements for the establishment of the Ram Janmabhoomi temple in Ayodhya, Krishna Janmabhoomi temple in Mathura and the Kashi Vishwanath temple in Varanasi. What is intriguing is that the fringe groups like the Bajrang Dal always helped sponsor a saffron tide in favour of the BJP as part of their electoral strategy and received tacit approval from the sadhus backed by the RSS–VHP. The sadhus from a non-VHP background did not always come in support of the Hindutva politics promoted by the Sangh Parivar. In Madhya Pradesh, Namdeo Das Tyagi, a high-profile sadhu popularly known as Computer Baba, waged a protest against the then BJP government in the state and asked people to protect their 'dharma' by voting out the BJP government. He had strong objections against the Bajrang Dal, VHP and BJP, which he accused of creating divisions among the sadhu *samaj*.[63] Computer Baba was offered the Minister of State status in the ruling BJP government in the state along with four other fellow sadhus, namely Narmadanand Maharaj, Hariharanand Maharaj, Bhaiyyu Maharaj and Pandit Yogendra Mahant, but he drifted apart as soon he realized that 'there is a class among sadhus who receive preferential treatment. This class is backed by the RSS and its sole objective is to promote the politics of the BJP'.[64] Computer Baba might have had the backing of the opposition parties, and the questions that he raised, which were not new, created enough uproar inside the BJP circle. VHP sadhus were often made culpable for provoking pro-BJP sentiments in the name of promoting dharma, but what happened in Madhya Pradesh pushed Hindutva interlocutors towards new strategic arrangements.

The relationship between the BJP and the VHP sadhus did not remain the same forever. BJP recruited the sadhus in political rank mainly because of the latter's mass appeal. Formerly excluded groups, especially women, responded quickly to the sadhus, and the same sadhus who renounced worldly regulations and the struggle for material power were often found seeking votes in the name of caste and creed. Sadhus campaigning for a political party and asking for votes based on one's identity, while being held in high esteem, suggests the paradox of representative democracy that creates the illusion that everybody has the right to wield their own authority, when necessary. The tensions around having sadhus as the face of the party gradually made the BJP cautious of its electoral decisions. When the issue of Ram Mandir could no longer remain the centre of attraction, the party had to decide in what capacity the sadhus would be incorporated into the election process. It was a tough choice indeed. There were individualist–egoist sadhus who could have changed their political loyalties or demanded a sadhu quota to create a 'sadhudom' inside the party circle. The BJP and the VHP continued to send the message that in spite of major disagreements, the sadhus would always be with the Sangh Parivar because no other party or organization would ever satisfy the political desires of the sadhus. It was the only platform available to be used as a launch pad for the sadhus to enter mainstream politics. Interestingly, the Congress had never claimed its agency in the sadhu *samaj* in the way the Sangh Parivar did. There were instances when sadhus were roped in to campaign for the Congress against the BJP; however, the entire exercise proved to be meaningless for the Congress brand of politics in general. In its campaign to counter the Hindutva propaganda by Sadhvi Pragya during the Lok Sabha elections in Bhopal in 2019, the Congress resorted to performing religious rituals with saffron-clad sadhus and bequeathed its so-called claims of being secular to the growing religious ardour to fetch Hindu votes in favour of the party. Over the years, North Indian Hindutva faces were caught up in political imbroglios caused by extreme religious fervour over various issues. No one can forget the examples set by BJP's firebrand leaders like Sadhvi Uma Bharti and Sadhvi Rithambara and relatively newer faces, such as Yogi Adityanath, Sakshi Maharaj, Sadhvi Pragya Thakur and others.[65] Many of them were found indulging in objectionable speeches, as reported; however, they contested elections and even won with gracious margins.

What characterized this shift was the rise of a Hindutva brand based on the democratic credentials of the state. It served as more than a militant Hindutva with nationalist ideals being nurtured by ideologues; it invested in India's spiritual resources as 'capital' to gain global recognition in a world where geopolitical negotiations using old strategies were crumbling. Forged as a counter-theory to 'pseudo-secularism', the new Hindutva model strived to offer an all-inclusive space but continued to feed the majoritarian impulse. The articulation of an all-inclusive political culture increased the demand for Hinduism in India and abroad. E. Anderson and A. Longkumar called it a Hindu renaissance that had developed extensive relations with diverse institutions from the worlds of media, culture, education, business, finance, film and environment (Anderson and Longkumar 2018, 371–377). Now, Hindutva is not being judged on the analogy of the so-called Islamic onslaught on Hinduism. It desires to capture the labyrinth of global imaginations and expects to pervade the thought world of the English-speaking elites through corporate-style guru-based organizations. The traditional *maths* or the old *parampara* ties no longer seem flexible to cater to the needs of brand Hindutva, and the 'ownership' of Hindutva's ideology is continually contested and reshaped. The sadhus too, in the process, are often found adapting to the changing connotations of Hindutva. Now, we can trace a bunch of confident and virulent sadhus who could take the challenge of a political party not simply as a latent force but as a dominant voice in politics. Hindutva's new expressions of malleability and pliability have offered the sadhus new spaces and ideas that could enable them to explore what makes one a 'Hindu' or what it means to be Hindu in the changed circumstances. The VHP sadhus might have collaborated with the Modi government for tactical reasons, but what is captivating is that they are the same people who dare to question Modi for allegedly deviating from the path of Hindutva. One can easily notice how the VHP sadhus drove a hard bargain with the BJP government on the Ram Mandir issue and even threatened to withdraw their support if Modi failed to commit to the core causes of Hindutva. The VHP sadhus often hit a nerve when they referred to the Ram Mandir issue; Modi, however, seized the very opportunity to promote himself as a 'Vikas-purush' committed to the cause of valorizing *Bharatiyatva* through endorsing those elements of Indian history which are indigenous and free from alien influences. Modi appeared to be a sharper player than what the sadhus could ever imagine him to be, and he was the first person who refined the democratic political culture of India in simplistic Hinduized terms. After the Supreme Court's verdict on the definition of Hindutva in 1995, it became far easier for him to propagate Hindutva as a 'secular' principle that could be interpreted synonymously with 'Indianization or *Bharatiyakaran'* of Indian culture. The VHP sadhus and the activists took much time to realize the real implications of this brand Hindutva that incorporates all dissensions, differences and divergences into one singular fabric of the nation.

NOTES

1. 'Prayag main Dharma Sansad adhiveshan' (The Dharma Sansad conference at Prayag), Hindu Vishva, March–April 1989, p. 16.
2. The Margdarshak Mandal was constituted by the VHP to chalk out policies and programmes for the organization, and accordingly the Dharma Sansad was started in 1982 through involving Hindu religious figures from different monastic traditions. The fundamental principles of the VHP were laid down as: (a) It is the VHP's duty to organize all those people, whether residing in India or abroad, who adhere to the *sampradayas* that originated in India; (b) The VHP should work towards freeing Hindu society from meaningless rites and customs that hamper the society's progress. It should restore the self-esteem of Hindu society and make it attuned to the present age; (c) The VHP must propagate the message of harmony and mutual respect among the adherents of various ways of worship—Sikhs, Jains, Buddhists, etc.—within the vast Hindu society; (d) The VHP is an organization of Hindus worldwide and is distant from the practice of politics of any type; (e) In its attempt to serve society, the VHP should not discriminate between individuals on the basis of caste, colour, religion, sect, sex, etc.; (f) The VHP should try to elicit and encourage support from different regional, community, social and political leaders, industrialists, etc.; (g) The VHP should endeavour to bring sadhus, *sants* and *matha adhyakshas* of various sects and orders onto one platform; and (h) The VHP should make efforts to make the age-old Hindu dharma compatible with the present requirements of society, so that it is able to face the challenges of the modem world. See, Narayan Rao Tarte, *Vishva Hindu Parishad Ki Kalpana (Formation of Vishva Hindu Parishad), Hindu Vishva*, Silver Jubilee Issue, 1989–1990, pp. 14–15 (Hindi edition).
3. Despite fragmented references in most studies on Hindu nationalism, the ideological and chronological developments of the VHP have been recorded by very few scholars. Manjari Katju provides a detailed historical account of the organization, identifying its transformative characteristics from being a fragmented body of Hindus to a mass organization involving multifarious programmes and movements prior to the Babri Masjid affair and in its

immediate aftermath (Manjari Katju, *Vishva Hindu Parishad and Indian Politics* [New Delhi: Orient Blackswan, 2010]). Professor Chetan Bhatt incorporated a thoughtful analysis of the VHP in his book on Hindu nationalism, focusing mainly on its policies and programmes and their implications on the Babri Masjid demolition incident (Chetan Bhatt, *Hindu Nationalism: Origins, Ideologies and Modern Myths* [London: Bloomsbury Academic, 2001]). Dhirendra K. Jha, a journalist by profession, published an account of an inside view of the VHP-inclined sadhus as men who desired for money, power and influence. This book does not treat the sadhu–ascetic imbroglio from the VHP's perspective but places greater emphasis on the conflicting nature of power politics inside the *akharas akharas* (Dhirendra K. Jha, *Ascetic Games: Sadhus, Akharas and the Making of the Hindu Vote* [New Delhi: Westland Publications Private Limited, 2019]). In his multiple studies on Hindu nationalism, Christophe Jaffrelot, one of the leading scholars on the subject, has devoted much of his energy to illuminating the growth of the VHP as part of the Sangh Parivar politics around the Hindutva agenda and has revealed interesting facts on the strategic involvement of the VHP with the larger political compulsions in contemporary India (Christophe Jaffrelot, *Religion, Caste and Politics in India* [London: C. Hurst Co. Publishers, 2011]). In almost all those studies, the VHP's Babri Masjid involvement remained central to the fundamental propositions other than the issues of religious conversion, cow slaughter, Kumbh Mela politics and the VHP's community-oriented works in the Dalit–*adivasi* regions.

4. Erstwhile Maharaja of Mysore Jayachamarajendra Wadiyar, Bhagwat Singh of Mewar and Karan Singh, son of Maharaja Hari Singh of Kashmir, joined the VHP. Wadiyar became the governor of Karnataka and Madras after India's independence and, realizing the importance of reviving the spiritual essence of the Hindu dharma, helped the VHP propagate the message of Hinduism among the masses. Bhagwat Singh remained instrumental behind the dharma *sammelans* and the *ekatmata* yatras organized by the VHP in later years. Karan Singh, the ex-governor of Jammu and Kashmir and a pro-chancellor of Banaras Hindu University spearheaded the VHP movement in multiple ways; however, he lost his insignificance later. Shraddhanjali Smarika, *Commemorative Volume* (New Delhi: Vishva Hindu Parishad Foundation, 1986–1987), 22.
5. World Hindu Conference, 1966 (WHC-I), 2–3.https://vhp.org/conferences/world-hindu-conference
6. Ibid, pp. 2–5.
7. It was proposed that 'Sanskrit Bhasha is not merely a most ancient of languages, but it is a carrier of Sanskriti of Bharat also. The entire gamut of science and knowledge has been finding expression soon only through this language. Hence this Sammelan passed a resolution and enjoined there to Govt. to expand the facilities of teaching Sanskrit Bhasha inside and outside the country to strengthen the unity among the Hindus spread all over the

world; so that the Hindus living abroad may take advantage of their Dharmic and cultural knowledge freely'. Ibid, p. 5.

8. See, Emily Tucker, 'Identity, Religion and Dialogue: The Rearticulation of Hinduism in America' (BA thesis, Radcliffe College, Harvard University, 1993).
9. Bhatt, *Hindu Nationalism*, 181–185.
10. Deoki Nandan Agarwal, former vice president of the VHP, in a personal interview on 15 November 1993. Cited in Katju, *Vishva Hindu Parishad and Indian Politics*, 48.
11. 'To keep up the purity of the Race and its culture, Germany shocked the world by her purging the country of Semitic races—the Jews. Race pride at its highest has been manifested here. Germany has also shown how highly impossible it is for Races and cultures, having differences going to the root, to be assimilated into one united whole, a good lesson for us in Hindustan to learn and profit by.... The foreign races [i.e., Indian Muslims] in Hindustan must either adopt the Hindu culture and language, must learn to respect and hold in reverence Hindu religion [which they renounced], must entertain no ideas but those of glorification of the Hindu race and culture [which they left]...or may stay in the country, wholly subordinated to the Hindu nation, claiming nothing, deserving no privileges, far less any preferential treatment-not even citizen's rights'. Tapan Basu, Pradip Datta, Sumit Sarkar, Tanika Sarkar, and Sambuddha Sen, *Khakhi Shorts and Saffron Flags: A Critique of the Hindu Right* (New Delhi: Orient Longman, 1993), 26–27; Also see, Madhav Sadashiva Golwalkar, *We, or the Nationhood Redefined* (Nagpur: Bharat Publication, 1939).
12. 'The term *akhara* designates a place where the young men of a locality gather daily for body-building, exercise, and sportsmainly wrestling-and weight lifting. In this guise the *akhara* retains a ritual dimension-even a spiritual one. It includes a temple-when not attached to one-that is generally dedicated to Hanuman [the monkey god, a symbol of strength and devotion, in the epic *Ramayana]*; it is placed under the authority of a *guru* who instructs the members of the *akhara* in physical and mental discipline, giving them a certain balance that also implies abstinence...[of a sadhu]. Members of an akhara are recruited from all social milieus and develop a strong collective attachment to it'. Christophe Jaffrelot, *The Hindu Nationalist Movement in India* (New Delhi: Viking Penguin India, 1996), 35.
13. The VHP was entrusted with the task of 'defending, protecting and preserving' the Hindu society from the insidiously spreading clutches of alien ideologies. Editorial, *World Hindu Conference* (Bombay: Vishva Hindu Parishad publication, 1979), vii.
14. William Gould, 'Contesting Secularism in Colonial and Post Colonial North India Between the 1930 and 1950s', *Contemporary South Asia* 14, no. 4 (2005): 482.
15. Mukta, Parita, 'The Public Face of Hindu Nationalism', *Ethnic and Racial Studies* 23, no. 3 (2000): 446.

16. R. Manchanda, 'Militarized Hindu Nationalism and the Mass Media: Shaping a Hindutva Public Discourse', *Journal of South Asian Studies* 25, no. 3 (2002): 8.
17. Basu et al., *Khakhi Shorts and Saffron Flags*; Bhatt, *Hindu Nationalism*.
18. Jaffrelot, *Religion, Caste and Politics in India*, 66.
19. H. McLeod, 'The Religious Crisis of the 1960s', *Journal of Modern European History* 3, no. 2 (2005): 205. [Christian Churches and Religion in the 20th Century]
20. H. McLeod, *Religion and the People of Western Europe, 1789–1990* (Oxford: Oxford University Press, 1997), 15–21.
21. Akeel Bilgrami, 'Secularism: A Genealogical Analysis', *American Book Review* 39, no. 5 (July/August 2018): 11–15.
22. The successful establishment of the European model of a nation state based on a 'homogeneous culture' of 'single languages' and 'predominant religious communities'. Professor Sudipta Kaviraj holds that 'an Indian nation state could be securely based on a single culture of Hinduism, and the usual collar of this was that Hindi of a particularly Sanskritized variety should be given precedence over other vernaculars as India's national language'. Sudipta Kaviraj, *The Trajectories of the Indian State: Politics and Ideas* (Ranikhet: Permanent Black, 2010), 30.
23. Kaviraj, *The Trajectories of the Indian State*, 31.
24. Partha Chatterjee, *Nationalist Thought and the Colonial World* (Delhi: Oxford University Press, 1986), 30.
25. David Arnold, *Science, Technology and Medicine in Colonial India* (Cambridge: Cambridge University Press, 2000), 17.
26. Secularism as *dharma-nirapeksata* indicates neutrality of the state towards religions. Misconceptions were created around the real implications of the term, since the Indian state had never been following any policy of non-interference in religious matters in the actual sense. Gandhi preferred to use the phrase *sarva dharma sama bhava*, reflecting the true spirit of that neutrality and denoting equal flourishing of all religions under the state's neutrality. van der Veer, Peter, 'Secularism and National Development in India and China', *Third World Quarterly* 13, no. 4 (2012): 725.
27. An impatient Nehru could be heard sarcastically speaking at the Constituent Assembly, 'May I beg with all humility those gentlemen who use this word (secularism) often to consult some dictionary before they use it? …It is right in all contexts, as if by saying that we are a secular state we have done something amazingly generous, given something out of our pocket to the rest of the world, something we ought not to have done, so on and so forth'. See, Jawaharlal Nehru's speech at the Constituent Assembly, CAD, Vol. 9, p. 401.
28. Atal Behari Vajpayee, 'The Bane of Secularism', in *Jana Sangh Souvenir*, ed. S. S. Bhandari (Delhi: Bharatiya Janata Party, 1969), 55–63, quoted in

Christophe Jaffrelot, *Hindu Nationalism: A Reader* (Ranikhet: Permanent Black, 2007), 328.

29. Sampurnanand, *Congress Ideology and Programme in Memories and Reflections* (Bombay: Asia Publishing House, 1962), 645–655.
30. William Gould in one of his easy described the debates around the Cow Slaughter issue in U.P as one of the best revealing stories of secular hypocrisy in India. 'A petition to the court of 12 UP Muslim butchers questioned the constitutional validity of UP Prevention of Cow Slaughter Act. Their counsel pointed to chapter IV, article 48 of the Indian Constitution, Moreover, it was claimed that the bill undermined and offended fundamental rights guaranteed to them.... The debate moved onto whether the slaughter of cattle was a tenet of Islam, or whether the complaint was about the ruination of the petitioners' business. What came through clearly in the judgement were the repeated references to religious customs, particularly those of Vedic times. Juxtaposed to this religious history was discussion of milk production, milk consumption per hand, the production of dung, the science of human nutrition and the cost of cattle protection compared with state expenditure on education'. Gould, 'Contesting Secularism in Colonial and Post Colonial North India', 490. For details on the cow slaughter debate in state assemblies see, 'Supreme Court Judgement, Uttar Pradesh, Bihar and Madhya Pradesh Prevention of Cow Slaughter Acts, on 23 April 1958', Tandon Papers, file 277 (New Delhi: National Archives of India).
31. It is highly conspicuous whether in India the so-called secular public sphere purified and empowered religion through religions' disconnection from theology and authentic culture. The theory developed by influential French anthropologist Olivier Roy makes a real case in India, because here every possibility was created to disconnect religion from culture, thereby making it radicalized and 'de-ethinicized' or globalized after a certain period of time. In that case, secularism should be viewed as dysfunctional in that religion got entrapped in fundamentalism, divorced from its cultural acumen. It is an impressive and intriguing analysis on the revival or re-invention of religion through the preconditions of a secular public sphere. See, Olivier Roy, *Holy Ignorance: When Religion and Culture Part Always* (London: Hurst & Co, 2010).
32. Basu et al., *Khakhi Shorts and Saffron Flags*, 37.
33. Tapan Raychaudhuri, 'Shadows of the Swastika: Historical Perspectives on the Politics of Hindu Communalism', *Modern Asian Studies* 34, no. 2 (May 2000): 271–272.
34. Radhika Desai, in her excusive analysis on Indian bourgeoisie, further explained that 'by the 1980s, if not earlier, it was clear that the character and aspirations of this class were no longer exclusively rural...their investments are not confined to agriculture...'. Other than investing in the business of various descriptions in towns—trade, finance, hotels or cinemas—a young, bright child of this facility could have continued as a doctor, engineer

or even a professor at one of the small-town universities. Radhika Desai, 'Cultureless and Contemporary Right: Indian Bourgeoisie and Political Hindutva', *Economic and Political Weekly* 34, no. 12 (20–26 March 1999): 695–697+699–712. For details see, K. Balagopal, 'An Ideology for the Provincial Propertied Class', *Economic and Political Weekly* XXII, nos. 36 and 37 (September 5–12, 1987): 1546–1547.

35. Vibha Pingle and Ashutosh Varshney, 'India's Identity Politics: Then and Now', in *Managing Globalization: Lessons from China and India*, eds. David A. Kelly, Ramkishen S. Rajan, and Gillian H. L. Goh (Singapore: World Scientific Publishing Co Pte Ltd, 2006), 6–7.
36. Swami Chinmayananda did not represent any exclusive Hindu school of thought, rather endeavouring to spread the knowledge of Advaita Vedanta and the Bhagavad Gita. Born as Balakrishna Menon in Kerala in 1916, Swami Chinmayananda Saraswati spearheaded a Hindu spiritual renaissance across the world and established one educational–philanthropic organization called the Chinmaya Mission to reach the Hindus in India and abroad. He was an academically sound sadhu who attained excellence in Indian philosophy, literature and journalism and contributed to the dissemination of the knowledge of Vedanta among the common Hindus all over the world. He was one of the most influential sadhus in the post-independence time who left a permanent impact on the interfaith dialogues at different national and international platforms and received the highest applause from different sectors of the Hindu society. See, Rudite Emir, *Swami Chinmayananda: A Life of Inspiration and Service* (Mumbai: Central Chinmaya Mission Trust, 1998); Radhika Krishnakumar, *Ageless Guru: The Inspirational Life of Swami Chinmayananda* (Mumbai: Central Chinmaya Mission Trust, 2008).
37. Swami Chinmayananda, *World Hindu Conference 1979* (Bombay: Vishva Hindu Parishad Publication, 1979), 100.
38. The second meeting of the VHP was held in November 1964 in New Delhi and chaired by Swami Chinmayananda, with Jayachamarajendra Wadiyar, the Maharaja of Mysore, accepting presidentship of the VHP. Shivram Shankar Apte became the VHP's general secretary at its inauguration, starting a tradition in which senior RSS executives, rather than religious leaders, would hold this office.
39. In the historic World Hindu Conference at Allahabad in 1966, over 25,000 delegates from all parts of the country and about 250 Hindu representatives from foreign lands arrived. Thousands of these delegates were women. The galaxy of spiritual and religious luminaries who adorned the dais presented a sight that thrilled every votary of Hindu unity and strengthened their faith in the bright future of the Hindu society. Present were: the revered Jagadguru Shankaracharyas of Dwaraka Peeth, and of Govardhan Peeth, Purl; Swami Naradanandji of Naimisharanya, Swami Chinmayananda of the Sandeepani Ashram, Bombay; Swami Advaitananda of the Bharat Sewashram Sangh,

Satguru Shri Jagjit Singh of the Namdhari Sikh sect, Mahant Guru Charan Das, President of the Bharat Sadhu Samaj; Jain Muni Shri Ashok, Shri Hemachandra Deb Goswami of Assam, Jagadguru Swami Shri Vishveshwar Teerth of the Pejawar Math, Shri Sant Tukdoji Maharaj, Jagadguru Swami Raghavacharya, Mahamandaleshwar Swami Maheshwarananda Giri. Sant Prabhudutt Brahmachari of Jhusi, Swami Atmananda of the Vivekananda Ashram, Raipur; and Brahmachari Dattamurti of Masurashram, Bombay (collected from the Digital acrive of the VHP. https://vhp.org/orgnization/historic-world-hindu-conference/ [accessed 4 April 2019]).

40. According to Professor Chetan Bhatt, 'The presence of two *shankaracharyas* at the 1966 *sammelan* was significant. The importance of the "four" *shankaracharyas* for the VHP is related to the power they wield within (especially Brahmanical, Sanatanist and northern Indian) Hinduism. However, the *shankaracharyas* cannot be conceived as an ecclesiastical structure *of* Hinduism. The legitimacy of the *shankaracharyas*, or the authority of any one of them, can be questioned. Indeed, the authority of the *shankaracharyas* is often not acknowledged either within their own ostensible spheres of influence or from within a broader Indian Hinduism. The Brahmanical strictures, limits to "theological" influence, and the competition between *shankaracharyas* can create obstacles for the VHP's integrationist project' (Bhatt, *Hindu Nationalism*, 182–183).
41. Bhatt, *Hindu Nationalism*, 181.
42. Bhatt, *Hindu Nationalism*, 182–183.
43. In 2011, one Sanatan Dharm Manch was formed challenging the rights of the VHP to construct the Ram temple under the banner of its Ram Janmabhoomi trust. The new platform discarded any individual or organization generating orchestrated politics on the mandir issue, and none of the four officially recognized Shankaracharyas attended the conference organized by the VHP; even some of the *akharas* stayed away from the VHP's platform and expressed their disappointments over the VHP's failure to expedite the matter due to sheer political interest (see the coverage from Kumbh Mela, 27 January 2001, https://www.rediff.com/news [accessed 3 July 2020]).
44. P. R. Ram, *Hindutva Offensive: Social Roots and Characterization* (Mumbai: Centre for Study of Society and Secularism, 1996), 9.
45. Shivram Shankar Apte, the first general secretary of the VHP, mentioned, 'The declared object of Christianity is to tam the whole world into Christendom—as that of Islam is to make it "Pak." Besides these two dogmatic and proselytizing religions, there has arisen a third religion, communism. For all of these the major target of conquest is the vast Hindu society living in this land and scattered over the globe in small and big numbers. ...It is therefore necessary in this age of competition and conflict to think of, and organise, the Hindu world to save itself from the evil eyes of all the three'. (Shivram Shankar Apte, *Why Vishva Hindu Parishad*, Organiser, Diwali issue [2 November 1964]: 15)

46. VHP Executive Committee Resolution, 27 April 1966.
47. 24 September 2015. https://www.worldhindunews.com/swami-dayananda-sarsawati (accessed 3 April 2019).
48. For details see, http://shivallibrahmins.com/great-acharyas/sri-sri-vishvesha-theertha-swamiji/ (accessed 25 April 2021).
49. The main resolutions adopted in the Sansad included: (a) 'Devotthan Ekadashi be celebrated as Ekatmata Diwas for perpetual consolidation of National Unity and Integrity and it should be accepted and observed as a National Day'; (b) 'Sanskrit Language, Spirituality and Yoga Education should be made compulsory in all the schools'; (c) 'A campaign be undertaken for eradication of the evil practices in the society like untouchability, corruption and dowry. Dharmacharyas, Mathadheeshas, Sant-Mahatmas etc. should come forward and extend their support in this regard'; (d) 'All the classes of people should be linked with the work of upliftment of our Vanavasis, Girivasis and neglected brethren below the lowest line of normal sustenance, so that a sense of confidence would be awakened among them to think that they too are the part and parcel of Hindu society'; (e) '[a] Shriram Janmabhumi, Shrikrishna Janmasthan and Kashi Vishwanath temple : these three places be immediately handed over to Hindu society. [b] A country-wide campaign should be undertaken, if the Uttar Pradesh Govt. does not acquire Shriram Janmabhumi and hand it over to Shri Ramanandacharya'; and (f) 'Dharmacharyas should come out of their Mutt-Mandirs and strive for making Bharat, as Vishwa Guru [world master] by humanizing the man for human welfare and world peace'. See, *Second Dharma Sansad*, The digital archive of the VHP, https://vhp.org/conferences/dharma-sansad
50. See, The Report by Darshan Devaiah, *Indian Express*, Bengaluru, 9 December 2019, https://indianexpress.com.
51. Nilanjan Mukhopadhyay, *The Demolition. India at the Crossroads* (New Delhi: Indus, 1994), 32–33.
52. 'The (Ramjanmabhumi) RJB Nyas was established by VHP on February 3, 1986, and did not have a fixed membership except for the involvement of senior sadhus listed above. These sadhus were drawn from a bigger pool of sadhus who had associated themselves informally with VHP's Dharma Sansad (Parliament of Religion), an informal platform established in 1984. RJB Nyas was established to press the Congress government to transfer the property rights of the Ayodhya site for building the "world's biggest temple."' Rajesh Pradhan, 'When the Saints Go Marching in Sadhus in Democratic Politics in Late 20th Century India' (PhD thesis, Department of Political Science, MIT), 126.
53. There is no contemporary record of the origin and history of the different *akharas* except a few scattered materials on the subject. The most prominent of the akharas are: Shri Panch Dashnaam Juna Akhada, headed by Acharya Mahamandaleshwar Swami Avdheshanand Giri; Shree Panchayati Akhada Niranjani, headed by Swami Mahant Ravindra Puri (the secretary

of the *akhada*—Swami Narendra Giri is the president of Akhil Bharatiya Akhara Parishad [ABAP]); Shree Shambhu Panchayati Atal Akhada, headed by Acharya Mahamandaleshwar Swami Vishwatmanand Saraswati; Shri Panchayati Akhada Mahanirvani; Shri Panchayati Akhara Bada Udasin; Shri Panchayati Akhara Naya Udasin; Shree Panch Nirmohi Ani Akhada; Shri Panch Digambar Ani Akhada; Shree Panch Nirvani Ani Akhada; Shri Panchayati Akhara Nirmala, headed by Mahant Pandit Gurudev Singhji Vendantacharya; Shri Shambhu Panchagni Akhara, headed by Sabhapati Brahmchari Mukttanandji Maharaj; Shri Panchdashnaam Aavahan Akhara, headed by Acharya Mahamandaleshwar Shivendra Puri Ji Maharaj; and Taponidhi Shri Anand Akhara Panchayti, headed by Acharya Peetadheeshwar Balkanand Giri Ji Maharaj. For a detailed reading of the akharas, see, Ananda Bhattacharya, eds., *A History of the Dashnami Naga Sannyasis* (London: Routledge, 2018).

54. Narendra Giri of the Niranjani akhara became the chief of the ABAP in 2016. He played a keen role in dispelling scandalous and fraud sadhus from the sadhu *samaj*. Radhe Maa, Asaram Bapu, Narayan Sai and Swami Aseemanand were some of the sadhus who made the list of fake sadhus by Narendra Giri. His relation with the VHP was caught in sheer ambiguity, especially when he did not object to BJP's move of turning the Ardh Kumbh Mela into a mega affair through changing its name through the Prayagraj Mela Authority Bill. It was done only to get extra political mileage in favour of the BJP in the forthcoming Lok Sabha elections in 2019. Direndra K. Jha informs, 'The last straw probably was the attempt by the RSS and its various outfits to hijack the religious spectacle. In the Kumbh Mela area the VHP set up a campus city with several hundred tents housing leaders of the Sangh Parivar as well as sadhus attached to it. Other RSS outfits—BJP, Akhil Bharatiya Vidyarthi Parishad, Vidya Bharati, Sanskar Bharati and Vanvasi Kalyan Ashram—had their own separate camps. This overbearing Sangh Parivar presence turned off the *akharas*. The spectre of a rival focal point in Kumbh Melas has always been an issue of concern for them'. Dhirendra K. Jha, *RSS and the Akharas*, 8 March 2019, https://fountainink.in/reportage/rss-and-the-akharas
55. van der Veer, '"God Must Be Liberated!" A Hindu Liberation Movement in Ayodhya', *Modern Asian Studies* 21, no. 2 (1987): 294–297.
56. 'The first abbot of the Goraksanath Math with political ambitions was Digvijayanath, who was born in 1884 and was Mahant from 1934 until his death in 1969. In 1967 he won the Gorakhpur seat, standing officially as an independent.... Digvijayanath was the key figure who changed the identity of the Math. His adoption of the Hindu Right ideology was intimately connected to his participation in electoral politics. ...Avaidyanath counted the "eradication of untouchability" as his biggest achievement in politics and felt that it was important for (uncorrupt) people like him to enter politics to ensure "people's faith in the nation".... He was also a strong advocate of Hinduism and a supporter of the Ramjanmabhumi movement'. Shashank Chaturvedi,

David N. Gellner, and Sanjay Kumar Pandey, 'Politics in Gorakhpur Since the 1920s: The Making of a Safe "Hindu" constituency', *Contemporary South Asia* 27, no. 1 (2019): 40–57.

57. Chaturvedi et al., 'Politics in Gorakhpur Since the 1920s', 52.
58. Ali Sharib, 'Clean Chits, Deaths, Acquittals: The Unending "Tricks of Fate" in Saffron Terror Cases', *Economic and Political Weekly* 53, no. 17 (28 April 2018); Leena Gita Reghunath, 'The Believer: Swami Aseemanand's Radical Service to the Sangh', *Caravan*, 2014, http://www.caravanmagazine.in/reportage/believer
59. For newspaper reports and articles on Shankaracharya Jayendra Saraswathi, see, *Acharya Sri Jayendra Saraswathi Swamigal Who Melded Spiritualism with Social Outreach* (accessed 1 March 2018); *Jayendra Saraswathi: An Acharya with a Difference* (accessed 1 March 2018); Jayendra Saraswati, The Seer Who Tried to Resolve the Ram Janmabhoomi-Babri Masjid Dispute (accessed 1 March 2018); http://www.justicenews.co.in/jayendra-saraswathi-1935-2018-spiritual-leader-who-expanded-kanchi-mutts-business-services/; Kanchi Seer Jayendra Saraswathi, 'A Spiritual Colossus Till His Arrest in 2004, Dies', *Times of India* (accessed 1 March 2018).
60. *Indian Express* reported, 'In January 1999, Australian missionary Graham Staines was burnt alive with his two sons by a murderous mob led by Dara Singh. Though the Orissa Freedom of Religion Act was passed by the state Government in 1967 to prohibit conversions by inducements, it could not come into effect till 1989 when the Government framed the Rules of the Act. It was only in 1993 that the Orissa police first booked 21 pastors in tribal dominated Nowrangpur district under the Act'. See, Debabrata Mohanty, *Slain VHP Man Was Conversion King*, Bhubaneswar, 26 August 2008.
61. The state government under the Congress remained fairly ineffective in checking the successful growth of the RSS in the social, religious and cultural domains in the area. Today, the spread of the Hindutva organizations is wide. The RSS runs more than 6,000 *shakhas* in Orissa, with a membership of 150,000-plus, while the VHP has a base of 125,000 members in the state. Another rabidly communal organization, the Bajrang Dal, has more than 50,000 members who serve in 200 *akharas*, and the women's wing, Durga Vahini, has 25,000 members. Both the organizations are working in close coordination with the RSS and VHP cadres. Angana Chatterjee, 'Hindutva's Violent History', *Tehelka Magazine*, 2000.
62. Pralay Kanungo, 'Hindutva's Entry into a "Hindu Province": Early Years of RSS in Orissa', *Economic and Political Weekly* 38, no. 31 (2 August 2003): 9.
63. In an interview with Telegraph reporter Sanjay K. Jha, Computer Baba pointed out that the Sangh Parivar associates like the RSS-VHP and the ABAP threw him out of their circle alleging that he supports the Congress. 'What are you doing by supporting the BJP? Is the Akhara Parishad ready to issue an order saying 'don't oppose BJP', asked the Baba. The outrageous Baba

anticipated that, 'If politics and religion should be strictly kept separate, why are some babas appealing to vote for the BJP? They are doing politics to interfere in religious matters. ...The Parishad withdrew my Mahamandleshwar title and barred me from entering the upcoming Kumbh in Allahabad. Is opposing the BJP a crime in Hinduism?' See, Sanjay K. Jha, 20 November 2018, https://www.telegraphindia.com/india/computer-baba (accessed 4 February 2020).

64. Angry with the RSS, sadhus campaign against the BJP in Madhya Pradesh polls, November 24, 2018, https://hindi.caravanmagazine.in/politics/madhya-pradesh
65. Tanika Sarkar, 'Aspects of Contemporary Hindutva Theology: The Voice of Sadhvi Rithambhara', in *Hindu Wife, Hindu Nation: Community, Religion, and Cultural Nationalism*, ed. Tanika Sarkar (Bloomington: Indiana University Press, 2001); Brenda Cossman and Ratna Kapur, 'Secularism: Bench-Marked by Hindu Right', *Economic and Political Weekly* 31, no. 38 (1996): 2613-2617+2619-2627+2629-2630; Sudha Pai, *Political Process in Uttar Pradesh: Identity, Economic Reforms, and Governance* (Uttar Pradesh: Pearson Education India, 2007), 97, 124–125. Accessed 6 October 2015; Sikta Banerjee, 'In the Crucible of Hindutva: Women and Masculine Hinduism', in *Make Me a Man!: Masculinity, Hinduism, and Nationalism in India*, ed. Sikta Banerjee (Albany, NY: State University of New York Press, 2005); Christophe Jaffrelot, *The Hindu Nationalist Movement and Indian Politics: 1925 to the 1990s: Strategies of Identity-building, Implantation and Mobilisation (with Special Reference to Central India)*. (London: C. Hurst & Co. Publishers, 1996); *The Worldly Ascetic*. Business and Economy. (Accessed 6 December 2013); 'Election 2019: "It Is Sedition": Digvijaya Singh Points To Pragya Thakur's Godse Remark', *NDTV.com*. (Accessed 28 November 2019).

New-Age Gurus

The Votaries of Universal Hindutva

To ponder how a new bunch of sadhus who turned into spiritual gurus[1] and preachers stepped into new-age Hindutva politics, one would do well to mull over first the innovation possibilities of modern media technology that has facilitated creation of new identities and a cultural space of one's own over the last two decades or more. This new cultural space is very much controlled by the worlds of market and media, which made communities behave in a certain manner and redefined the conventional political terms to create room for the logic of cultural reproduction. Claims that Hindutva is an overtly political ideology combined with Hindu majoritarianism and militancy lost their grounds at the turn of the 20th century when liberal economic reforms and cyberspace revolution in the country ushered in a new era of cultural transformation. At the onset of these changes, the centrality of state-centric national territories came under scrutiny, and the new cultural space of technology, media and market gradually reshaped the frontiers of Hindutva at a global scale. The exclusive media climate created after Hindutva's universal ambitions of pervading new spaces provided the primary impetus to reframing the existing perceptions of Hindutva and its hitherto existing narratives, and one unique mode of 'non-participatory' politics evolved with time. This new-age Hindutva, partly negotiated at the virtual space and partly at the vernacularized performative space, gathered momentum around the market patterns of a commodity society for which politics itself has become a trope to de-politicize the expressions of individual actors and organizations. New-age Hindutva and 'non-participatory' politics have evolved as natural partners, mostly through the ways and means the ruling Hindu nationalist party has made use of media platforms for electoral gains, and the guru-led movements have appropriated some everyday performative acts that speak for the idea of Hindu nationalism in general. Mostly flourishing since the 1990s, these gurus and their organizations emerged as key players in 'transnational capitalism' in India and added to the growing support for Hindu nationalism in India and abroad. 'As producers and purveyors of spiritual commodities, gurus assist in propagating Hindu nationalism, an ideology that relies on referents to Hindu India's unparallel spiritual prowess and moral authority'.[2] Hindu spirituality as a cultural trope has been sanctioned by multinational corporations for market expansions and for the promotion of corporate capitalism—an alternative form of spirituality which is being 'sold' as 'trendy, transformative and radical' spirituality to bring about a fundamental change in one's lifestyle behaviour.[3] The new-age Hindu nationalists in India quickly realized that religion could no longer become more than a service sector in the periods succeeding globalization and that religion would soon be reframed as spirituality to support the trends of market capitalism.[4]

This spiritualism would best be manifested not in isolation from politics and economy but through continuing to operate from a similar cultural space, because all these so-called categories would be conditioned by the ethics of media and the market in the age of neoliberalism. It signified the emergence of a dominant economic ideology that unfolded major political shifts and a slow taking over of the cultural space by a certain economic agenda. In place of the nation states of earlier times, now it is the market state, mentioned Phillip Bobbitt,[5] which would 'maximise the opportunity of the people and thus tends to privatise many state activities and to make voting and representative government less influential and more responsive to the market'. With the importance of the representative government fading away from public discourse, alternative modalities of politics would become the prevailing form of reality. Here, the individuals would embrace spirituality as a resourceful commodity while keeping strong links with their traditions and religious heritage and ancient wisdom. Approaches leading to the integration of consumerism and renunciation, incorporation and denial of worldly desires, came out as a plausible stereotype to outline the actual spectrum of the new structure.[6] It is this analysis of new-age spirituality which gave a new impetus to the idea of 'non-participatory' politics under changed circumstances.

Importantly, the thought of a 'non-participatory' politics does not necessarily signify a kind of lackadaisical attitude by the citizens in a liberal democracy; rather, it brings up an alternative to traditional representative democracy. Here, politics becomes a non-competitive act of self-appropriation through creating limitless spectacles of mass media images and invoking some vernacularized Hindu practices to create a self-conscious Hindu nationalist subject. In the non-participatory politics of Hindutva, both the media spectacles and vernacular performative practices initiated by the gurus and their disciples create permeable boundaries, with some traditions being similar to those popularized by the mainstream Hindu nationalist organizations. For instance, other than providing spiritual messages and lifestyle teachings to a cosmopolitan audience over media platforms, the new-age gurus often indulge in social service projects, such as healthcare programmes, rural development programmes, yoga and meditation programmes, caste–class empowerment programmes and such. In their respective ashram premises, religious performative activities, such as *pujas*, *prarthanas* and *kirtans*, are held on a regular basis. All these performances are indicative of the approaches instrumental to the political project of Hindu nationalism and equally suggestive of the development of Hindu identities—what John Zavos has labelled as 'informal politics of social action'. My primary aim in this chapter is to look for the ways in which the dynamics of new-age Hindutva have been produced with the emergence of the new-age gurus and their respective traditions in both the virtual and real cultural spaces. The major problem with new-age Hindutva is that, so far, the subject has always been treated mostly in the realms of political statecraft, as a *sangathanist* strategy of the RSS, and any serious engagement with the alternative cultural spaces operating on the edge of the Sangh Parivar network is excluded.

Gurus and their network of followers function from an ideologically high pedestal, leaving enough room for exclusionary discourses and invoking hybridity in their nature and approach. They have shown every potential to shift towards a Hindutva agenda in a neoliberal regime that encourages 'guru-led and Hindu-inspired movements to extend their mandate of social operations and that in turn elicits favourable behaviours such as institutional social services from them' (Pandeya 2016, 401–423). Interestingly, non-participatory politics may explain the essentials of the so-called spectacle politics—a theory developed by French Marxist theorist Guy Debord in 1967 in his book *The Society of the Spectacles*.[7] The allegory of 'non-participation' hardly cast the citizens as a passive audience lacking real political concern for the issues of collective socio-economic interests or removed from the realities of life. It is not a 'one-dimensional society'[8] ruled by a commercialized media culture; rather, in the case of new-age Hindutva in India, multidimensional networks have been utilized on both national and transnational platforms to ensure greater mass participation in the process. The advocates of new-age Hindutva are not driven by the ethics of any voluntary entertainment business, rather rearticulating the ideological space of Hindutva with the 'desire to transform Indian public culture into a sovereign, disciplined national culture rooted in what is claimed to be a superior ancient Hindu past, and to impose a corporatist and disciplined social and political organization upon society' (Hansen 1999, 4). Simultaneously, the participants of new-age Hindutva best utilize the opportunities for social communication available on various media platforms and attempt to connect the virtual with the real in the vast domain of a public culture where political discourses meet with commercial and cultural expressions of an existing regime (Hansen 1999).

The recent history of Hindu politics in India brings out an interesting picture of how people's religious perceptions and affiliations have been exploited in media networks and the entire context in which politics is conceived as an experimental affair.[9] Scholars and researchers contributed to the rise of mass media in the 1980s, its alleged connection with the Ram Janmabhoomi movement and subsequent communal upsurges in the early 1990s.[10] Despite laying conflicting claims over Hindu nationalism as being a patriotic movement or a communally charged campaign, the Indian media has treated the issue with utter importance, and both the English and vernacular media platforms have helped to create a national public sphere of its own. It was within this public sphere that the new-age sadhus, or more specifically the new-age gurus, appeared and initiated an era of new spirituality, emphasizing a break or turn from the 'old' or traditional to the 'new'.[11] The new-age gurus fitted well with the attributes of new-age Hindutva—indexed by modern technologies, open markets, worldwide movements and a universal audience 'cutting across regional, linguistic, and cultural divides' (Rudert 2010, 630). These new-age gurus came out as the most trusted agents of non-participatory politics by virtue of their reframing of the boundaries of organization-based Hindutva and embrace of the virtual space of communication with a universal cosmopolitan audience in a less religious but more spiritual language.[12] The so-called 'non-political' spirit present in the language and expressions of these gurus indicated the power of new-age Hindutva, which attained a new kind of social justification and validation from a larger audience, especially from the urban middle classes in India and abroad. The gurus innovated and modified the traditional forms of social communication such that it resonated with a new kind of late-capitalist modernity.[13] New-age Hindutva bears the spirit of the ancient past, 'carries with it a nostalgia for the pre modern and a hope that ancient traditions can help in re-enchanting the world, through, ironically, their own kind of "sciences" and "technologies."'[14] The gurus discarded the disillusionment over modernity, revived the authentic spirit of the ancient Hindu traditions and took up leadership roles in various fields, such as health, medicine, education, academics and even politics, though in a different manner.[15] Their irrefutable presence in the public arena and unvarnished way of disseminating knowledge of various forms of Hinduism to audiences around the globe revealed their zeal to get represented through a 'publicly visible uniqueness that sets them apart from established tradition, a uniqueness that inherently includes novelty and innovation'.[16]

A whole lot of 'global gurus' and their followers appear to be the whistle-blowers of 'an ecumenical form of spirituality'[17] in India and abroad. The ecumenical impulses present in their teachings in fact allowed them to rule out the 'ecclesiastical hierarchies' of Hindu society and challenge all sorts of inequalities present in the socio-religious structure, so that a liberal–progressive aura of reputability could be created around their respective personalities. The universal appeal of ecumenical spirituality cutting across caste, class and gender divisions endorsed one 'de-ethicized' form of Hinduism[18] which helped resuscitate the spirit of Hindu spirituality once again for a cosmopolitan audience. It was expected that the ethnocentric, exclusionary narratives of a Hindu nationalist party like the BJP would become incredulous of these gurus and that the universal–humanist appeal of Hindu spirituality would get flattened out in the real political discourse. Much earlier than the emergence of these global gurus in India, the Sangh Parivar had wrestled with how the sadhus and gurus could supplement their own brand of politics. Despite manifesting their global dream on different international platforms, the VHP sadhus reflected their sectarian or *sampradayik* desires in overseas missionary movements and kept their voice alive to 'rouse the Hindu nation against the "menacing conversions to Christianity and Islam."'[19] Unlike the VHP sadhus, the new-age gurus, however, registered their commitment to a secular value system, embraced the cultural roots to a theosophical universalism, adopted new patterns of communication and appeared to be flourishing in the urban Indian market.[20] For the RSS–BJP bosses, it would not be the best idea to grapple with the shifting patterns of Hindutva in India when dozens of closely connected groups in the Sangh Parivar were already reframing Hindutva through an extensive network. The ever-changing face of Hindutva mapped out the growing importance of media and the market, quickly sold its brand to the tech-savvy population of new India and tracked down routes to integrate the new-age actors and their voices into its operations and use them to broadcast itself. What makes it more intriguing is the fact that new-age Hindutva offered its space to both the VHP and non-VHP sadhus; however, the latter attempted to cover up any direct association with the RSS. The approaches of new-age Hindutva suggest that the idea of being and becoming a Hindu must resonate with the politics of familiarity rather than extremism, and any sort of overt connection with the Hindu chauvinist groups from the RSS network could spoil the free–liberal spirit of its brand ambassadors. Various diasporic Hindu organizations,[21] especially those of high intellectual calibre, turned out to be ideal partners of new-age Hindutva, while the Sangh Parivar-oriented fringe groups such as the Hindu Yuva Vahini, Bajrang Dal or Sri Ram Sena[22] failed to get into the zone of plausibility. For obvious reasons, the sadhus-turned-gurus walked the path that led them away from militancy and extremism. Drawing a line between 'hard' and 'soft' Hindutva (Anderson 2015), the new-age sadhus choose not to get identified with any particular organization or network but always remain aroused for the cause of Hindutva in terms of reclaiming an authentic Indian culture, spirituality and national identity.

The most crucial part of the story involves the question—in what ways could these gurus contribute to Indian politics? The question is reminiscent of the ways in which one concludes that sadhus and gurus have nothing to offer politics. In the case of new-age Hindutva or new-age gurus, the issue is not of exploring the ethics of virtue politics or defining the rationale behind spirituality in Indian politics. The issue is understanding how the gurus made spirituality and universality a product of public consumption and claimed their authority over a vast political audience in India. Knowing the fact that Indian politics is a peculiar ecosystem that legitimizes diverse phenomena from bizarre backgrounds, these new-age gurus employed media spectacles to create conditions specific to Hindutva perspectives.[23] The political parties, especially the Hindu nationalist BJP, seized maximum advantage from the spectacles of mass media images, and the party bosses have never been in denial about how these gurus helped in making those images convenient. This is the power of new-age Hindutva, which has achieved mastery over social media branding, with a range of individual actors, like the gurus, knowingly or unknowingly lending their support to the political project of a party which has nothing to do with the message of spiritual wisdom or universal salvation. It is an irony that the contradiction present in Hindutva is itself contradictory. If one goes by the interpretation provided by the Supreme Court of India,[24] no precise meaning could be ascribed to the word Hindutva when seen within the narrow limits of religion alone, since Hindutva manifests as a way of life of the people of the subcontinent. The contradictory pulls of Hindutva look more apparent on online media platforms because the disagreements over the actual connotation of the term often get livid and abusive to an extent. The twin aspects of new-age Hindutva being an Indian way of life and a communally charged hate campaign of the majoritarian community made it an arduous job for the gurus to minimize the tensions over the debate on Hindutva, as well as to sound motivational and 'secular' for the cosmopolitan audience. The welfare services provided by these gurus and their organizations in healthcare, food distribution, education, childcare, employment and other sectors increased the social visibility of their movements, and with the increasing inequality in India, these welfare services have become extensive.

The idea of new-age Hindutva drew increasingly on the new cultural space through media and the market, expanding the possibilities of greater mass participation in the process, which had never been the case in the decades after independence. Moving far beyond the organizational network of the RSS, and motivated by the incentives given to consumer markets, new-age Hindutva appeared to permeate into innovative domains of knowledge dissemination mostly in psychological conformity with the established ideology. What is clear is that at the onset of the present civilizational conjuncture, mainly with the advance of market reforms, the monopoly of the Hindutva elites had been challenged, if not refuted; the multi-polarity of Hindutva helped it pervade the political landscape and manifest as the political symbolism of the new age. The ecosystem of this new age is inhabited by knowledge and information[25]—the chief resources to index ideas, values and even belief systems in a new world order where 'individuality and freedom ensured the success for "third wave civilisation,"'[26] which equally reshaped old-world ideologies, like Hindu nationalism, with idiosyncratic expressions. With new forms and ways of communicating to a larger audience, new-age Hindutva in fact absorbed local knowledge systems into the process of what is called 'vernacularization' of Hindutva with a different set of political interests.[27] It is ironic that while new-age Hindutva attempted to enfranchise certain sections of the society through various means of accommodation, it also infused a more ominous design of racism, misogyny, communal hatred and casteism into the body politics of the nation. Individual actors and organizations who were considered outlandish or had so far existed only at the margins might have found ways and means of speaking their minds, but the loosely defined perception of Hindu nationalism often served the interests of the traditional elites. It is mostly because of the fact that new-age Hindutva emerged to be an unregulated, decentralized zone that a cluster of individuals and institutions mainly flourished in the public sphere, sometimes with tacit approval from the Sangh Parivar, and were mostly excluded from being identified with Hindu majoritarian politics as such.[28] The votaries of new age Hindutva found a larger audience both among the Indian diasporic communities and in the middle class public sphere of India; however, they espoused a sense of autonomy in both the real and virtual spaces, which blended easily with political actions and aspirations. The articulation of autonomy depended largely on how the proponents of new-age Hindutva kept exploring the art of being non-political in nature and explicitly political in ambitions. It is a highly volatile zone where anonymous actors and organizations deploy a self-styled module of public mobilization—relying on hyper-visible popular symbols and mediated mostly by a middle-class public culture in urban India.

Right from the time of the Hindu resurgence in the 19th century, universal diffusion of Upanishadic and Vedantic knowledge had already set the stage for the reification of Indian spirituality by Hindu nationalists who theorized it as a transnational reflection of Hindu interests. The trajectory of Hindu spirituality, however, differed from place to place, 'as it is inserted into different historical developments'. One must not see the Hindutva trends of the Sangh Parivar as similar to those of the Hindu renaissance of the 19th century; however, in both nationalist discourses, Hinduism has been linked with Indian identity, which is closely tied up with India's intrinsic spirituality. There are scholars who prefer to see the VHP movement as an incarnation of the neo-Hindu movement of the 19th century; mention must be made about Swami Dayananda—one of the disciples of Swami Chinmayananda of the VHP—who attracted devotes simply by propagating Vedantic philosophies.

Fuller and Harrias note that a traditional guru like Swami Dayananda criticized the BJP for not propagating Hindutva properly and expressed that the BJP's emphasis should be on spirituality, not on 'new-age fantasies'.[29] The failure of the VHP in popularizing the universal–spiritual essence of the Hindu dharma could be explained partly in terms of its struggle for organizational control and partly by its failure to define the connection between the secular state and religion in India. Despite that, it set the stage for a global Hindu society that got structured by the 'territorial imaginations of the nation state', even though 'nation state' lost its relevance as a category of analysis in the age of globalization.[30] New-age Hindutva played well with these imaginations of a nation state on various media platforms, reshaped the idea of nationhood and helped in endorsing what Sahana Udupa has called 'enterprise Hindutva'.[31] The actual paradox of new-age Hindutva relates to the fact that it revived the notion of superiority claimed by Hindu/Indian spirituality over Western materialism, claimed a real scientific basis for Indian religious traditions, emphasized everyday performative acts, like yoga and meditation, as analogous to true ancient wisdom. Continuing with the theme of reshaping the nation and nationhood in both the virtual and real spaces, the messengers of new-age Hindutva often infused political meaning into the prescribed performative acts like yoga and meditation which resonated with the militant–masculine project of Hindu nationalists endorsed by the Sangh Parivar. The social service schemes, yoga programmes and long series of performative acts offered by the new-age gurus proved productive in circulating spirituality and Hindu nationalist themes, and most notably, they contributed to the formation of a middle-class public space where a variety of actors participated, mostly due to their attraction to an ecumenical–universal Hinduism. The new-age gurus happily connected spirituality with Hindu nationalist themes but rejected any direct association with the big bosses of the Sangh Parivar. They made it possible partly because of their adjustment with the virtual world in the real world and partly because of their popularity on transnational platforms. They have the power to work for an agenda without even being identified with any specific political ideology. Thus, an alternative reading of new-age Hindutva could be outlined using the contributions made by the gurus and their disciples. Following from this point, I weave my narrative around three interlinked issues: (a) the gurus and their networks; (b) modalities of their functioning; and (c) the politics of new-age Hindutva in a transnational setting.

GURUS AND THE KNOWLEDGE TRADITION

Angela Rudert, in her thoughtful essay on new-age gurus, mentioned:

> Throughout the long history of Indian religious life, gurus, seers, rishis in India have oftentimes been innovators and facilitators of intercultural exchange. Through their words, their songs, and their teachings—which often form eclectic scriptural canons—they have always sought to teach to the very temporal setting in which they lived and to meet people where they are..... Even before the colonial encounter, the settings in which people lived were always expanding beyond the known, inherited religious-cultural boundaries to include varying worldviews. In this sense, there have always been gurus who in some ways saw themselves as teaching in a new age, setting, or context. And some perhaps saw themselves as ushering in a New Age in a time of conflict or repressive social or political regimes making Truth accessible yet again.

The tradition of knowledge passed on by the gurus was not identified with a monolithic system but represented diversity all through the ages. Brahmanical tradition remained strong in articulating one authoritative tradition; however, lived religious experiences always influenced the Hindu way of believing and experiencing traditions. In the guru lineage, the word 'tradition' has always been called '*parampara*' in Sanskrit, which refers to the succession of knowledge from one generation to another or from one space to the other. In India, the idea of traditional knowledge took a hold on every aspect of community life, including healthcare practices, belief-oriented practices, spiritual practices and even knowledge from the lived experiences of everyday politics. The *parampara* of knowledge did not ever see any severe clash between the elites and the masses; rather, a wonderful cohesion had been maintained. With the advent of the so-called modern science and technology and English education in India, this *parampara* of traditional knowledge first clashed with a different system and was relegated to a point of inferiority. The orientalist construction of a backward India and the civilizing mission of the early imperialists prepared the blueprint of colonial contròl, and all the survey operations or natural explorations established a new pattern of knowledge production in India. The attempts to replace the vast gamut of traditional knowledge with one hegemonic pattern of knowledge resulted in the emergence of two worlds of knowledge: one dominated by the spirit of reason, modernity, science and technology and the other by belief systems, emotions, religious practices and metaphysical forces and 'unscientific' perceptions.[32] Interestingly, the Indian gurus who spoke in a universal spiritual language tried to live on the ecumenical and egalitarian spirit of Hinduism and assiduously attempted to connect the word of Western modernity with Eastern spatiality. In doing so, 'the majority of the modern gurus drew on *bhakti* sensibilities (Kabir, Sri Aurobindo, Ramana Maharshi, Maharishi Mahesh Yogi)—each propounded aversion of universalized ecumenical spirituality based in a variety of Hindu philosophical roots'.[33] The depth and range of Indian spirituality, however, should not be judged by a monolithic model, because the spectrum of traditional spiritual knowledge is based on the patterns of the dualities of Brahmanical and non-Brahmanical knowledge, which controlled the common people's perception of life. Negotiating with the dualities of the Brahmanical and the non-Brahmanical often become problematic for the traditionalists who wanted to visualize the world of Indian spiritual knowledge tradition as an unsystematic but homogeneous construction against the hegemonic world of the modern Western knowledge system. This notion of homogeneity helped produce the one-Hindu nationalist rhetoric, which resulted in espousing Hindu cultural supremacy with well-augmented political agenda.[34]

Putting the qualitative East in direct contrast to the quantitative West seems lackadaisical and reluctant to the complex structure of interconnectedness between different perspectives of spiritual knowledge coming from different cultures and traditions. Creating the 'other' in Western modernity appeared to be helpful in mothering everything that was traditional and Indian, and at the same time, it opened up the possibilities of a dialogue between the primary components of traditional spiritual knowledge, that is, religion, culture, identities and belief systems. Traditionalism did not necessarily introduce conservatism or any specific religious–cultural version of spirituality; however, drawing inspiration from Brahmanical sacred texts or symbolizing Hindu cultural metaphors as the epitome of self-conscious purity might have led the Hindu nationalists to project a sacred–uninterrupted Hindu/Indian past essential to the construction of Indian nationhood through the Hindutva lens. Since the fundamental attribute of spiritually is tethered to the development of the self, they often portrayed institutional religion as a place where authoritarianism, mendicancy and dogmatism had replaced the authentic, living religious experience. 'Therefore, new age gurus when echoing I's spiritual but not religious' hold to a conception of a 'highly individualised, very psychological' form of spiritual knowledge which looked 'predictably capitalist in it stress on human potential and techniques for growth, and so attractive to so many—that interests us'.[35] In this highly individualistic zone of 'gurudom', different institutions, such as families, castes, business corporations, the military, criminal gangs and even political parties, enter for their own benefits, because having a guru often helps them get the necessary recognition and appreciation from others. The structure of 'gurudom' works in sync with a psychological model of Hindu culture which 'emphasises to human dependence and vulnerability to feelings of estrangement and helplessness'.[36] However, the situation was not the same always. During the early decades after independence, the importance and visibility of gurus were much less in comparison to those after later developments. The Nehruvian deployment of secularism as the state policy of India might have challenged the rise and growth of the guru movements and the gradual capturing of public imaginations by the Hindu nationalists to a large extent; however, the efficacy of the gurus and their networks in the political sphere needs to be explored. Framing Hindu nationalism as a useful political strategy was symptomatic of a range of new meanings to the approaches of Hindutva, which started dominating the public sphere from the 1980s, and a bunch of sadhus-turned-gurus appeared crucial to the politics of Hindutva then onwards. In his soulful analysis on gurus, Mckean noted that the Hindu nationalists projected themselves as the defenders of democracy…linked democracy with the stability of Indian society, 'a stability founded on the spirituality taught by the Hindu sages'. Simultaneously, they proclaimed that because of its uniquely tolerant spiritual nature, Hinduism should be taken to be the actual basis of Indian secularism, 'which calls for the state support to all religions and denies any strict separation of the state and religion'.[37]

This new interpretation of an indigenous secularism could have had its impact on the growing importance of sadhus in Indian politics. The real saga of the politics of new-age gurus started with the waves of neoliberal economic transformation in the 1990s. It involved a thorough deregulation of Indian industry, trade liberalization and growth of the private sector, among other changes. Commenting on how economic growth is associated with increasing secularization, Professor Sriya Iyer observed that after the economic liberalization of the Indian economy in 1991, religious-service provision in the country changed. The religious organizations that 'viewed their religious services as faith propagation and religious education' brought many changes in service provision after 1991, especially in the competitive market. Special attention was given to raising funds and using funds in a more systematic manner so that services could be provided to the people more effectively through various means, mostly using online technology. In return for their religion marketing, the organizations, especially those run by the gurus, gained 'goodwill, monetary contributions from the country, increased number of adherents, greater political influence and other benefits'.[38] Here, the theoretical insights mark the notion of a spiritual capital created by the gurus and their organizations following the rules of democracy and market freedom. Spiritual capital suggests one interesting form of 'social capital' surrounding 'the spaces of power, influence, knowledge and dispositions created by participation in a particular religious tradition'.[39] This notion of a social capital, nay spiritual capital, translated the dominant class interest of that period into the cultural–ideological space of new-age Hindutva. Determining how the so-called new-age gurus responded to the new-age Hindutva would form the conceptual understanding of Hindutva as part of the economic transformations in the late 20th century. The proponents of new-age Hindutva supported trade liberalization, opposed trade unionism, favoured the trading class's uninterrupted reflection of interests in the domestic markets, etc. Critics have often pointed out its petty-bourgeoisie character, as well as its efforts in disqualifying class and caste struggles while promoting big-capital interests at a later stage.[40]

The rise of big-capital investment expanded market opportunities, and the growth of individual opportunities under state-sponsored reforms outlined the features of an era that endorsed one absolute notion of the state/community. Within this all-pervasive notion of state/community, 'individualisation constitutes the material expression in capitalist bodies of the existing relations of production and the social division of labour...and the "individual" forms the conceptual terrain on which class relationships within capitalism are defined'.[41] Already in the 1980s a small class of capitalist farmers emerged in most states of India except the Northeast, especially after the abolition of *zamindari* and the Green Revolution, and these classes contributed to the formulation of regional parties, as well as the 'subsequent OBC mobilizations'.[42] Communities asking for their share in state resources and creating a political culture of competition and contestation unfolded a complex challenge to individualization of Indian polity, showing the lack of common-interest politics by the state. The ideology of Hindutva had the most suitable political response to the questions arising out of the new economic transformations in the country. It provided the option to incorporate and accelerate individual choices in a hegemonic social structure where 'real' Hindus would be entrusted with the right values, and these 'real' Hindus would collectively form the notion of Indian polity. Collective Hindu interest signified the idea of a *parivar*, where individual potential would not be appreciated at the cost of collective interests. These collective interests would not be threatened by community interests; rather, a common understanding of the Indian (Hindu) society would prevail. The notion of a common understanding sought to explain the individual traits needed to become a good, virtuous Hindu and condemned the 'foreigner/invaders', or the so-called 'religious others', for having the malicious intention to disrupt the so-called common understanding of the Hindu society.[43] The state, therefore, would have to take initiatives to maintain a harmonious balance in the society and take necessary actions to preserve the conditions in which the ideal of a nation would flourish. Hindutva as a political–economic project of action positioned itself amid multiple combinations of forces with a kind of 'intellectual and moral' leadership that reflected the interest of the dominant class as the general will of the society.[44] The primary tensions between Hindutva and economic linearization played much of a role not in class contestations but in Hindutva's celebration of social collectiveness over individual preferences.

Furthermore, economic liberalization depended largely on opening markets to international projects and responding to the call of globalization at the earliest. Hindutva in its primordial form placed much emphasis on 'swadeshi', or to be precise, adopted a conservative way of dealing with the idea of Hindu nationalism. Despite that, the new-age Hindutva model surmounted the pigeonholing of Hindu nationalism as an indigenous, class-biased phenomenon, instead utilizing the neoliberal marketing strategies to make Hindutva a global brand. The success of economic liberalism and new-age Hindutva depended much on the reflection of their shared political interests, especially when the realities of Indian politics remained allusive to the potential clash of interests.[45] Interestingly, the proponents of new-age Hindutva, including a section of the Sangh Parivar bosses, approved twin strategies to address the issues of economic liberalization. New-age Hindutva's constant focus on swadeshi economy or on the ideal of *atmanirbharta* somewhat evolved analogous to its pro-poor policy, particularly when discussed in terms of its electoral strategies. Welcoming of foreign investments or opening up of Indian markets to global economic fortunes stood in sharp contrast to the policy of self-reliance or development of a sense of patriotism/nationalism among the masses. One may recall what L. K. Advani had declared in late 1980s, '...the solution to our economic problems does not lie in credits or technology from abroad, but in giving a boost to domestic production and exports based on total mobilization of national resources...'. Tariq Thachil, in his study on the BJP, has shown that voters from low-income groups found the privatizing reforms of the Congress regime in the late 1980s frustrating, and the Hindu nationalists promoted their policy of swadeshi economic policy as the right alternative liberalization initiative. Subsequently, it was presumed that the BJP would turn completely antagonistic to privatization and foreign capital investment in Indian markets, but in reality the party grew increasingly concerned 'about losing its upper caste base, who were being won over by the opportunities neoliberal reforms were unleashing for them', and very soon the BJP too started favouring neoliberal reforms (Thachil 2009, 56).

The trajectory of new-age Hindutva in the 1990s unveiled the enigma of popular politics, especially in the ways it brought back traditions and swadeshi in 'new India' as commodities of consumption, thus feeding into the political project of Hindu nationalism.[46]

The new-age gurus invested much on this project of reviving 'true Indian civilization' in their respective innovative styles. The everyday performative acts in their ashram premises too offered the aesthetic of cultural nationalism through bodily discipline, dietary restrictions, spiritual practices or by others means. The modes by which these normative approaches to spirituality and Indianness/Hindu-ness constituted the individual disciple indicated the power of the gurus in mobilizing a patriotic–ideal citizen figure—an apolitical character who could 'plunge into politics to cleanse it of its various "corruptions," rid the nation of its residual colonial structures and revive/restore the glory of the nation'.[47] The entire narrative of how new-age Hindutva permeates politics remained central to the understating of the process of vernacularization of Hindutva, which started a dialogue with different regional actors, organizations and groups. Simultaneously, the vindication of new-age Hindutva stood on the grounds of its multifarious political actions at different locations through multiple means. This highly fragile but ideologically cohesive project of new-age Hindutva utilized the market and media to their fullest extent, while the new-age gurus represented a powerful position in that discourse—'emerging within and shaping a constellation of political practises and aspirations'.[48]

It is a fact that other than a section of the urban middle classes, the rest are not so familiar with the high-profile guru landscape of India. Most of these urban classes reaped benefits from neoliberal economic transformations, and a large segment of these classes hailed from white-collar-job backgrounds. Highly skilled technocrats, information technology (IT) professionals, doctors, multinational magnets, industrialists, engineers and even scientists took the cue sooner or later, and many of them developed solid transnational connections with time. These people came out as the best buyers of the spiritual commodity market in India and abroad and got involved in various performative programmes in both the virtual and the real world. Modern means of communication over online media platforms provided them the best possible opportunity to participate in high-profile spiritual programmes and connect with spiritual networks all over the world. Maya Warrier, one of the leading scholars in this field, explained,

> the particular appeal of modern gurus to India's urban educated middle classes often perceive a supposed gap in their lives that these persons purportedly seek to fill by attaching themselves to a guru. This 'gap' is described in terms of their inability to cope with modern India's fast paced and rapidly changing urban environment, their lack of anchoring in a closely knit community, and their sense of losing touch with their Hindu religious traditions. While the resulting sense of 'rootlessness', 'alienation', and 'anomie', as these scholars describe it, may be true for some middle-class urbanites in contemporary India, it is certainly not a characteristic feature of them all.[49]

Undoubtedly, the urban middle classes extracted the highest amount of benefits from the economic reforms; seeking spiritual peace also came out as an ambitious project of their lives. If treated simply as a consumer of the commodity society, their individual cognizance of freedom, liberty and well-being could have been threatened. Despite drawing a handsome salary and living a comfortable life, people may experience themselves only as reproductive tools of a system that works and functions not as an integrated whole but in a fractured manner just to keep the producers and consumers busy in the business. I would call this a kind of civilizational crisis, if not a spiritual crisis, whereby individual creativity and the capacity to feel connected with the universe seem as gullible as one's abstract momentary survival in this world. Various vernacular performative practices, such as yoga,[50] meditation, self-healing, *bhajan-kirtans* and others, have been invoked by the new-age gurus as immediate solutions to these problems and also as the preconditions for attaining life-changing benefits, such as health, energy, youthfulness, strength and happiness. The urban middle classes have consumed the teachings and message of the gurus mostly through various media platforms or sometimes in the spiritual congregations organized within or outside ashram premises. The art of consumption shown by the urban middle classes implies the celebration of economic transformations in the country followed by a series of political profit-making endeavours.

The trajectory of the new-age guru movements tracked down the same cultural-economic space which delineated the politics of Hindutva under the agencies of globalization and comic liberalization. This was a unique combination that quickly grew in appeal with narratives and symbols of collective belonging and the slow-but-steady Hinduization of the people. This particular aspect of enunciating the highest values of Hindutva made it an imperative to be loyal to the Hindu culture and Hindu nation against all sorts of negative effects of Westernization or, to be specific, Americanization. Now, this development can be interpreted as being paradoxical. Out of a purely tactical reason, the trends of new-age Hindutva have benefitted from the waves of economic liberalization, market reforms and globalization. Despite the initial inertia to the 'invasive and exploitative' foreign capital investment in India, the Hindutva bosses gradually became increasingly concerned about the opportunities created by such reforms, especially when the BJP 'shifted towards internal economic liberalization or the relaxation of restrictions within India. The party believed this position would strike a balance between a *swadeshi* line favoured by its Sangh affiliates and its electoral concerns with losing elite support' (Thachil 2009, 56). It was mainly due to electoral concerns that the BJP leaders and the new-age Hindutva proponents faced extreme conflicts with the old bosses of the Sangh Parivar circle. Unlike those of other political parties, the BJP leaders had to act per the command of the RSS to a great extent; concurrently, BJP, being the democratic wing of the Sangh Parivar, had the responsibility to respect people's choice and especially the will of its voters. The old guards of the Sangh Parivar might have shown a kind of anathema to neoliberal economic policies, but the urban-middle-class support base of the BJP pushed the party leaders to take decisions in their favour. As soon as the market possibilities of economic liberalization became apparent, the business and trading community and a section of the corporate professionals brought its fruits at home, and the BJP too moved a step further for plausible outcomes. This might have strained the BJP–RSS relationship for a while. The Swadeshi Jagran Manch—an RSS platform—also started promoting economic nationalism. The foundational principles of Hindutva, however, continued to be used as a base for sketching out the dominant ideology of *Bharatiyatva* or Indianness in both cultural and political practices.[51]

In spite of a selective defence against economic liberalization, the proponents of new-age Hindutva attempted to arrive at an understanding or make an adjustment between *Bharatiyatva* and universalism, between the swadeshi policy and globalization. They in fact sought to produce a new modus operandi to appeal primarily to the urban middle classes, followed by the elite classes and later the Hindu diaspora. The influence of the gurus remained crucial to these endeavours—the gurus successfully projected brand Hindutva encompassing spiritual–universal values for a wider audience on various platforms and through multiple channels. It was obvious that the relatively privileged sections of the Hindus would be attracted to the new-age gurus; however, the low-caste subaltern poor of the country received the benefits of the *seva* projects undertaken by the gurus and their disciples. The subaltern poor stood at the receiving end of the *seva* projects carried on by the local ashrams—which witnessed a sharp increase in the wake of the economic liberalization process. Ecumenists have shown how income inequality among the masses forced them to ask for education, jobs, healthcare, food distribution and other services from the state, while in the absence of such service provisions by the state in adequate quantity, the religious and spiritual organizations started all-round social service activities. In a highly competitive 'religion market', some of the organizations came out to be 'more radical and the others more liberal over time'.[52] Radicalism, when explained in terms of Hinduization, constructs the necessary conditions for politicizing the domain of vernacular performative acts, including *seva*, over a passive marginalized population; however, the dominant discourse of new-age Hindutva stood strong as an elite-centric ideology for long.[53]

Given the media's important role in socializing Hindu/Indian culture and spirituality as the collective choice of the nation, the new-age gurus and their messages travelled far and wide through printed and audio-visual material. The availability of spiritual alternatives, as well as the chronic proliferation of the new religious movements in the West, provided the devotees with different choices (Graham 1988, 224).

Such choices were not available in India for long. It was only since the late 1980s that a plethora of guru literature and networks of guru organizations could be seen occupying the urban-middle-class public sphere. Almost parallel to the rise of news media has been the astonishing growth of the new-age Hindutva movement, endorsed and extended by the new-age gurus in India and abroad. The political insinuations present in the ideology of Hindu nationalism often portrayed these gurus as the face of soft Hindutva; however, the nuances of their universal spiritual appeal often contradicted the Hindu supremacist overtone of Hindutva politics. The ways they surpassed the exclusionary rhetoric of Hindu nationalism underlined the power and influence of Hindu spirituality and culture as an inimitable resource for the nation, as well as for the media and market. Each and every performative component of that spiritual discourse was displayed as not less than a product of consumption, in order to gain a Hindu majoritarian consensus. For instance, scholars working on yoga referred to Swami Ramdev's yogic health regime as 'seeking to discipline the body while simultaneously indexing it to a particular kind of majoritarian nationalism'.[54] Widely displayed on various media platforms and sponsored by corporate investments, yoga-based health regime, meditation and certain dietary practices proposed by Swami Ramdev accentuated the individual and collective well-being of the nation, helped situate him at the centre of non-participatory politics and made yoga the quintessential symbol of national unity, a product of national consumption, an embodiment of scientific spirituality[55] and the epitome of Indianness or *Bharatiyatva*.[56]

Almost all the fast-growing popular guru movements in the 20th century introduced a kind of soft revolution against some of the elements of the existing traditions but retained the basic spirit of the tradition with a focus on the service of the nation. The dialectic of tradition and globalization denoted the problematic of oneness to individuality or differences to universality and homogeneity. The global political culture of sameness often contradicts the particularities and uniqueness of local/regional cultures and makes globalism–universalism a sacrilege to traditions. However, what is forgotten in the discourse of the spirit of recognition generated by the global culture of universalism is that it calls for a space for exclusionary ideas, like Hindu nationalism, as components of globalization.[57] The new-age gurus, as flag-bearers of globalism and universalism, demanded recognition of their traditions in the name of an authentic Hindu/Indian spirituality and culture. Hindutva, claiming global recognition, attracts the attention of critics, for whom it is an art of public imagination which 'sought to compensate for the loss of economic importance of their nation in the world, or the loss of coherence and efficiency of the ruling political project, by the worship of strength, masculinity, cultural purity and radical difference from the west'.[58] It may sound quite harsh and insensitive to say that the new-age gurus as part of the Hindutva project attempted to mirror the growing influence of a majoritarian political party and paved the way for it to emerge as a global player in alternative cultural spaces. One must not forget the fact that these gurus and their movements crafted the synergy of the spiritual, the social and the economic sprit of the nation following civil society dispositions. They did not behave like reformers or rebels, or agents of the BJP, nor were they in any way attached to the Sangh Parivar networks. They have their own innovative domains of operation which undoubtedly fuelled the visions of new-age Hindutva as an integral part of globalism and universalism. Issues crop up when the post-colonial nostalgia of ancient wisdom becomes subjected to the micro-politics of production and consumption—a strategy of influence, however with different ambiguities and anomalies. In the next section, I focus on two highly influential new-age gurus to validate my narrative in a precise manner.

SADHGURU JAGGI VASUDEV

Isha Foundation, a volunteer-run organization, was founded in 1992 near Coimbatore[59] by Sadhguru Jaggi Vasudev, who has emerged as one of the most influential new-age gurus in contemporary India with millions of followers around the world. Sadhguru—a yogi and a mystic—has spoken at different international leadership forums, has been a delegate at the US Millennium Peace Summit and the World Peace Congress and frequents the World Economic Forum at Davos.[60]

Acknowledging his authority as a global guru and a celebrated author of this century, Sir Ken Robnson declared,

> By any measure, Sadhguru is a remarkable man. For countless people around the world, he is a luminous spiritual guide. He is as well a pragmatic social activist and compassionate campaigner for human rights, for universal education, and for global peace and well-being.... More than that, he offers a practiced program for personal transformation that also draws from the venerable teachings of the yogic masters who continue to inspire him. Throughout the ages there have been no more insistent questions than 'Who are we?' and 'What is our purpose in living at all?' Contrarian and consistent, ancient and contemporary, Inner Engineering is a loving invitation to live our best lives and a profound reassurance of why and how we can.[61]

Sadhguru and his Isha Foundation claim to not adhere to any particular ideology or religion but 'transmits inner science of universal appeal'. This inner science resonates with spiritual science only to 'awaken the human beings to their ultimate possibility so that they become complete human beings and live a full life on all levels—physical, mental, emotional and spiritual'. Emerging as a self-styled new-age guru, Sadhguru Jaggi Vasudev developed his own 'gurudom' mainly through followers from the urban middle classes and the tech-savvy generation from India and abroad. Packaged in academic sophistry and fluent English, Sadhguru's brand of spirituality nurtures the spell of scientific wisdom, astute intelligence and the cognition of superior knowledge. He himself has acknowledged that unless pragmatism is not blended with profundity, the knowledge of spirituality as a science would not reach the technologically advanced public. Being a poet, author, motivational speaker, human rights activist and budding environmentalist, Sadhguru has picked up issues of global importance and weaved Hindu spirituality into science for the self-transformation of the individual through scientifically innovative programmes and performative acts. Leaving much scope for further speculations and ambiguities, Sadhguru has answered the question raised by each and every individual in a troubled world to realize what the 'body' is and what the 'mind' is...

> Your body, you accumulated over a period of time. What you call 'my body' is just a heap of food that you have eaten. What you call 'my mind' is just a heap of impressions that you gathered from outside. So these two things are

> still outside. Your mind is just society's garbage bin. Anybody who walks by you, stuffs something in your head and goes. The accumulative part of the mind is subject to all kinds of social, religious and cultural situations, you are being exposed to. (*Ancient Technology for the Modern Mind*, 70)

The inward-looking guru here talked of the hollowness of the mind and body unless they were being channelized for a real spiritual journey from within. In almost all his messages, Sadhguru speaks of the ongoing battle between the consciousness of the body and the consciousness beyond the body, that is, between the material and the spiritual....

> All the struggles of humanity in terms of 'should I be spiritual or materialistic?' come from this ignorance. It seems like a conflict between the instinct of self-preservation and the longing to become boundless. These two forces are not against each other, but when you look at it from a physical perspective, when your whole perception is limited to the physical; they seem to be in conflict. (*Deccan Chronicle*, 30 November 2011)

At the primary level, Sadhguru's emphasis on the 'soul' over the mind and body contests the corporeal understanding of the body as the primary site of discipline and control—an instrument of experimentation with a rigorous fitness regime that in turn feeds on the symbolic rhetoric of a nationalist masculinity—a locus of Hindutva politics through the ages. Integrating the bodily consciousness with the mind or making the physical analogous to the spiritual validates the importance of yoga—an art of 'breaking the limitations of this dimension and moving into a totally different sphere of life—from the physical world to another existence by itself'.[62] In Sadhguru's own narrative, the body becomes a disembodied subject because human aspirations work fully when a human connects the body with the mind through the 'technology' called yoga and meditation. Sadhguru has avoided using any hypersensitive religious or philosophical jargon to reinforce the conquest of the mind over the body, because he himself has admitted that yoga is nothing but mastery over the mind—a spiritual science to 'elevate a person to an experience beyond all sorts of carnal senses and desires'. Unlike Swami Ramdev, who makes the 'body' a site for nationalist regeneration and the yogic health regime a theme of refurbishing Hindu wisdom towards an useful orientation, Sadhguru prefers to depart from the so-called saffronizing stereotypes of ascetic–nationalist masculinity. He chooses to speak for a scientific discourse of spirituality—a rightful union of the mind and body, an interesting ploy to overcome the burden of religiosity in an age of globalization. 'The moment man became religious, it should have been the end of all conflict, but unfortunately, everywhere in the world, religion has become the main source of all the conflict', concludes Sadhguru. It is astonishing to note that Sadhguru, while speaking as a teacher and mystic before his followers, replaced the idea of self-consciousness with self-appropriation and asked, 'Are our identities becoming an impediment or our identities an empowerment that is the question?', while the same Sadhguru, when speaking at public events or giving interviews to various media platforms, has asserted,

> The first and foremost thing is that our people should have a strong sense of belonging, identity and pride in the nation. Nation is something we made up. It's just an idea. But if we don't own the idea, if we don't feel strongly for it, if we don't have passion and pride for it, it will fail. In 1947, when we got freedom from our occupiers, the citizens of this nation, despite what they had or did not have felt proud.... Today though, there are debates about whether we should keep this nation at all or not.... This is happening because we did not bring that strong sense of pride that this is my nation and I must make this a great place to live.[63]

The contradictions present in the Sadhguru's speeches became relevant when he started sharing opinions on various issues of sheer political importance. He was an instant hit on media platforms, especially on social media. His expertise in mooring Hindu spiritual thoughts to themes of Hindu politics made the latter look much more universal and engaging for the middle-class Hindus who liked his peaceful demeanour. The RSS pattern of somatic nationalism is absent in his approaches, nor has he demonstrated the micro-politics of bodily practices to emanate power and authority, instead using sombre expressions for the hyper-nationalist–militant ideology of Hindutva. At this point, new-age Hindutva comes out to be related to the virtual world of non-participatory politics—a special playground owned by the new-age gurus who ask one to control anger, hatred, emotion, fear and all sorts of emotions to connect with the inner spirituality. The

VHP sadhus or those who rallied for the Ram Janmabhoomi movement in Ayodhya eulogized militancy and heroism, reinvested in a collective past and called for a thorough masculinization of the Hindu race. They often stigmatized the so-called foreigners in India but looked for support from the Hindu diaspora. The allegations of militancy during the VHP-led Ayodhya movement grabbed media attention for long, and reports came out in abundance about how the VHP and its fringe group Bajrang Dal organized numerous camps for their cadres 'which impart training in the use of arms and close combat, and include gory rituals based on trishuls and swords'.[64] Critics have pointed out that the imaginings of the RSS and VHP's reconstruction of Hindu manhood depended largely on the 'celebration of Hindu warrior myths', to 'initiate the values of a new social order, to rework the meanings of patriotism, and to authorise the violence of Hindu nationalism'.[65] Use of the phrases like 'violence of Hindu nationalism' against the VHP–RSS duo is uncalled for, because all they had done was just make Hindus believe in a collective nation building project by putting their nationalist–masculinist valour to use. However, Hindu nationalists' call to 'militarise the Hindudom' and 'Hinduise all politics'[66] offered lucrative opportunities to their critics to point out the rise of 'Hindutva terrorism' in a tense political climate in the country.[67] Being charged with challenging India's quintessential character as a multi-ethnic, multilingual, multi-religious society with the malicious intention to convert India into a Hindu Rashtra, the advocates of new-age Hindutva shifted their allegiance to the moderate voices inside the Sangh Parivar and carried on with a new language of politics.[68]

In the same way as his contemporaries, Sadhguru centralized his vision on the empowerment of the underprivileged in terms of health, education and environmental well-being. In order to get the best results from the transformation projects, Sadhguru first addressed the question of individual self-transformation through scientifically structured spiritual programmes. In the early years of his career as a spiritual guru, he wisely refrained from making political statements, but with time he started sharing his opinions on some issues that are very political. He has spoken on various subjects on which he has no expertise and is often seen talking about democracy and politics around the time of elections. Through various media platforms, he enters into the collective consciousness of his audience and markets himself in a tailored style. He has been interviewed by Bollywood celebrities, and he frequently uploads videos on social media sites, appears on television channels and intelligently plants his ideology of Hindu spirituality by making the philosophy widely appetizing for the new-age followers. He did not seem much problematic as long as he stood away from propagating the majoritarian narratives on different political issues; the moment he started talking in the same tune as the Hindu nationalist parties, critics of the Sangh Parivar fumed at this yogi. Several newspaper articles alleged that Sadhguru was selling Hindutva in the name of spirituality and attempting to drive communal tensions in the country. For instance, articles published in *The Wire* used headlines like 'An (Un)Enlightened Sadhguru in King Modi's Court' (*The Wire*, 1 January 2020), 'Why Hindutva Nationalists Need a Sadhguru' (*The Wire*, 9 March 2019), etc., with the conclusion that

> Jaggi Vasudev allows one to be a businessman or a politician or a Lutyens potentate, one golf swing at a time. His late burst of tweeting about democracy and nationalism has provided a more palatable alternative to hyper-nationalists who now often find them cringing at the extreme ardour of BJP's telly evangelists (*The Print*, 16 March 2019).

The terms 'telly-evangelist' and 'Hindu nationalism's in-house mystic' point to the amount of backlash he has faced for allegedly peddling an agenda similar to the BJP in the media; however, it has made practically no difference to this guru.[69] Sadhguru's recent comments on the 'Citizenship Amendment Act' (CAA) controversy[70] created enough media outrage that a section of the journalists addressed him as 'BJP's 'henchman' and indicted him for being 'seeming unaware (or unconcerned) that the Act is exclusionary, discriminatory and the discriminatory and the information upon which his views rest is deeply flawed'. The media houses could have had their own stances on the CAA; it however seems completely gratuitous to conclude that 'His words do not enlighten the audience but instead radicalize and desensitize them to the suffering of the victims of the citizenship law'. Sadhguru's presence in the media domain must not be discarded on the grounds of mixing of spirituality with politics, because there have been a number of such sadhus or gurus who have shown perfect harmonization with the ruling party of their time.

Sadhguru's individual legitimacy and acceptance as a self-styled god-man fell into further jeopardy when Prime Minister Modi posted a tweet on the video message of Sadhguru speaking in favour of the CAA. Sadhguru's 'lucid explanations' of the CAA appeared to be popular among the ruling party who found in this guru a spiritual master who could corroborate the Hindutva politics of Modi and push it to a bigger audience. Sadhguru came up to the expectations of the BJP once again when he took an indirect jibe at Pakistan with regard to the Pulwama terror attack and declared,

> National boundaries should have been settling but we didn't do that. We had Line of Control (LOC) which is always out of control. We must settle to what our nation is and what not our nation is and until we do so we will bleed for years to come.... Article 370 is leaving people confused not knowing of where they belong. (*DNA* 21 February 2019)

Tagging Prime Minister Modi's microblogging account in his tweet, Sadhguru called for striking down Article 370 in Kashmir. Amid massive protests and controversy over the CAA and Article 370, Sadhguru's speaking in favour of these issues gave BJP support and enough reasons to rejoice at their good fortune; however, a large number of online users did not get convinced by the explanations of Sadhguru. It seemed quite astonishing for them why Prime Minister Modi promoted a mystic's explanations of the CAA on Twitter instead of those of a constitutional expert or lawyer who could have driven the issue towards a logical conclusion. The followers of Sadhguru may find nothing remotely political in his opinions on these politically sensitive issues. Sadhguru's ostensibly symbiotic relationship with the BJP makes it quite clear that it is the BJP that relies profoundly on the popularity of this yogi who has established a tangible spiritual empire in both the virtual and the real world simultaneously.

What made this new-age guru a fashionable choice in the virtual world? His mixing of myths with history or spirituality with science might have fitted well with the Hindutva agenda, because on no occasion did Sadhguru admit that spirituality has any business to do with organized religion. Hindutva, being an incarnation of *Bharatiyatva*, gets perfect ideological moorings in his writings and speeches in American-accent English—which, unfortunately, many Indians still consider a symbol of sophistication and astuteness. With thousands of followers around the globe from multiple nations, Sadhguru has got across to the people with his inner-engineering programmes and fetched huge amounts of funding for his other projects. With his easily marketable yoga–meditation programmes, Sadhguru has commoditized his own brand of spirituality for the benefit of his universal audience, who felt energized and rejuvenated after going through his courses, like Shambhavi or Mahamudra. Sharing her experience with Sadhguru, one of the NRI (non-resident Indian) followers of Sadhguru wrote,

> It is true—all of us adults do get caught up in a maelstrom of responsibilities and soon feel bogged down by the meaninglessness of what life holds. At such a juncture, it is common to feel deflated and isolated.... A modern mystic like Sadhguru makes Indian yogic discipline and spirituality accessible to the mainstream in a way that is awe-inspiring. Every word that he utters is not meant to be esoteric and out-of-reach—quite the opposite actually. We can identify with the challenges that lie within ourselves and his words serve to help us seek lasting solutions inside of us.

The sagacity and judiciousness of new-age gurus rest on their easily accessible messages, along with the desire to live up to the teachings of Hindu philosophical traditions, presented as a result of thorough performative practices. The feeling of insecurity and isolation starkly threw light on the realities of life endangered by capitalism, especially after the neoliberal economic transformations. Globalization and laissez-faire were expected to stress on equality and social mobility, but in reality they heightened anxiety[71] and alienation—a 'social symptom of the neoliberal phase of capitalism'.[72] Anxiety is induced when people are forced to communicate or 'commanded to be communicable and "networked" within in neoliberal systems'. In this context of declining social communications, spiritualism has claimed to be a panacea for the anxiety of humans across the globe and teach them to wield power over the mind. This process of thought control (what Noam Chomsky has described as the control of the public mind) 'is associated with the rise of new institutions and dominant ideologies within society...and an ideology that sees everything (and we mean everything) as a commodity that can be bought and sold and which promotes corporate rights over respect for individual and community rights'.

Western societies have been receiving the Indian tradition of yoga for long. The secular perception of yoga attracted a large audience there when many yoga teachers started giving lessons on yoga and promoting it as a physical regime to gain good health and reform the self through different meditation practices. Two streams of yoga—one for spiritual self-transformation and the other for physical benefits—have been popularized by yoga teachers and Indian mystics since long; however, the physical attributes of yoga became the centre of attraction in the West in the contemporary neoliberal era. The ancient tradition of self-evolutionary yoga as an art of mind control might have been in practice for long in post-Second World War societies in the West, but it gradually lost its relevance to the more body-oriented and stress-relieving techniques of yoga. The new-age gurus from India have attempted their best to accommodate both streams of yoga in a single package to overcome the fear, anxiety and pressure of a consumerist lifestyle. They have challenged the superficialities of consumerism but used consumerist tropes of the market and media to popularize their own brand, especially focusing on yoga, meditation, Ayurveda and a few other performative practices. Central to their arguments is not that all these Hindu spiritual performative practices emerged as esoteric disciplines in the past but that they are based on a universal science for the consumption of a technology-oriented society.

Almost all new-age gurus have reflected the fabric of soft Hindutva through a kind of psycho-political engagement with the living trends of corporatization of all aspects of life. A confident Sadhguru once proclaimed,

> in the next 100 years, business leadership will be the most important aspect of society; and in the next 25 years, company CEOs will rule the world! ...Greed is good: I say it as well. I say why not has it all...you want the world, and then you must have that.... My greed wants the entire world to live in prosperity and abundance, that's how big it is. It's an unabashed greed. In that sense, spirituality is still about the 'me'—but the context of 'me' is enlarged. What I, as a spiritualist, consider as 'mine', is the whole universe. (*DNA*, 6 November 2013)

Sadhguru represents an interesting example of spiritual capitalism, which pays equal attention to the questions of social justice, community rights and politics. For him, profit-making and spirituality do not have any conflict of interest, because 'the success of a nation is largely determined by the success of its business houses, hence the responsibility is more on businessmen to think of society at large, and not about quarterly results alone' (*Economic Times*, 27 September 2019). The new-age gurus have in fact provided the rubric for the alliance between corporatism and spirituality, leading to an understanding between Hindutva and corporates. Noted economist Professor Prabhat Patnaik has pointed out the kind of unholy alliance between these two in reference to the discourse on the abolition of Articles 370 and 35A and the NRC (National Register of Citizens), which 'stokes Hindutva hyper-nationalism' and helped the government introduce corporate tax concessions to overcome the growing economic crisis in the country. Tax concessions, Professor Patnaik believes, have a gross negative impact on the economic stricture, but the cheering brigade of Hindutva nationalists would be able to divert attention from the economic mistakes of the BJP government. Good marketing of the Hindutva slogans through media platforms would 'continue to hype the Hindutva projects until the craze turns' (*Hindu*, 3 October 2019). Marxist scholars have remained highly critical of the political propagandas made by the supporters of Hindutva in the name of settling the historical mistakes done in the past, while the support of big businesses for the BJP, especially for Modi, rattle the opposition parties by a massive extent. The narrative of a Modi wave[73] was pushed wisely by the media backed by the corporate houses acting for their respective business interests. The Modi wave thus became the signature trend of corporatization of Hindutva, which subtly endorsed a business-friendly narrative of development and good governance based on the twin concepts of *Bharatiya sanskriti* and *Bharatiya maryada*.

To ensure good governance based on Indianness or *Bharatiyatva*, the new-age gurus played an important part in favour of the ruling party. Setting a bizarre example of being politically perfect, the BJP and its allies looked for some non-political players to settle some of the highly controversial issues that required 'unbiased' intervention from third-party actors. Hindutva's Sadhguru connections might have helped increase its social accountability, mostly in the virtual space. Modi's efforts to involve spiritual gurus in matters of governance have perhaps worked to reduce the negativities growing rampant in a highly polarized society.

SRI SRI RAVI SHANKAR

In the case of Sri Sri Ravi Shankar, one may recall how Prime Minister Modi tried to engage this man[74] in various peacekeeping missions, especially in Kashmir, in the Northeast and in Ayodhya. Sri Sri's engagement with mainstream politics should not be counted in the array of events where new-age gurus/sadhus/yogis have appeared crucial for the success of the Hindutva agenda. Be it in making the political class conscious of their importance in policymaking or in setting up peace agreements between mutually conflicting groups or in breaking the boundary between spirituality and politics, Sri Sri has always been active. It would be pointless to make any comparison between Sadhguru and Sri Sri or between either of them and Swami Ramdev, because all the new-age gurus set out on their own journey of spirituality and accordingly responded to mainstream political developments.

Sri Sri Ravi Shankar, best known as Sri Sri Guruji or Gurudev to his followers, established the Art of Living Foundation (AOL) in 1981—an educational–philanthropic organization working under a special consultative status with the Economic and Social Council of the United Nations. According to his official biography,

> present in 156 countries, it formulates and implements lasting solutions to conflicts and issues faced by individuals, communities and nations.... He has pioneered and supported movements to revive ethics in public life such as India Against Corruption and the World Forum for Ethics in Business. He has reached out to an estimated 450 million people worldwide through personal interactions, public events, teachings, Art of Living workshops and humanitarian initiatives. Not since Mahatma Gandhi has one person united people of different traditions and faiths into a spiritual communion across the length and breadth of India.[75]

Among the wide range of literary works on Sri Sri Guruji, the biographies written by his foreign disciples Francois Gautier[76] and Frederique

Lebelley[77] are considered to be the most authentic sources available so far on the life of this spiritual leader. In compliance with the idea of generating Vedic propositions along with the ancient practices of the Samkhya Yoga, the AOL initiated spiritual courses on Sudarshan Kriya (a powerful breathing technique), which evolved as Sahaj Samadhi meditation and the Sri Sri Yoga. Different self-improvement techniques have been designed by Sri Sri Guruji for one to get rid of anxiety, depression, fear and suicidal tendencies. With the strength of a bunch of full-time staff based in Bangalore and at various centres, AOL conducts multifarious activities for women's empowerment, rural development, self-development for prisoners, disaster relief works, etc. as acts of *seva* and simultaneously works for the publicity of Sri Sri's spiritual messages all over the world. As per one estimate produced by *Business Standard* (2016), Sri Sri's successful translation of Indian spirituality into a universal package has landed him over 370 million followers across 155 countries and around 1.43 million followers across social media sites.[78] Much of his initiatives have a distinct economic push through his investment in the Ayurvedic business, along with that in various lifestyle products. His marketing strategy is similar to that of Patanjali Ayurved of Swami Ramdev and akin to the model of Swami Ramdev's on Aastha television (TV) channel; he lapped up Anandam Active—a Dish TV channel—to promote the teachings and products of AOL in different parts of the country.

The construction of wider patterns of Hindu spirituality by Sri Sri Guruji exalted the plethora of universalism through embracing the ancient Vedic idea of 'Vasudhaiva Kutumbakam'—the call for one global family—frequently eulogized by new-age Hindutva preachers to bring about world peace and harmony. Revered as a neutral preacher, Sri Sri Guruji has never ever been castigated as the flag-bearer of Hindutva in India; however, it is astonishing to note that new-age RSS *pracharaks* and a section of Modi followers in particular speak in the same universal language used by Sri Sri Guruji on various national and international platforms. Pointing towards India's age-old contributions in tying up everything through the adage of 'Vasudhaiva Kutumbakam', RSS chief Mohan Bhagwat asked RSS *pracharaks* to 'connect with people irrespective of their caste, language, religion or region'. 'We live for each other, not for ourselves.... We believe that the world has made us and we have to give back to it and we look at the world with gratitude'. The newly acquired spirit of universality and globalism invoked links between the ethical self of Hindutva and the horizontally organized global community on the principles of Indianness or *Bharatiyatva*. It indicated a swift transition from Hindutva to *Bharatiyatva*, or vice versa. This became much clear when Bhagwat claimed, 'Bharatiya sanskriti (Indian culture) is also known as Hindu sanskriti, reflecting its values, conduct and culture'.[79] Despite having the public image of a neutral mediator in some highly sensitive political debates in India, Sri Sri Guruji's frequent emphasis on the stereotyped Hindu performative acts and his banking on the antiquity and exclusivity of *Bharatiyatva* have allowed the visualization of a universally structured Hindu community. The spectacle of non-participatory politics gets into shape in the imagination of a community through continuous linking of the performative acts with perceived national interest.[80] The idea of a collective 'national interest' gains further legitimacy in the discourse of Hindutva through giving the consciousness of a spiritual Hindu self utmost priority. Trivializing the universal appeal of this 'spiritual Hindu self' further, political leaders, especially the BJP, have displayed 'friendly' relations with Sri Sri Guruji on various occasions. Following from Foucault, I want to call this the art of governmentality—leaving no stone unturned to exercise sovereign power over the management of life through organizational networks and practices. Prime Minister Modi successfully exhibits shades and patterns of governmentality, especially when he creates an aura of 'friendship' with the new-age gurus or shares pictures and tweets hailing their contributions, or even when these gurus come to the support of Modi and his regime. 'Modi has been bashed unjustly for years and years', said an overly exuberant Sri Sri Guruji at the swearing-in ceremony of the prime minister and declared,

> In ancient days, the gurus used to do the rajyabhishek to the raja, administering the oath. Today, it is the president. Still, in many countries, it is the bishop or cardinal who places the crown on the head of the king or queen. That is because wisdom is given first place.... We spiritual leaders are not there to give Narendra Modi any advice but to give moral and ethical support and ask him to be accountable for moral and ethical wrongs. (*Times of India*, 30 May 2014)

Unlike his fellow spiritual leaders, Sri Sri Guruji has made it quite clear that providing moral and ethical support to Prime Minister Modi would be something of a responsibility, since both politics and spirituality care for people's welfare, and spirituality 'alone can make a leader samadarshi, one who sees everyone as being equal; satyadarshi, who moves with the Truth; paradarshi, who is transparent in action; doordarshi, being farsighted; and priyadarshi, embodying love and compassion'.[81] Modi might have endeavoured to become a *samadarshi* leader while chanting the mantras like *sab ka sath, sab ka vikas*, but his government has often showed lack of enthusiasm to live up to his words. His claims of being *samadarshi* raise questions all around; however, he has proved his worth of being a *doordarshi* leader on various grounds. Investing in spirituality as a soft-power strategy for India in international politics has offered him greater chances to glorify India and Indianness for a new world order. His mixing with new-age, universal gurus, like Sri Sri Guruji, has increased the possibility of further recognition of Modi by a global 'secular' audience who hold a deep reverence for Sri Sri Guruji's teachings and messages.

Under the compulsion of being a *samadarshi* leader, Modi has persisted with being adoptive of the culture of pluralism and continued to embrace the spirit of Vasudhaiva Kutumbakam. In order to validate this new ideology both in India and abroad, Modi needed the universal gurus on his side to manage the performative nature of the new discourse of Hindutva. Marketing strategies and media support brought this new discourse of Hindutva into a dialogue with a larger audience, especially with the urban classes who appeared to be crucial to negotiating the power dynamics of Hindutva with *Bharatiyatva* through regular display of and participation in spiritual performative acts. In this new discourse, spirituality has become easily available for consumption through social media sites, YouTube channels, television channels, pamphlets, newsletters, posters, audiotapes, video cassettes and advertisements on print and electronic media.

Defining the essentials of Hindutva has become the search for the collective cultural resources—a readily consumable product for the global market. These transformational dimensions of ancient Hindu wisdom have never been properly explored, not even by the Hindu nationalists, because the 'trans-formative' dimensions of Hinduism always preoccupied the critical approaches to the question how a certain religious practice could have the source of social injustice and how it prevents people from realizing their potential as a liberating force for the society. New-age Hindutva, even if employed as a social camouflage for or an apologetic version of Hindu supremacy, pushes the narrative of a transcendental–transformative Hindu tradition, if not a religious belief, which claims to bring out the excellence of human endeavours through the art of spirituality.[82] It could sound thrilling and stimulating for the overambitious project of Hindutva, which has already been caught in the political compulsion to grow 'secular' to live up to its slogan of *sab ka sath, sab ka vikas*, being mocked by its Marxist critics on a regular basis. Interestingly, contrary to its claims of being 'vocal for local' or representing a socially cohesive policy, the corporate bias of new-age Hindutva has denied any kind of agency to this ideology in producing an alternative language of resistance. It falls into the same repetitive terrain of individualism when marketing for Hindu spirituality and ancient wisdom in the name of brand India and deviates from its potential to be transformative or renitent to the so-called dogmatic–supremacist tendencies of Hindu religious traditions.

Mostly because of the fact that the notion of individual consumption or the so called corporatization of spirituality made its hazardous for new age Hindutva to become counter-productive to capitalism and its allied socio-cultural ideologues. Equally problematic are the approaches to spirituality and religion adopted by the new-age gurus for whom being spiritual does not necessarily mean to line up with a particular religion. One can be spiritual without having registered with a religious tradition. Spirituality minus religiosity has been an option for the new-age gurus because in an individualist market/society such a distinction remains useful, though it seems problematic for an ideology like Hindutva. New-age gurus, while having a dialogue with their global audience, present themselves as universal teachers, not simply as Hindu or Indian. Their teachings appear timeless and timely, applicable to all contexts and in turn setting off a 'new age' in every period of history. This new-age concept looks much convincing when judged as a response to some conflicts or sociopolitical despotism; however, in no way should the new-age gurus from India be located within the wider spectrum of anti-globalization resistance movements. They offer remedies to lifestyle hazards aggravated by economic transformations in the society, but they themselves use the most hyped channels of globalization, that is, the market and media, to reach their global audience. Unlike the modern anglophone gurus of the earlier generation, the new-age gurus employ new consumption patterns when it comes to spirituality, and this includes India's rising spiritual marketplace, mostly controlled by the aspirations of the urban middle class that defines itself with new identities through consuming Hinduism in a new format.[83]

To what extent this new format of Hinduism would be conducive to the ideology of Hindutva creates the enigma of putting spirituality and religiosity in their respective terrains. The enigma of Hindutva, which has so far survived on the perfect blending of spirituality and religiosity, now appears a bit perplexed because of the newly emerged space between spirituality and religiousity—the space of 'secular universalism', which has reframed and repackaged the former sometimes in isolation and sometimes in adherence to the latter.[84] Now the question is, can Hindutva survive without being engaged with religious traditions and practices, since the political journey of Hindutva in India has never been a 'universal–spiritual' affair? Despite showing different shades and patterns, the logic of Hindutva has stood on the linkage of the cultural tradition of Hinduism with the political form of the nation state.[85] The Hindu-ness of a Hindu depends on three prerequisites—geographical unity, common racial heritage, and common culture—all of which are provided for within the interpretation of Hindutva. It has even been expected that people of a foreign race should get assimilated into the 'body of the mother race and inextricably fused into it…for otherwise such foreign races may be considered at best members of a common state, but they can never form part and parcel of the National body'.[86] The idea of a common bloodline for the unification of the Hindu society could have had its own implications for Hindu nationalist politics in India, but it hardly matched with the proposed universal–secular appeal of new-age Hindutva. Consequently, the new-age gurus who have grabbed every opportunity to make Hindu spirituality a commodity for universal consumption are likely to face a dilemma with regard to going global with the ideology of Hindutva if it continues to remain faithful to its original perspectives even in changed circumstances. Modi and his supporters would attract sadistic criticism from the sceptics if Modi fails to satisfy the vision of a proposed Hindu Rashtra in future India; however, his relentless tactic of exploring the inner dynamics of soft Hindutva or going global with Hindutva/*Bharatiyatva* keeps him closer to a transcendental–corporeal mode of politics.

NOTES

1. In *A Dictionary of Hinduism*, Stutley defined that 'The guru is a religious guide or a teacher, who especially gives initiation to disciples'. The actual meaning of the term guru is 'the heavy one'. 'The reason for this meaning is that gurus were specialists in their chosen scriptures and were often involved in debating contests. They mostly tended to win and were called "the heavy ones." The term "Guru" is commonly used in a derisory manner in the west Etymologically the "Guru" is a Sanskrit term. It is made up of two syllables "Gu" and "Ru." "Gu" means darkness or ignorance and "Ru" means dispeller or remover, so the guru is one who removes or dispels ignorance of the disciple'. See, M. Stutley and J. Sutley, *A Dictionary of Hinduism* (London: Routledge, 1977); Paras Shridhar, 'The Guru Disciple Relationship in Diaspora' (Unpublished PhD thesis, Derby University, 2005), 15–16.
2. L. McKean, *Divine Enterprise: Gurus and the Hindu Nationalist Movement* (Chicago, IL: University of Chicago Press, 1996), 1.
3. Jeremy Carrette and Richard King, *Selling Spirituality: The Silent Takeover of Religion* (Abingdon, NY: Routledge, 2004), 5.
4. Jeremy Carrette and Richard King presented an interesting picture of how religion had been taken over by spirituality silently in the business world. 'Today, in most British cities, you will find old church buildings that have been sold off to become business offices, supermarkets, public houses, nightclubs and private apartments. However, it is not primarily the sale of buildings that we are concerned with here, but rather the exploitation of the "cultural capital" of the religious for the purposes of consumption and corporate gain…the promotion of management courses offering "spiritual techniques" for the enhancement of one's work productivity and corporate business-efficiency, the sanitized religiosity of "the spiritual" sells'. (Carrette and King, *Selling Spirituality*, 16).
5. Phillip Bobbitt, *The Shield of Achilles: War, Peace, and the Course of History*. Foreword by Michael Howard (New York: Alfred A. Knopf, 2002).

6. Carrette and King, *Selling Spirituality*, 21.
7. See, Guy Debord, *The Society of the Spectacle*, translation by Fredy Perlman and Jon Supak, (Detroit, MI: Black & Red, 1970; rev. ed. 1967, 1977). The idea of the 'society of the spectacle' was developed by French theorist Guy Debord and has had a major impact on a variety of contemporary theories of society and culture. For Debord, spectacle 'unifies and explains a great diversity of apparent phenomena' (Debord, *The Society of the Spectacle*, 10). Appearing in the 1960s, Debord's concept continued to influence academia—it explained the importance of a media and consumer society developed around the production and consumption of commodities, performances, display of images, etc. M. L. Smith, L. Miller-Kahn, W. Heinecke, and P. F. Jarvis, *Political Spectacle and the Fate of American Schools* (New York: Routledge Falmer, 2004).
8. *Fax Horkheimer* and Theodor W. *Adorno*, *Dialectic of Enlightenment*, translation by John (New York: Cumming Seabury, *1972*).
9. A. Rajagopal, *Politics After Television: Religious Nationalism and Reshaping of the Indian Public* (Cambridge: Cambridge University Press, 2001); Ram Puniyani, *Communalism: What is False, What is True* (Bombay: Sarvodaya Friendship Centre, 2005).
10. Purnima Mankekar, in her work on ethnography of television viewing in India, suggests that 'the political ascendency of Hindu militancy was also facilitated by its seizure of the public sphere'. P. Mankekar, *Screening Culture, Viewing Politics: An Ethnography of Television, Womanhood, and Nation in Postcolonial India* (Durham: Duke University Press, 1999). Scholars, like Arvind Rajagopal and Shanti Kumar, have argued that the emergence of the national broadcaster Doordarshan's national programming as a pan-Indian genre was 'crucial for the post-colonial project of nation-building'. S. Kumar, *Gandhi Meets Prime Time: Globalisation and Nationalism in Indian Television* (Champaign, IL: University of Illinois Press, 2006), 35; Rajagopal, *Politics After Television*; A. Rajagopal, 'The Public Sphere in India: Structure and Transformation', in *The Indian Public Sphere*, ed. A. Rajagopal (New Delhi: Oxford University Press, 2009).
11. Angela Rudert, 'Research on Contemporary Indian Gurus: What's New About New Age Gurus?' *Religion Compass* 4, no. 10 (2010): 629–642, 630.
12. Paras Shridhar, in his thoughtful study on gurus and diaspora, raised a very crucial point. He noted, 'During the last two centuries Hinduism has spread from India to other parts of the world through a process of migration. The most recent diaspora studies place Hindus in all of the world's continents in visible minorities. As a result of the diasporic spread, Hinduism has moved away from the patriarchal culture of extended family dependent networks, of restraints and safeguards, to a more materially orientated Western society, with its emphasis on individual freedom of choice and independence'. This is a very important observation on the diasporic presence of the Hindus in the

early ages. However, what is equally noteworthy is that 'During the last three decades, between 1970 and 2000, the situation in diaspora has registered a dramatic change for the better as far as many migrant Hindus are concerned'. In the case of the United Kingdom, 'there was a mass movement of Asian migrants from Southern African countries to the U.K during this time; many were very skilful and enterprising people. They settled in run-down inner city areas, tried their hands in business ventures and through sheer hard work and dedication made the ventures undertaken into going concerns'.
Paras Shridhar, 'The Guru Disciple Relationship in Diaspora' (Unpublished PhD thesis, Derby University, 2005), 12, 21.

13. David L. McMahan, in his seminal work on Buddhist modernism, identifies the sense of modernity adopted by the gurus to fit their expressions and messages in different environments. The new-age gurus innovated their own style of communication in continuity with the tradition that 'allows them to participate in the conversations of the day'.
David L. McMahan, *The Making of Buddhist Modernism* (New York: Oxford University Press, 2008), 28.
14. McMahan, *The Making of Buddhist Modernism*, 13.
15. Sudhir Kakar suggests that despite modernity's propensity for individualization in Western cultures, 'The guru-disciple relationship has shown extraordinary resilience and adaptability to retain its hold on the minds of people despite challenges of modernity and the process of individualisation'
Sudhir Kakar, *The Analyst and the Mystic: Psychoanalytic Reflections on Religion and Mysticism* (Viking: University of California, 1991), 11.
16. Amanda Lucia, 'Innovative Gurus: Tradition and Change in Contemporary Hinduism', *International Journal of Hindu Studies* 18, no. 2 (August 2014): 225.
17. Ibid., 236.
18. Ibid., 237.
19. Chetan Bhatt, *Hindu Nationalism: Origins, Ideologies and Modern Myths* (London: Bloomsbury Academic, 2001), 181.
20. Smriti Srinivas, in her study on the Sai Baba movement, finds how the new-age gurus espoused the message of pluralism in their teachings while emphasizing the basics of Indian spirituality. Maya Warrier, in her monograph on Mata Anandamayi, looked for similar traits of spirituality, humanity and plurality in the teachings of the Mata followed by numerous disciples in India and abroad. The tech-savvy followers got impressed and influenced by the jargon-free language used by the gurus in their preaching—it created one de-Sanskritized modern lingua franca, either in English or in vernaculars that appeared quite intelligible to the audience. See, M. Warrier, 'The Seva Ethic and the Spirit of Institution Building in the Mata Amritanandamayi Mission', in *Hinduism in Public and Private: Reform, Hindutva, Gender and Sampraday*, ed. A. R. H. Copley (New Delhi: Oxford University Press, 2003),

254–289; S. Srinivas, *In the Presence of Sai Baba: Body, City, and Memory in a Global Religious Movement* (Leiden, Boston: Brill, 2008); Rudert, 'Research on Contemporary Indian Gurus', 635–636.

21. The Hindu Forum of Britain, the National Council of Hindu Temples (UK), the Art of Living Foundation, the Hindu American Foundation and the Vedic Foundation in the United States are some of the popular organizations in a diasporic setting. For a detailed discussion, see, John Zavos, 'Stamp It Out!' Disciplining the Image of Hinduism in a Multicultural Milieu', *Contemporary South Asia* 16, no. 3 (2008): 323–337; John Zavos, Pralay Kanungo, Deepa Reddy, Maya Warrier, and Raymond Brady Williams, eds., *Public Hinduisms* (New Delhi: SAGE Publications, 2012).
22. Christophe Jaffrelot, ed., *The Sangh Parivar: A Reader* (New Delhi: Oxford University Press, 2005).
23. Jacob Copeman and Aya Ikegame, 'The Multifarious Guru: An Introduction', in *The Guru in South Asia: New Interdisciplinary Perspectives*, eds. Jacob Copeman and Aya Ikegame (London: Routledge, 2012), 1–46.
24. See, 'Supreme Court to Consider Revisiting Hindutva Definition Case', *Times of India*, 28 February 2020, https://timesofindia.indiatimes.com/india/sc-to-consider-revisiting-hindutva-definition-case/articleshow/74347376.cms (accessed 12 October 2020).
25. Jeremy Carrette and Richard King, in the their much-discussed book *Selling Spirituality*, have cleverly contextualized the information age in terms of the global proliferation of technology and ideas. 'The explosion of information and ideas on the internet, for example, is such that the transfer of ideas, and even money, can no longer be controlled by any single institution or nation-state. If we are now moving into a world that moves beyond the traditional boundaries of the nation-state, the rapid spread of information technology is presenting us with a new knowledge-based economy. In the new "information age" ideas become even more important as forces of economic change and resistance. It is important to realise that change is always possible' (see, Carrette and King, *Selling Spirituality*, 13).
26. Alvin Toffler and his associates (Esther Dyson, George Gilder, Jay Keyworth, and Alvin Toffler, 'A Magna Carta for the Knowledge Age', *New Perspectives Quarterly* 11, no. 4 (1994): 32) proposed the information civilization to be the Third Wave of civilization. The first wave of civilization was the agricultural revolution, the second wave ushered in the age of industrial production, and with the third wave we saw the cyberspace revolution. '… the exploration of that land can be a civilization's truest, highest calling' and 'demassification, customization, individuality, freedom—these are the keys to success for Third Wave civilization'. Dyson et al., 'A Magna Carta for the Knowledge Age', 32.
27. D. Reddy, 'Hindutva as Praxis', *Religion Compass* 5, no. 8 (2011).
28. Edward Anderson preferred to describe new-age Hindutva as 'Neo-Hindutva' having the two categories of hard and soft Hindutva. The first one did not

show any reluctance or sensitivity to the RSS brand of majoritarian Hindutva; the latter always maintained a safe distance from the established Hindutva network for realistic reasons. Edward Anderson, 'Neo-Hindutva': The Asia House M. F. Husain Campaign and the Mainstreaming of Hindu Nationalist Rhetoric in Britain', *Contemporary South Asia* 23, no. 1 (2015): 45–66.

29. Travis D. Webster, 'Secularization and Cosmopolitan Gurus', *Asian Ethnology* 75, no. 2 (2016): 351.
30. Ibid., 332.
31. Sahana Udupa, 'Enterprise Hindutva and Social Media in Urban India', *Contemporary South Asia* 26, no. 4 (2018).
32. The three dominions of knowledge—experiencing, knowing and enjoying—give an integrated understanding of the environment in everyday life. This integrated vision helps human beings develop dialectical reasoning on the cause-and-effect relationships in the world. Problems appears when reasoning or rationality occupies an omnipotent position in the thought world, rejecting alternative ways of dealing with the world. Rejection of alternative means to reach the truth often denies ethics and morality any agency to human existence, and the attributes of rationality trim down the possibilities of knowledge to get transformed into wisdom. It happens only when the superiority of an instrumental rationality dominates human mind and knowledge, for example, when knowledge becomes an instrument of power and control. This is the fundamental problem with modernity in India. Despite having a long-drawn legacy of community beliefs and practices at every stage, modernity tended to reject each available alternative of knowledge systems, especially those of the traditional or *parampara*-based knowledge, to build its undisputed sovereignty over nature. Mahatma Gandhi, one of the early 'traditionalists' in India, called out this particular aspect of Western modernity which he believed had placed man as the Supreme Being on earth controlling and regulating nature. Putting man at the top of the material world, Gandhi believed, would encourage man's exploitation of the rest of the world and nature. In his idea of civilization, the knowledgeable man should have the power of self-control, so that he can voluntarily check his wants of raw materials and commodities. Ramchandra Guha, *Environmentalism: A Global History* (New Delhi: Oxford University Press, 2014), 20.
33. Lucia, 'Innovative Gurus', 236.
34. Mukul Sharma, *Green and Saffron: Hindu Nationalism and Indian Environmental Politics* (New Delhi: Permanent Black, 2012).
35. William B. Parosons, 'Psychoanalytic Spirituality', in *Spirituality and Religion, Psychoanalytic Perspectives*, eds. Jerome A. Winter and James William Anderson (Chicago: Mental Health Resource, 2007), 86.
36. Kakar, *The Analyst and the Mystic*, 124.
37. McKean, *Divine Enterprise*, 5–6.
38. Sriya Iyer, *Economics of Religion of India* (Cambridge: Belknap-Harvard, 2018), 102–112.

39. P. Berger and R. Hefner, 'Spiritual Capital in Comparative Perspective', Paper prepared for the Spiritual Capital Planning Meeting 2003. http://www.metanexus.net/spiritual capital/pdf/Berger.pdf (accessed 29 March 2006).
40. The political ambitions of Hindutva and neoliberal economic transformations had some equal social political agendas. Their shared interests were put to use to shape Indian politics in the desired manner. In one way or the other, Hindutva appeared to be the most effective ideology 'that capital has picked up for its purposes'. See, Shankar Gopalakrishnan, 'Neoliberalism and Hindutva: Fascism, Free Markets and the Restructuring of Indian Capitalism', *Radical Notes* (29 October 2008).
41. Ibid, 2–13.
42. Ibid, 7.
43. In his unequivocal manner, Madhav Sadashiv Golwalkar explained, 'Even if there be people of a foreign origin, they must have become assimilated into the body of the mother race and inextricably fused into it…for otherwise such foreign races may be considered at best members of a common state, but they can never form part and parcel of the National body'. See, Christophe Jaffrelot, ed., *Hindu Nationalism: A Reader* (New Delhi: Permanent Black, 2007), 102.
44. Chantal Mouffe, ed., *Gramsci & Marxist Theory* (London: Routledge & Kegan Paul, 1979).
45. Referring to the situation, Shankar Gopalakrishnan pointed out, 'Both Hindutva and neoliberals truly emerged on to the national scene during the 1980s, a decade that saw a critical process of change in Indian political discourse…. Pushed by these movements and driven by its own political collapse, the Congress Party in particular and other political formations as well began giving increasing centrality to the notion of "community rights," including allusions to "Hindu" communities, as the driving force of Indian politics'. Shankar Gopalakrishnan, 'Defining, Constructing and Policing a "New India": Relationship Between Neoliberalism and Hindutva', *Economic and Political Weekly* 41, no. 26 (30 June to 7 July 2006): 2806.
46. The rise of the new-age gurus by the late 1980s indicated the gradual erosion of the Nehruvian socialist culture that rose to prominence in the decades after independence and intensified during Indira Gandhi's regime. By the end of the century, corporate entrepreneurship occupied a dominant position in economy, and the upper-caste rhetoric of Hindutva lost its previous agency. By creating a welfare network through provision of economic subsidies to the poor, the Modi–Shah rule in India have tried to employ government schemes and policies to bring these hitherto unattended groups into the fold of Hindutva. See Thachil (2009, 55–58).
47. Bhuvi Gupta and Jacob Copeman, 'Awakening Hindu Nationalism Through Yoga: Swami Ramdev and the Bharat Swabhiman Movement', *Contemporary South Asia* 27, no. 3 (2019): 322.

48. Udupa, 'Enterprise Hindutva and Social Media in Urban India', 465.
49. Warrier, 'The Seva Ethic and the Spirit of Institution Building', 38.
50. Maintaining yoga as one of the so-called six schools of Indian philosophy, Joseph Alter, one of the prominent writers on yoga, described it as an union between the individual self and the universal cosmic self through the transcendence of all things, recognizing the full range of possible meaning and explicitly concerned with placing it in 'its proper historical and philosophical context. .... Man adepts have said that yoga cannot be understood. It can only be experienced as such. What it is only becomes clear from a perspective wherein self and cosmic self are one. Thus it cannot be understood until true understanding is achieved. ...yoga is the full range of practises that lead to this paradoxical end, including intellectual training meditation, strict standards of moral and ethical behaviour, along with rigorous physical training'. See, Joseph S. Alter, *Yoga in Modern India: The Body Between Science and Philosophy* (Princeton, NJ: Princeton University Press, 2004), 10–11.
51. Walter K. Andersen and D. Damle Sridhar, *Brotherhood in Saffron, The Rastriya Swayamsevak Sangh and Hindu Revivalism* (New Delhi: Westview Press, Vistaar Publications, 1987); P. Kanungo, *The RSS's Tryst with Politics* (New Delhi: Manohar, 2002; K. Jayaprasad, *RSS and Hindu Nationalism: Inroad in a Leftist Stronghold* (New Delhi: Deep and Deep, 1991).
52. Iyer, *The Economics of Religion of India*, 239–240.
53. It was only after the failure of the BJP in different regional legislative assembly elections in 1993 that the party desperately sought to gain lower-caste poor voters' support and devised the strategy of 'social engineering'. Commenting on the strategical change in the BJP's policy, Praful Bidwai mentioned, 'It would give prominence to leaders from the intermediate and low castes in campaigning for Hindutva. This would at once help the BJP to free itself from the confines of its traditional identification with upper-caste Hindus, sink roots among the lower castes, and further an ideological-political vision'. Praful Bidwai, 'End of Social Engineering', *Frontline* 22, no. 26 (17–30 December 2005); Also see, Thachil (2009, 75).
54. Gupta and Copeman, 'Awakening Hindu Nationalism Through Yoga', 314.
55. Ibid., 15.
56. For details on various aspects of yoga, see Joseph S. Alter, 'Somatic Nationalism: Indian Wrestling and Militant Hinduism', *Modern Asian Studies* 28, no. 3 (1994): 557–588; Alter, *Yoga in Modern India*; Jacob and Ikegame, 'The Multifarious Guru', 1–46; Swami Ramdev, 'Vedas- The Proponent of World Fraternity', *Yog Sandesh* (15 January 2003a): 14–19. Swami Ramdev, *Jeevan Darshan* (Haridwar: Divya Prakashan, 2008); Lawrence Cohen, 'Science, Politics, and Dancing Boys: Propositions and Accounts', *Parallax* 14, no. 3 (2008): 35–47.
57. I. McDonald, 'Hindu Nationalism, Cultural Spaces, and Bodily Practices in India', *American Behavioural Scientist* 46 (1 July 2003): 1565.

58. *Thomas B. Hansen, 'Recuperating Masculinity: Hindu Nationalism, Violence and Exorcism of the Muslim Other', Critique of Anthropology* 16, no. 2 (1996): 613.
59. As per the information shared by its official website, 'The Isha Yoga Center situated at the foothills of Velliangiri, on the outskirts of Coimbatore, is the headquarters for Isha Foundation. Isha is a sacred space for self-transformation, where you can come dedicate time towards your inner growth. The centre offers all four major paths of yoga *kriya* (energy), *gnana* (knowledge), *karma* (action), and *bhakti* (devotion), drawing people from all over the world. The Center is dedicated to fostering inner transformation and creating an established state of wellbeing in individuals. The large residential facility houses an active international community of Brahmachari, full-time volunteers and visitors. Isha Yoga Center provides a supportive environment for you to shift to healthier lifestyles, seek a higher level of self-fulfilment and realize your full potential' (https://isha.sadhguru.org/ [accessed 12 February 2020]).
60. The official website of the Isha Foundation declares, 'Sadhguru has a unique ability to make the ancient yogic sciences relevant to contemporary minds, acting as a bridge to the deeper dimensions of life. His approach does not ascribe to any belief system, but offers methods for self-transformation that are both proven and powerful. Through powerful yoga programs for inner transformation and inspiring social outreach initiatives, Isha Foundation has created a massive movement dedicated to addressing all aspects of human wellbeing'. (https://isha.sadhguru.org/ [accessed 12 February 2020]).
61. Sir Ken Robinson is the author of *The Element, Finding Your Element, and Out of Our Minds: Learning to Be Creative*, https://isha.sadhguru.org/booktour/ (accessed 1 January 2020).
62. Sadhguru, and Cheryl Simone. *Midnights with The Mystic*. Mumbai: Jaico Publishing House, 2012.
63. Sadhguru Jaggi Vasudev, 'Sense of National Pride is Need of the Hour', *Economic Times*, 22 February 2019, https://economictimes.indiatimes.com/ (accessed 28 April 2020).
64. Praful Bidwai, 'Confronting the Reality of Hindutva Terrorism', *Economic and Political Weekly* 43, no. 47 (22–28 November 2008): 12.
65. Chandrima Chakraborty, *Masculinity Asceticism, Hinduism: Past and Present Imaginations of India* (Ranikhet: Permanent Black, 2011), 185.
66. Ibid, 186.
67. Bidwai, 'Confronting the Reality of Hindutva Terrorism', 10.
68. BJP's old guard, like L. K. Advani, advanced the modern views and proposed that the acolytes of real Hindu nationalism could never promote violence or, to say, terrorism. In 2005, *Outlook* reported, 'To a query that idea of formation of separate Hindu Political Front mooted out by the VHP after the last Lok Sabha election by citing the reason that BJP under NDA regime had failed to fulfil the agenda of "Hindutva" like abolition of Article 370 and construction of Ram Mandir, Acharya said VHP still stood by the idea that time was

ripe for all Hindus to come on a united platform to take their rights. Kishore attacked the NDA saying "It was NDA which damaged the Hindu Andolan causing great hurt to the Hindus." On issue of Ram Mandir, he said that the Parishad was hopeful that before this year ended "justice" would be done in favour of Hindus'. (https://www.outlookindia.com [accessed 12 August 2020]). Interestingly, on the issue of delaying the agenda of a Ram Mandir at Ayodhya, VHP leader Acharya Giriaj Kishore accused BJP Prime Minister Atal Bihari Vajpayee as a 'pseudo-Hindu' (*Hindu*, 3 January 2003) and blamed L. K. Advani for 'betraying the Hindutva cause after having ridden to power in the name of Ram' (*Hindu*, 25 April 2003).

69. It has been reported that 'Through a combination of an active YouTube channel with over 2.5 million subscribers, regular tweets to his nearly two million followers, an Isha Foundation programme on campuses called Youth and Truth, several wealthy patrons whose homes he often commandeers, and prolific appearances at media summits, Jaggi Vasudev has built a reputation as a mystic with the mystic'. Kaveeri Bamzai, *The Print*, 16 March 2019.
70. Rajshree Chandra, in one of her articles published in the *The Wire*, went on to criticize Sadhguru in an extravagant manner. 'He says that the CAA is a compassionate move to extend citizenship to persecuted minorities from the three surrounding Islamic countries. He doesn't question, why these three, and why not the persecuted Muslims and Sri Lankan Tamils but we'll let that be for the moment. ... He ignores what legal experts, historians, political analysts have been saying over and over again about the text and intent of the law; he plants calibrated doubts about "certain people who misinformed illiterate Muslim masses" who then have got "misled"; he ignores the psychic, the material, the economic costs and sociological impact of this law and felt free to talk of compassion... He repeats each homily and each exaggeration of the ruling party so unabashedly that one is almost forced to wonder who the *guru* here is'. Rajshree Chandra, *The Wire*, 1 January 2020.
71. See, LaMothe, R. The Colonizing Realities of Neoliberal Capitalism. *Pastoral Psychol* 65, 23–40.
72. Slavoj Zizek, *The Ticklish Subject: The Absent Centre of Political Ontology* (London: Verso, 1999), 138–140.
73. Hailing Modi's selection for the prime ministerial candidacy, RSS mouthpiece *The Organiser* wrote, 'The nation, especially the youths, is looking for decisive, credible and dynamic leadership and popular mood vividly exhibits the undisputable alternative in the form of Modi' (29 September 2013). Narendra Modi was elevated to the position of a *vikas purush*—the leader who would deliver development and 'good governance'. For a detailed Marxist critique of BJP's ascendency to power and its growing presence in the corporate world, see Prakash Karat, 'The Rise of Narendra Modi: A Joint Enterprise of Hindutva and Big Business', *The Marxist* XXX, no. 1 (January–March 2014).
74. 'Gurudev Sri Sri Ravi Shankar is a universally revered spiritual and humanitarian leader. His vision of a violence-free, stress-free society through the

reawakening of human values has inspired millions to broaden their spheres of responsibility and work towards the betterment of the world'. Gurudev Sri Sri Ravi Shankar, *Uniting the World into a Global Family*, p. 1, https://www.srisriravishankar.org (accessed 6 September 2020).

75. Ravi Shankar, *Uniting the World into a Global Family*, 2.
76. F. Gautier, *The Guru of Joy: Sri Sri Ravi Shankar and the Art of Living* (Sydney: Hay House India, 2010).
77. F. Lebelley, *Walking the Path: Narrative of an Experience with H. H. Sri Sri Ravi Shankar* (Bangalore: Sri Sri Publications Trust, 2010).
78. Sri Sri Guruji's spiritual courses found buyers in corporate houses. The Art of Living's (AOL) specially designed 'Achieve Personal Excellence' programme is meant to enhance skills at the workplace. Several big corporate houses, such as Reliance Industries, Wipro, JPMorgan and Google, have participated in these courses. It helped increase Sri Sri Guruji's online visibility to a great extent (2 April 2016, https://www.business-standard.com, [accessed 3 May 2020]).
79. The excerpts are taken from the speech delivered by RSS chief Mohan Bhagwat at the Metropolitan Meeting organized by the RSS in Ranchi. For details, see https://www.ndtv.com/india-news [accessed 10 August 2020]).
80. B. Anderson, *Imagined Communities* (London: Verso, 2006), 27.
81. For details on Sri Sri Guruji's take on politics, see, *Why Modi's Sri Sri Ravi Shanhar Connection is Good for Politics* (https://www.artofliving.org [accessed 18 September 2020]).
82. Carrette and King, *Selling Spirituality*, 175–176.
83. *Brian A. Hatcher,* 'Bourgeois Vedanta: The Colonial Roots of Middle-Class Hinduism', *Journal of the American Academy of Religion* 75, no. 2 (*2007*): 301.
84. Angela Rudert, in her study on contemporary Indian gurus, observed, 'many contemporary Indian gurus do provide "alternative spiritualities" in the neo-Hindu meditation and yoga movements that they offer to global constituencies today. These spiritualities may take varying positions vis-a-vis religion in defining the identities of gurus and disciples. Gurus' teachings and devotional traditions may be grounded in Indian religiosity and at the same time speak to universal longings'. Rudert, 'Research on Contemporary Indian Gurus', 635.
85. See, Vinayak Damodar Savarkar, *Hindutva: Who is a Hindu* (New Delhi: Bharatiya Sahitya Sadan, 1923).
86. Jaffrelot, *Hindu Nationalism*, 102.

Epilogue

On 17 April 2020, the nation woke up to one horrifying press coverage. Two sadhus, Kalpavriksha Giri and Sushil Giri, reportedly from the Juna Akhara, were beaten to death by a group of villagers in Palghar district of Maharashtra. The horrifying incident trigged a massive war of words between political parties; especially, the BJP and the Congress started slamming each other on various media platforms. The outcry of the Hindutva forces triggered a social media protest, and the television channels got engaged in heated debates on the issue. What is intriguing is the fact that for a long period of time, the saffron-clad sadhus got remarkable attention from the media and the Hindutva forces. Earlier, such killings of sadhus largely went unnoticed or remained less politicized unless the victims came from similar organizations or groups as those promoted by the Sangh Parivar. Sadhus had never been properly represented in the media, except during the occasions when they collectively raised their voice for the Ram Mandir movement or for some selective issues affecting the unity and integrity of the Hindu society. The sense of freedom and self-control enjoyed by the sadhus remained decisive for the society, and this idea of individualism separated the sadhus from the so-called religious leaders. This is the reason why sadhus, spread across a vast network of *sampradayas*, ashrams and *maths*, unfolded their own course of actions in spite of being closely involved with the Babri Masjid–Ram Janmabhoomi movement and worked for different aspects of Hindutva politics. This brings us to the fact that Hindutva has so far been explained mostly as an atypical and twisted expression of Hinduism, though dominant and hegemonic in manifestation. Now, it is completely misleading to propose an archetype of Hindutva, particularly that which has been sanctioned and popularized by the proponents of present-day Hindutva politics. Sadhus have always welcomed diversity of opinions, practices, traditions and expressions, and Hindutva, or to be precise the art of espousing Hindu-ness, never became a doctrinal–monochromatic identity for them. Therefore, when exposed to the world of political Hindutva, the sadhus often chose to offer their individual mode of political activism and responded according to their own individual perspectives. Importantly, the Sangh Parivar too adopted and promoted sadhus having similar ideological perceptions and expected them to offer a Hindu tinge to sociopolitical matters. In the case of the Palghar lynching, the BJP responded quickly mostly because of the victims' proximity to the ruling establishment, with the Juna Akhara being itself a very strong supporter of the VHP and by far the biggest monastic society of sadhus and a vocal defender of Sanatana Dharma.

Asceticism, or 'sadhuism', emerged as crucial to the celebration of the ideal of *karma* yoga to serve the nation in a selfless manner. The sadhu, as a *karma* yogi, aimed at exploring his true *Bharatiyatva* and reinstated the imageries of a *janasevak* who could strive to reform society as part of his spiritual–nationalist endeavours. It was a unique combination, often eulogized by the votaries of Hindutva mostly to bring out the fallacy of Hindu identity formation as a complex interweaving of religion and politics. Ascetic nationalism and its subsequent drive to politicize Hindu identity formation as a historically conditioned affair proliferated the possibilities of sadhus joining politics out of their ethical responsibilities to society. Power relations inherent in the political activism of the sadhus revealed the authoritative context of mass politics to illustrate how the sadhus showed individual stamina to carve their own niche in the mucky world of rivalry, sectarianism and orthodoxy and often bargained over gender, caste, class, religion and ethnic identities. Theoretical arguments aside, the sadhus under consideration expected to champion the cause of promoting Hindu-ness, along with Indianness or *Bharatiyatva*, with or without the Sangh Parivar, for building a Hindu Rashtra in the near future. However, the rhetorical efficacy of the transformation of the nation into a Hindu Rashtra was overwhelmed by the heroic self-image of ascetic masculinity which valorized allegiance to the nation and its people through self-disciplinary practices, scholastic exuberance and impetuous articulation of a Hindu self through political activism, when necessary. 'Politics' is a natural choice for the sadhus—not a forced consumption or displaying of resentment against the 'non-Hindu' others—but a set of behavioural practices claimed to be legitimate and spontaneous at times. Their innate desires to be independent from the rigid, codified entity called political Hindutva often restrained them from submitting to a political party or showing unconditional devotion to a particular leader. The ideological underpinning of political Hindutva might have provided them critical insights into the narratives of Hindus constituting the real sprit and self of the nation, but the sadhus themselves tried to permeate the consciousness of the nation with alternative versions of the 'truth' through an ephemeral but persuasive collage of varied political expressions, dialogues, texts and imageries. The sadhus could be traced also producing and manipulating the knowledge dissemination mechanism used by the Hindutva ideologues, especially the networks of television media, education and cyberspace, as a means of reconstructing the Indian/Hindu self—a long-lost identity of the nation.

This book emerged out of a discomfort about the way sadhus have been treated in contemporary Indian politics. Anything related to sadhus is considered with the suspicion of its being harmful to the secular fabric of the country. What stimulated it further was the imposition of an authoritarian ethno-religious structure in the name of Hindu dharma completely subverting the flexible, all-inclusive philosophy called Sanatana Dharma that accommodates different *sampradayas* or sects and traditions at the core of the Hindu religion. Sadhus/gurus/*sants* as conscious agents of this diverse structure need special attention, since the authoritarian project of Hindutva is being presented since the 1960s as the only alternative to the secularist culture in Indian politics. The new political culture, better known as Hindutva, conceived India less as a geographical entity and more as a spiritual, esoteric space defined by Hindu culture and traditions. It is to be noted once again that the word 'Hindu' was coined out of an intellectual obsession with defining the features of a classical past, denoting the population lying beyond the river called Indus—an ideological construct to signify the collective identity of the people of this land. It is just like what a physical body is to a yogi—the seven sacred sites of Hinduism have been embellished as the sensitive centres or chakras of the kundalini which one must unite through yoga to attain *moksha,* or the ultimate spiritual experience (Jaffrelot 2011, 36).[1] What encouraged the sadhus towards the ideal of Hindutva is not clear. It was not simply the lure of wealth or political power, or to capture the *gaddi* at Delhi, because had there been such a concrete desire or intentions, the sadhus would have come out as a collective entity irrespective of their sectarian differences. The art of being a Hindu was never a political choice for the sadhus even before Hindutva appeared as a political project, because the heresy of 'Hindu-ness' as a qualitative choice always sought to explore the unique spirit of liberty, creativity and spirituality within the psychosomatic world of an individual. All though their spiritual journey, the sadhus responded with rapture to this absorbing experience of Hindutva and celebrated the nuances of a universal–cosmological–spiritual experience with selective religious–cultural idioms not in isolation from the political or social dimensions of human life. Dealing with Hindutva as a single bogey project hints at the enigma of 20th-century Hindu politics, when contemporary Hindutva forces were themselves divided into ideological factions. The factionalism present in the so-called Sangh Parivar does not necessarily signify the conflict of interests between the liberals and radicals but repeatedly uncovers the predestined vacuity of an idea that had replaced the individualism of the spiritual with a kind of shadowy collectiveness of the 'political'. This book seeks to contest the monochromatic rendering of Hindutva by the so-called honchos of Hindu nationalist politics investing on the most unpredictable agents of the movement—the sadhus who remained committed to the absoluteness of their transcendental 'self', cherished a sense of superiority over their political associates and delved into deciphering new connotations and meanings of Hindutva. As a latent but persuasive political force, the sadhus had the potential to manipulate the fate of the Hindutva movement in a desired way; especially, those with organizational representation could have enjoyed some extra mileage than the rest of the fraternity. The former *swayamsevaks*, *pracharaks* or Hindu activists might have had the backing of the Sangh Parivar even after they opted to become full-time sadhus, and these sadhus often worked as 'linkmen' between the sadhu *samaj* and the Sangh Parivar. Very obviously, these sadhus persuaded the sadhu fraternity to work for the political project of Hindutva in a seamless but varnished manner, while the others continued to face the dilemma of whether to go with a political party and submit to the will of a political leader, even though they spontaneously worked for the common interest of the Hindu society by choice. It seemed that both the *pracharak*-turned-sadhus and the insiders embraced the political project of Hindutva as part of their spiritual journey, but in reality the former defended a 'threatened' culture to keep up with the hierarchy and tradition and nurtured the idea of a Hindu revival, whereas the latter mainly supplied moral and social support to the Hindutva movement through putting the RSS–VHP–BJP agenda forward. Despite operating from mutually conclusive zones, they had their individual approaches to the question of promoting and defending the Hindu religion and society; eventually, they looked the same at the end of their journey. They registered their voices separately; however, these voices seem to have got lost within the whirlpool of the movement over the years. It is this charisma of the Hindutva movement that bolstered its attempt to grab almost all the individual voices and ideas with its emphasis on the affirmation of Hindu collective power. With its own rules and directives for a collective Hindu force, the networks of political Hindutva claimed a kind of autonomy over the multi-layered structure of the Hindu society, thereby turning the brand of Hindutva into a mass ideology. They spearheaded a sort of organic solidarity to resist all kind of threats to the Hindu society and worked arduously to make the syncretic Hindu society the real face of the nation.

Within this scrupulously crafted framework, if we talk about the sadhus as a homogeneous category, we must acknowledge how the Sangh Parivar, especially the VHP, provided them an opportunity to link the viscerally consecrated world with the pompous world of everyday politics. After having the sadhus align with it, Hindutva as a political project attained an amount of legitimacy that it had been missing earlier. However, the Parivar's attachment with fringe groups, such as the Bajrang Dal, Hindu Yuva Vahini or Hindu Jagran Manch, often caused serious embarrassment for the sadhus, because in no way did these organizations satisfy the criteria upon which ascetic–masculinized politics was imagined. Now, it is to be noted that the sadhus, especially those who were attached with the *akhara* tradition, could have been inducted into a warrior tradition of self-discipline and self-defence while being acquiescent to a guru. Warrior ascetics, generally referred to as *nagas*, were skilled fighters, defended their material interests always with violent gestures and got trained mainly through the *akharas* or wrestling arenas on various modes of fighting. They carried out their historical duty to defend and protect the Hindu religion; however, these sadhus did not easily mingle with the Hindutva project envisaged through a certain political ideology. For example, the VHP roped in the support of a section of the *akhara*-based sadhus during the Ayodhya movement, but the rest of the sadhus remained less responsive or sometimes antagonistic to the VHP-led initiatives. The *naga* sadhus of the Hanuman Garhi temple of Ayodhya seemed to have responded otherwise. They might have apprehended losing their wealth and position if the Ram temple came into existence; however, what made them more cautious about the movement was a sense of alienation from the sadhu fraternity itself. There is no reason to think that generally sadhus do not have a 'belief in Ram' while those sadhus who support the liberation movement do have that belief. The point is that the aims of the liberation movement are quite contrary to the real interests of these sadhus and that is why they prefer not to 'support', mentioned van der Veer.[2] The fact that 'there is no constant and static existence of Hindu feelings and values' could have offered the dynamics of intense emotional manifestation of popular support to the movement, but the changing configuration of the issues produced within the context of the movement remained volatile and vulnerable. As a natural corollary to the situation, the Hindutva forces worked hard to develop serious engagement with the movement through making it part of their political decision-making process in the near future.

Did the sadhus ever register their presence in the political decision-making process of the BJP? It is totally misleading to construct a unipolar analysis of the question, since the BJP did not necessarily conform to the same political legacy of Hindu nationalism shared by the other members of the Hindu Parivar. The BJP came into being in the 1980s as the rightful successor of the Bharatiya Jana Sangh and marked out to be a new experience arising out of situational exigencies. It contrasted with the Nehruvian project, innovated new meanings of being and becoming a true Indian and infused the virtues of Hindu-ness into the core of *Bharatiyatva*. The Meenakshipuram incident of 1981,[3] the Shah Bano affair,[4] the rise of separatist movements all over India and rising charges of corruption against the Congress government might have had their impact on the hasty but sharp rise of the BJP, but what is noteworthy is that the BJP itself brought out an essential logic for its success in the context of a failing democracy.[5] Congress's failure to satisfy the economic demands of the masses and its limitations with respect to quickly responding to the caste–class aspirations of social groups transformed the language of popular politics into one of discontent and disappointment, and the lower orders of the society looked somewhat indifferent or insensitive to the modernist project of state reforms in a secular–socialist model. State interference in matters of caste and religion caused immense discomfort for them, mostly because of the fact that these people had never been addressed or brought into an open dialogue in an upright manner. Living in a self-centred world of faiths, customs and beliefs made them get absorbed into the banality of a political discourse encumbered by the uncertainties of identity formation through different avenues. Here exists the fear and anxiety of being outnumbered by a certain community, alienated by certain castes, entrapped by the new social transformations or deprived of the new economic opportunities. Orchestrating the view that the secular–socialist messages of the Nehruvian government were anti-Indian or anti-Hindu in character helped the BJP invest much on its own agenda of Hindutva through feeding to the theory that '*Hindutva* and Indian nationhood are synonymous terms. All those living in the country are Bharatiya or Hindus. There is no contradiction between the two'.[6] The BJP could have had its own logic to work on the theory of *Bharatiyatva* as an incarnation of Hindutva for electoral exigencies. The so-called vanguards of the Hindutva movement, the RSS and the VHP, often showed lack of enthusiasm to promote the all-inclusive visions of Hindutva epitomized by the electoral objectives of the BJP since the late 1980s. Spreading Hindutva among poor Hindus required strategical innovations on the part of the BJP, which moved fast to create a mechanism of its own.

> A precondition for the BJP's meteoric rise was the ideological, political and organisational decline of the Congress and its numerous compromises with communalism of different denominations.... However, the Congress alone cannot be blamed for the BJP's rapid ascendancy. The ground was laid earlier, by the anti-Congress Nav Nirman and Jayaprakash Narayan movements of the 1970s, the imposition of Emergency rule, and the protest movement against it, which led to the formation of the Janata Party. Without the RSS-Jana Sangh's participation in the JP movement, facilitated by Narayan's own jaundiced view of the Hindutva groupings, the Jana Sangh could not have quasi-'mainstreamed' itself and acquired a degree of respectability. It exploited this to capture key positions in the Janata regime, including influence in the media.[7]

The other members of the Sangh Parivar took time to grasp the real implications of recruiting popular support while retaining the upper-caste support base intact. Despite this, the BJP and the VHP jointly organized several programmes to consolidate their position among the vast sections of the electorate. Apart from putting the highest amounts of energy into the Ayodhya movement, the Hindutva forces endeavoured to translate the fear, anxiety and ambitions of India's vast underclass into one nationalist–inclusive–all-encompassing project called Hindutva. Interestingly, the ideal of asceticism, particularly in its invigorated form of ascetic masculinity, coincided well with this project of Hindutva, especially in the semi-industrial urban centres of North India—in and around the cities of Ayodhya, Allahabad, Varanasi, Haridwar and others that were considered to be sacred and blessed in Hindu religious tradition. All these cities had been mapped as parts of a holy Hinduized territory, centres of ancient

Hindu learning and seats of *sanatani* ascetic traditions. A series of VHP *sammelans* and Dharma Sansads were held in these cities during the Kumbh Mela festival, keeping in mind the large congregation of sadhus and pilgrims from different parts of the country. Sadhus from different *sanatani* sects flowed into the VHP (and the BJP) in the first Ekatmata Yatra from Haridwar to Kanyakumari, followed by other countrywide processions mapping the holy Hindu sites from north to south and east to west. Crossing over the Char Dham, or the four holy temples in Puri, Rameswaram, Dwarka and Badrinath, the chariot yatras styled as Hindu pilgrimage processions and named as Mahadeva Ratha, Pashupati Ratha and Kapila Ratha provided the necessary boost to the VHP–BJP duo all over the country. Apart from their deep-rooted political significance, what made the yatras and the Kumbh Mela congregations a far more exciting experience for the political observers was the display of Hindu religious symbols and Hindu idols and the presence of some saffron-clad or white-clad sadhus in some of the occasions. Did it ensure all-round support of the sadhus to these organizations? Perhaps not. How could one forget the names of Mahant Lal Das, the head priest of the Ram temple in Ayodhya, and Baba Gyan Das, the *mahant* of the Hanuman Garhi temple? Both of them opposed the 'shrewd tactics' played out by L. K. Advani through the chariot yatras and asked the most relevant question, 'what business do sadhus have in pursuing politics?' The answers must be sought from within the context of how the patterns of Hindu politics have been conceptualized as an art of self-ennoblement, displaying the expanse of its cultural opulence and historical convenience. Sadhus as religious leaders hardly had any freedom or autonomy to channelize the movement in a desired course, because upon a broader analysis, religion emerged as a supplementary force to politics—an instrument of mobilization—a means to manage the mass psyche for political benefits. It did not become overpowering or superior to politics that the sadhus, when presented as religious actors, failed to claim any legitimacy of their own. Interestingly, sadhus, if represented simply as spiritual seekers or practising yogis, could have been found generating a new pattern of politics beyond the existing stereotypes. The dialectic of spirituality and religiosity often impacted the approaches leading to the involvement of sadhus in active politics; however, the overlapping categories of spirituality and religiosity often make it difficult to ascertain how an indifferent/other-worldly spiritual seeker or a yogi fit in the label of a religious leader or how a sadhu successfully registered his 'spiritual' presence in the political domain. The conflicting positions shared by sadhus in both politics and religion complicated the spontaneous interactions between these two domains.

Is it possible for sadhus to transcend the casteist and sectarian identities when viewed as part of any socio-economic or political process? In the Indian situation, is it possible for sadhus to ignore the impotence of identity formation or to be marked as a homogeneous group with a certain consciousness of their own? The response to this lies in developing a new language of power which could shape the cultural imagination of the critical segments of society and make people aware of their existential crises in this world. Religion, like it or not, worked as a major source of power for the sadhus, and they took full advantage of religion by recycling ideas to make them socially adaptive or economically accommodative to an alternative structure. One may call this structure 'sadhudom', or sadhu *samaj*, which sanctioned alternative forms of identity formation and group association, welcomed the so-called 'abnormal', or the dissidents, and even allowed them to establish their own *parampara*-based institutions. Sadhu-led institutions in India might have appeared to be a little clumsy because of their multifarious activities from pre-colonial times; the modern institutions evolved in a far more transparent way, mostly engaging in *seva*-based activities across different segments of the society. What is weird is that the sadhus from a purely *seva*-based organization did not get much importance in mainstream politics, but those coming with a monastic baggage or carrying an agenda-driven portfolio received much recognition from political parties. This book seeks to open up a space for both these categories not only through refereeing the narrowly individualistic or populist values of political involvement but also through exploring a new domain for critical reflection upon some of the existing patterns of how sadhus got engaged with the world of politics in different manners. This work does not aim to provide any sort of justification to Hindutva as an ideological resistance to other establishments but recognizes the inner tensions of a tradition that has faced challenges from within and in effect twisted the actual connotations of these perspectives that provided the best possible consciousness for building an alternative to the dominant ideology. In arguing for the importance of the alternative formulations of Hindutva, this book explores select sadhus to uncover new configurations of resistance, in terms that are not eclipsed by the so-called separation of the religious from the political, the religious from the secular or the spiritual from the religious. Furthermore, in the context of neoliberal economic transformations, this book delves into new forms of universal spirituality that places emphasis on new-age gurus who discarded monasticism and traditional forms of asceticism to recommend the implications of Hindutva as a sustainable life choice in the so-called modern secular society, confirming Hindu spiritual experiences and perceptions as the best possible tools to face the lifestyle challenges arising out of the neoliberal–capitalist upsurge in the post-globalization era.

NOTES

1. Chidbhavananda, *Facets of Brahman or Hindu Gods*, 136.
2. Van der Veer, 'God Must Be Liberated!', 299.
3. In February 1981, Meenakshipuram, a village in Tirunelveli district of Tamil Nadu with a population of 13,000, where almost all the people were 'untouchables', witnessed a mass conversion of 1,000 Dalits to Islam. This conversion was widely described as manipulated by the Muslim League and indicated to what extent the proselytizing religions could influence the Dalits. One Bharatiya Jana Sangh team led by Atal Bihari Vajpayee visited the place immediately after the incident, and the VHP launched the Sanskriti Raksha Yojana (Programme to Protect Culture) and the Jana Jagrana Abhiyana (Campaign for People's Awakening) soon after the incident only to make Hindus aware of the threats. Eventually, the Margdarshak Mandal of the VHP formed the Dharam Sansad—a kind of religious parliament to 'give society a "Hindu" perspective on social and political matters'. Releasing a press statement, Vajpayee condemned religious conversion of any kind and also criticized the practice of untouchability. Manjari Katju, *Vishva Hindu Parishad and Indian Politics*. New Delhi: Orient Blackswan, 2010, 33–35; 'Press Statement by Shri A. B. Vajpayee, President Bharatiya Janata Party, at Madras on 17 July 1981, NMML, and New Delhi Clippings Collection.

4. See the case details in Kirti Singh, 'Women's Rights and the Reform of Personal Laws' In *Hindus and Others*, ed. Gyanendra Pandey (New Delhi: Viking, 1993): 193–195.
5. Praful Bidwai pointed out, 'rise, especially after the Ayodhya movement, was its ability to incorporate new forces in Indian politics—namely, regional parties and segments of the Dalit-OBC self-assertion movement—into alliances or social coalitions. For many regional parties, which arose and grew in opposition to the Congress, the BJP was a "natural" ally. The BJP's OBC leaders like Kalyan Singh and Uma Bharati, as well as the Bahujan Samaj Party, provided a special ballast to the BJP'. Praful Bidwai, 'Understanding a Political Chameleon', *India International Centre Quarterly*, 32, no. 1 (Summer, 2005): 134.
6. *Hindustan Times*, 2 February 1996 quoted in Partha S. Ghosh, *BJP and the Evolution of Hindu Nationalism*, 114–115.
7. Bidwai, 'Understanding a Political Chameleon', 134.

Bibliography

PRIMARY SOURCES

Adgadanand, Swami. *Jeevanadarsh Evam Atmanubhuti: Ideals of Life & Self-Realisation*. Mumbai: Shri Paramhans Swami Adgadanand Ji, Ashram Trust.

Advaitananda, Swami. *Sri Panavananda Lila Smriti* (Memoirs on Swami Pranabananda's Holy Acts). Kolkata: Bharat Sevashram Sangha, 1364 BS.

Annual Report of the Bharat Sevashram Sangha, *Pranav*. Kolkata: Baisakh, 1342 BS.

Annual Report of the Bharat Sevashram Sangha, 1933–1934.

Atmananda, Swami. *Hindu Samaj Samannay*. Kolkata: Bharat Sevashram Sangha, 1386 BS, 120.

Bengal *District Gazetteer* B. volume: *Faridpur* District Statistics, 1911–1912 to 1920–1921. Calcutta: Government of Bengal, 1923.

Government of Bengal, *Fortnightly Report*, 1st half of August 1926.

Nirmalananda, Swami. *Śrīgurusaṅge, Śrīguruprasaṅge*—1915. Kalikātā: Bhārata Sebā śrama Saṅgha, 1397 [1991]. (British Library, India Office Library Records).

Nirmalananda, Swami. eds. *Sri Sri Pranabananda: Satarupe, Satamukhe*. Calcutta: B. S., 1395.

Pranav—The Mouthpiece Magazine of the BSS, 1342 B.S, collected from BSS archive.

Sri, Aurobindo. 'Sri Aurobindo Birth Centenary Library (30 vols.)'. Pondicherry: Sri Aurobindo Ashram, 1970–1972, Vol. 2.

The Complete Works of Swami Vivekananda. Calcutta: Advaita Ashram, 9 Vols, 1907–1997.

The Mission of the Vedanta, Complete Works of Swami Vivekananda. Calcutta: Mayavati Advaita Ashrama, Vol. iii, 1995, twenty first print.

The Sangha Geeta. Calcutta: Bharat Sevashram Sangha, 1967. (It's a collection of the speeches, letters or advice by the Sangha leader/guru).

The Selected Works of Mahatma Gandhi. Ahmedabad: VI Navajan Publishing House, 1968; *Truth is God*. Ahmedabad, 1955, 12.

Vedananda, Swami. *The Prophet of the Age: A Short Life Sketch of Acharya Swami Pranavanandaji Founder of Bharat Sevashram Sangha*. Calcutta: Swami Nirmalananda, [n.d.] (British Library, India Office Library Records).

Vedananda, Swami. *Ideals of Indian Education and Culture. Acharya Swami Pranavananda Memorial Volume* (2nd edition.) [By various authors.] Calcutta, 1967. (British Library, India Office Library Records).

Vedananda, Swami. *Sangher Hindu Jati Gathon Andoloner Suchona* (The Starting of Hindu Jatigathan by the Sangha) in *Sri Sri Pranabananda: Sata Rupe Sata Mukhe*, edited by Swami Nirmalananda. Kolkata, Bharat Sevashram Sangh Sangha, 1395 BS.

Vedananda, Swami. *Sangher Hindu Jati Gathan Andoloner Suchana*, 1934.

Vedananda, Swami. *Sri Sri Yugacharya Jivancharat* (Biography of Swami Pranabananda in Bengali). Kolkata: Bharat Sevashram Sangha, 1385 BS.

Vedananda, Swami. eds. *Sangha Geeta: Inspiring Teachings of Jagadguru Swami Pranavanandaji Maharaj*. Sangha, London: Bharat Sevashram Sangha (Swami Nirliptananda on behalf of the BSS), 2007.

Yuktananda, Swami. *Hindu Jati Gothone Jati Sangathak Yugachara* (The Nation Bulder Swami Pranabananda in Building the Hindu Nation). Kolkata: Bharat Sevashram Sangha, 1414 BS, Aswin.

Publication by the VHP

An All India Sanatana Dharma Conference. Samagra Savarkar Wangmaya, Vol. VI: Hindu Rashtra Darshan. Poona: All India, Hindu Mahasabha, 1964.

Editorial. World Hindu Conference. Bombay: Vishva Hindu Parishad Publication, 1979, p. vii.

Ekatmata Yajna 1983. New Delhi: Vishva Hindu Parishad Publication, 1984.

Goswami, Parshuram.

Narayan Rao Tarte. *Vishva Hindu Parishad Ki Kalpana* (Formation of Vishva Hindu Parishad), *Hindu Vishva*, Silver Jubilee Issue, 1989–1990.

'Prayag main Dharma Sansad adhiveshan' (The Dharma Sansad Conference at Prayag). *Hindu Vishva*, March–April 1989.

Sharma, Raghunandan Prasad, ed. *Vishva Hindu Parishad Ke Prastav* (The Resolutions of the Vishva Hindu Parishad). New Delhi: Vishva Hindu Parishad. Not dated but in print in 1995.

Sharma, Raghunandan Prasad. *Marg Darshak Mandal Ki Vibhinn Baithakain Chhati Dharma Sansad Ke Aayojan Par* (The Various Meetings of the Marg Darshak Mandal on the Occasion of the 6th Dharma Sansad), 1995.

Sharma, Raghunandan Prasad. *Satat Sadhna Yatra Ke Tees Varsh* 1964–1994 (Thirty Years of Devoted Meditation), not dated but in print in 1995.

Sharma, Raghunandan Prasad. *Nagpur Main Dwitiya Ekatmata Yatra Ka Samapan Samaroh* (The Closing Ceremony of the Second Ekatmata Yatra at Nagpur). New Delhi: Vishva Hindu Parishad Publication, January 1996.

Shivram Shankar Apte. 'Why Vishva Hindu Parishad'. *Organiser*, Diwali issue, 2 November 1964.

Shraddhanjali Smarika. (Commemorative Volume). New Delhi: Viswa Hindu Parishad Foundation, 1986–1987.

World Hindu Conference, 1966 (WHC-I), https://vhp.org/conferences/world-hindu-conference

World Hindu Conference 1979. Bombay: Vishva Hindu Parishad Publication.

Others

Activities of the Bharat Seva Asram Sangha (illustrated) ... in the year 1933-34-35. Bhārata Sebāśrama Saṅgha (Calcutta, India), 1935 (British Library, Indian Office Library Records).

Brahmachanni Sadhnaji. Short Biography of Swami Chinmayananda, internet, http://www. tazoat. com/-bnaik/biograph. html

Collected Works of Mahatma Gandhi. New Delhi: Publications Division, Government of India, 1958–1984, p. 28.

First Lok Sabha, Party Wise Details—Ram Rajya Parishad'. https://loksabha.nic.in/members/partyardetail

Jawaharlal Nehru's Speech at the Constituent Assembly, Constituent Assembly Debates Proceedings, Vol. 9, http://loksabhaph.nic.in/writereaddata/cadebatefiles/vol9.html

Report of the Hindu Law Committee. Madras: Government Press, 1947.

Sri Mahamandal ki Balyavastha. Bañaras: Shri Bharat Dharma Mahamandal Head Office, 1910.

Suryodaya, Special Trilingual Quarterly Edition, March 1941.

S. P. Mookerjee Papers, Installment II–IV, Subject File No. 168, pp. 15. New Delhi: NMML.

Tandon Papers, file 277, National Archives of India, New Delhi.

The Statistical Report on the General Election, 1951 to the Legislative Assembly of Rajasthan, Election Commission of India, New Delhi, https://eci.gov.in/files/file/3378-rajasthan-1951

Vajpayee, Atal Bihari. 'The Bane of Secularism'. In *Jana Sangh Souvenir*, ed. S. S. Bhandari. Delhi: Bharatiya Janata Party, 1969.

SECONDARY SOURCE

Ahmed, Hilal. *Muslim Political Discourse in Postcolonial India: Monuments, Memory, Contestation*. Oxon: Routledge, 2014.

Alter, Joseph S. *Yoga in Modern India: The Body Between Science and Philosophy*. Princeton, NJ: Princeton University Press, 2004.

Andersen, Walter K., and Sridhar D. Damle. *Brotherhood in Saffron, The Rastriya Swayamsevak Sangh and Hindu Revivalism*. New Delhi: Westview Press, Vistaar Publications, 1987.

Anderson, B. *Imagined Communities*. London: Verso, 2006.

Anderson, Walter K., and Shridhar D. Damle, 'RSS: Ideology, Organization, and Training'. In *The Sangh Parivar: A Reader*, edited by Christophe Jaffrelot. New Delhi: Oxford University Press, 2005.

Arnold, David. *Science, Technology and Medicine in Colonial India*. Cambridge: Cambridge University Press, 2000.

Baily, Susan. 'Hindu Modernisers and the "Public" Arena: Indigenous Critiques of Caste in colonial India'. In *Swami Vivekananda and the Modernisation of Hinduism*, edited by William Radice. Delhi: Oxford University Press, 1998.

Bacchetta, Paola. 'Hindu Nationalist Women as Ideologues'. In *The Sangh Parivar: A Reader*, edited by Christophe Jaffrelot. New Delhi: Oxford University Press, 2005.

Bandyopadhyay, Sekhar. *Caste, Protest and Identity in Colonial India; The Namasudras of Bengal, 1872–1947*. Surrey: Curzon, 1977 ; London: Routledge, 1997.

Bandyopadhyay, Sekhar. *Caste, Politics and the Raj, 1872–1937*. Calcutta: K. P. Bagchi and Co., 1990.

Basu, Tapan, P. Datta, S. Sarkar, T. Sarkar, and S. Sen. *Khaki Shorts Saffron Flags*. (Tracts for the Times-I). New Delhi: Orient Longman, 1993.

Beckerlegge, Gwilym. 'Saffron and Seva: The Rastriya Swayamsevak Sangh's Appropriation of Swami Vivekananda'. In *Hinduism in Public and Private: Reform, Hindutva, Gender and Sampraday*, edited by Anthony Copley. New Delhi: Oxford University Press, 2003.

Beckerlegge Gwilym. *The Ramakrishna Mission: The Making of a Modern Hindu Movement*. New Delhi: Oxford University Press, 2000.

Beckerlegge, Gwilym. 'The Rashtriya Swayamsevak Sangh's Tradition of Selfless Service'. In *The Politics of Cultural Mobilization in India*, edited by John Zavos, Andrew Wyatt, and Vernon Hewitt. New Delhi: Oxford University Press, 2004.

Berger, P. L. *The Sacred Canopy: Elements of a Sociology of Religion*. Garden City: Doubleday, 1969.

Berger, P. L. *The Social Reality of Religion*. London: Allen Lane, 1973.

Bhatt, Chetan. 'From Revolutionary Nationalism to Hindutva'. In *Hindu Nationalism: Origins, Ideologies and Modern Myths*, edited by Chetan Bhatt. London: Bloomsbury Academic, 2001.

Bhatt, Chetan. *Hindu Nationalism: Origins, Ideologies and Modern Myths*. London: Bloomsbury Academic, 2001.

Bhattacharya, Ananda, eds. *A History of the Dashnami Naga Sannyasis*. London: Routledge, 2018.

Boehmer, Elleke. *Colonial and Post Colonial Literature: Migrant Metaphors*. Oxford: Oxford University Press, 1995.

Bobbitt, Phillip. *The Shield of Achilles: War, Peace, and the Course of History*. Foreword by Michael Howard. New York: Alfred A. Knopf, 2002.

Campbell, John Oman. *The Mystics, Ascetics and Saints of India*. London: Fisher Unwin, 1905.

Carr, Anthony Watt. *Serving the Nation, Cultures of Service, Association and Citizenship in Colonial India*. New Delhi: Oxford University Press, 2005.

Carrette, Jeremy, and Richard King. *Selling Sprituality: The Silent Takeover of Religion*. Abingdon: Routledge, 2004.

Chakraborty, Chandrima. *Masculinity Asceticism, Hinduism: Past and Present Imaginations of India*. Ranikhet: Permanent Black, 2011.

Chaturvedi, M., and B. N. Tiwari. *A Practica, Hindi–English Dictionary*. Delhi: National Publishing House, 1970.

Chatterjee, Partha. *Nationalist Thought and the Colonial World*. Delhi: Oxford University Press, 1986.

Chatterjee, Partha. *Nation and Its Fragments: Colonial and Postcolonial Histories*. Princeton, NJ: Princeton University Press, 1993.

Chatterjee, Joya. *The Spoils of Partition: Bengal and India, 1947–1967*. New Delhi: Cambridge University Press, 2007.

Chatterjee, Prashanto Kumar. *Dr. Syama Prasad Mookerjee and Indian Politics: An Account of An Outstanding Political Leader*. New Delhi: Cambridge University Press, 2012.

Chidbhavananda. *Facets of Brahman or Hindu Gods*. Tiruchirapalli: Sri Ramakrishna Tapovanam, 1985.

Chowdhury, Indira. *Frail Hero and Virile History: Gender and the Politics of Culture in Colonial Bengal*. Delhi: Oxford University Press, 1998.

Copeman, Jacob, and Aya Ikegame, eds. *The Guru in South Asia: New Interdisciplinary Perspectives*. London: Routledge, 2012.

Dalmia, V. *The Nationalisation of Hindu Traditions, Bharatendu Harishchandra and Nineteenth Century Banaras*. New Delhi: Oxford University Press, 1997.

Dalmia, V. *The Nationalization of Hindu Traditions: Bharatendu Harischandra and Nineteenth Century Banaras*. New Delhi: Oxford University Press, 2010.

Daniélou, Alain. *The Way to the Labrinth, Memories from East and West*, translated by Marie Claire Cournand. New York: New Directions, 1987.

Dasgupta, Koushiki. *Electoral Politics and Hindu Nationalism in India: The Bharatiya Jana Sangh, 1951–1971*. London: Routledge, 2020.

Datta, Pradip. 'Dying Hindus: Production of Hindu Communal Common Sense in Early 20th Century Bengal', *Economic and Political Weekly* 28, no. 25 (19 June 1993).

Debord, Guy. *The Society of the Spectacle*, translation by Fredy Perlman and Jon Supak. Detroit, MI: Black & Red, 1970; rev. ed. 1977, 1967.

DeNapoli, Antoinette E. 'A Mandal of Their Own: Gender and the Reimagining of Community by Hindu Renouncers in Northern India'. In *Modern Hinduism in Text and Context*, edited by Lavanya Vemsani. London: Bloomsbury Academic, 2018. [Bloomsbury Collections Web. 8 May 2020.]

Dumont, Louis. *Homo Hierarchicus: The Caste System and Its Implications*. Delhi: Oxford University Press, 1966.

Emir, Rudite. *Swami Chinmayananda: A Life of Inspiration and Service*. Mumbai: Central Chinmaya Mission Trust, 1998.

Fanon, Frantz. *Black Skin, White Mask*, translated by Charles Lam Markmann. New York: Grove, 1967.

Farquhar, John Nicol. *The Crown of Hinduism*. London: Oxford University Press, 1913.

Farquhar, J. N. *Modern Religious Movements in India*. New York: Macmillan Company, 1915 reprint ed., Delhi: Munshiram Manoharlal, 1967.]

Farquhar, J. N. 'The Fighting Ascetics of India'. *Bulletin of the Royal Rylands Library* 9, no. 2 (1925): 431–452.

Fort, O. Andrew. *Jīvanmukti in Transformation: Embodied Liberation in Advaita and Neo-Vedanta*. Albany: State University of New York Press, 1998.

Frykenberg, Robert. 'The Emergence of Modern "Hinduism" as a Concept and as an Institution: A Reappraisal with Special Reference to South India'. In *Hinduism Reconsidered*, edited by Sontheimer and Kulke. Delhi: Manohor, 1989.

Gautier, F. *The Guru of Joy: Sri Sri Ravi Shankar and the Art of Living*. Sydney: Hay House India, 2010.

Ghosh Partha, S. *BJP and the Evolution of Hindu Nationalism: From Periphery to Centre*. New Delhi: Manohar, 1999.

Golwalkar, Madhav Sadashiva. *We, or the Nationhood Redefined*. Nagpur: Bharat Publication, 1939.

Gopal, Sarvepallil, ed. *Jawaharlal Nehru: An Anthology*. New Delhi: Oxford University Press, 1980.

Gould, W. *Hindu Nationalism and the Language of Politics in Late Colonial India*. Delhi: Cambridge University Press, 2005.

Graham, B. D. 'The Congress and Hindu Nationalism'. In *The Indian National Congress: Centenary Hindsights*, edited by D. A. Low. New Delhi: Oxford University Press, 1988.

Greenfield, Liah. *Nationalism: Five Roads to Modernity*. Cambridge: Harvard University Press, 1992.

Guha, Ramchandra. *Environentalism: A Global History*. New Delhi: Oxford University Press, 2014.

Halbfass, Wilhelm. *Tradition and Reflection: Explorations in Indian Thought*. Albany: State University of New York Press, 1991.

Halbfass, Wilhelm. *Philology and Confrontation: Paul Hacker on Traditional and Modern Vedanta*. Albany, NY: State University of New York Press, 1995.

Hansen, Thomas Blom. *The Saffron Wave: Democracy and Hindu Nationalism in Modern India*. Princeton, NJ: Princeton University Press, 1999.

Heehs, Peter. 'Bengali Religious Nationalism and Communalism'. *International Journal of Hindu Studies* 1 (April, 1997): 117–139.

Hingorani, Anand T., ed. *M. K. Gandhi—Towards Lasting Peace*. Albany, NY: Bharatiya Vidya Bhavan, 1966.

Horkheimer, Fax, and Theodor W. *Adorno*, *Dialectic of Enlightenment*, trans. John. New York: Cumming Seabury, *1972*.

Iyre, Sriya. *Economics of Religion of India*. Cambridge: Belknap-Harvard, 2018.

Jackson, Carl T. *Vedanta for the West: the Ramakrishna Movement in the United States*. Bloomington, IN: Indiana University Press, 1994.

Jaffrelot, Christophe. *The Hindu Nationalist Movement in India 1925 to the 1990s*. Delhi: New C Hurst & Co, 1996.

Jaffrelot, Christophe. 'The Vishva Hindu Parishad: Structures and Strategies'. In *Religion, Globalization and Political Culture in the Third World*, edited by Jeff Haynes. London: Palgrave Macmillan, 1999.

Jaffrelot, Christophe, ed. *The Sangh Parivar: A Reader*. New Delhi: Oxford University Press, 2005.

Jaffrelot, Christophe. 'Hindu Nationalism as a Social Welfare Stratergy: Seva Bharati as an Educational Agency'. In *The Sangh Parivar: A Reader*, edited by C. Jaffrelot. Oxford: Oxford University Press, 2006.

Jaffrelot, Christophe, ed. *Hindu Nationalism: A Reader*. New Delhi: Permanent Black, 2007.

Jaffrelot, Christophe. *Religion, Caste and Politics in India*. London: C. Hurst Co. Publishers, 2011.

Jayaprasad, K. *RSS and Hindu Nationalism: Inroad in a Leftist Stronghold*. New Delhi: Deep and Deep, 1991.

Jensen, J. S. *What is Religion*? Durham: Acumen Publishing Ltd, 2014.

Jha, Dhirendra K. *Ascetic Games: Sadhus, Akharas and the Making of the Hindu Vote*. New Delhi: Westland Publications Private Limited, 2019.

Jones, K. W. *Arya Dharm: Hindu Consciousness in 19th Punjab*. London: University of California Press, 1976.

Jones, K. W. 'Religious Identity and the Indian Census'. In *The Census in British India: New Perspective*, edited by N. Gerald Barrier. New Delhi: Manohar, 1981.

Jorden, J. I. F. *Swami Shradhananda: His Life and Causes*. Delhi: Oxford University Press, 1981.

Juergensmeyer, Mark. *Terror in the Mind of God: The Global Rise of Religious Violence*. Berkeley, CA: University of California Press, 2003.

Kaelber, William O. 'Asceticism'. In The Encyclopedia of Religion, edited by M. Eliade. New York: Macmillan, Vol. 1, 1987.

Kakar, S. *The Inner World: A Psychoanalytic Study of Childhood and Society in India*. Delhi: Oxford University Press, 1978.

Kane, P. V. *History of the Dharmasastra*, Vol. 2, Pt. 2. Poona: Bhandarkar Oriental Research Institute, 1974.

Kanungo, P. *The RSS's Tryst with Politics*. New Delhi: Manohar, 2002.

Katju, Manjari. *Vishva Hindu Parishad and Indian Politics*. New Delhi: Orient Blackswan, 2010.

Kaviraj, Sudipta. *The Unhappy Consciousness: Bankimchandra Chattopadhya and the Formation of Nationalist Discourse in India*. Delhi/New York: Oxford University Press, 1995.

Kaviraj, Sudipta. *The Trajectories of the Indian State: Politics and Ideas*. Ranikhet: Permanent Black, 2010.

King, U. *The Search for Spirituality: Our Global Quest for a Spiritual Life*. Norwich: Canterbury Press, 2009.

Krishnakumar, Radhika. *Ageless Guru: The Inspirational Life of Swami Chinmayananda*. Mumbai: Central Chinmaya Mission Trust, 2008.

Kumar, S. *Gandhi Meets Prime Time: Globalisation and Nationalism in Indian Television*. Champaign, IL: University of Illinois Press, 2006.

Lebelley, F. *Walking the Path: Narrative of an Experience with H.H. Sri Sri Ravi Shankar*. Bangalore: Sri Sri Publications Trust, 2010.

Lutgendorf, Philip. *The Life of a Text: Performing the Ramcaritmanas of Tulsidas*. Berkeley, CA: University of California Press, 1991.

Malkani, K. R. *The RSS Story*. New Delhi: Impex India, 1980.

Mankekar, P. *Screening Culture, Viewing Politics: Ethnography of Television, Womanhood, and Nation in Postcolonial India*. Durham: Duke University Press, 1999.

McDonald, I. 'Hindu Nationalism, Cultural Spaces, and Bodily Practices in India'. *American Behavioural Scientist* 46 (1 July 2003): 11.

McKean, L. *Divine Enterprise: Gurus and the Hindu Nationalist Movement*. Chicago, IL: University of Chicago Press, 1996.

McMahan, David L. *The Making of Buddhist Modernism*. New York: Oxford University Press, 2008.

Menon, K. D. *Everyday Nationalism: Women of the Hindu Right in India*. Philadelphia: University of Pennsylvania Press, 2012.

Mill, James. *The History of British India*, Vol. 1. New York: Chelsea, 1968.

Mouffe, Chantal, ed. *Gramsci & Marxist Theory*. London: Routledge & Kegan Paul, 1979.

Moyser, G. *Politics and Religion in the Modern World*. London: Routledge, 1991.

Mukherjee, U. N. *Hindus—A Dying Race*, edited by M Banerjee., Calcutta, 1909, reprint 1910.

Mukul, Akshaya. *Gita Press and the Making of Hindu India*. New Delhi: Harper Collins India, 2015.

Nagappa Gowda, K. *The Bhagawat Gita and the Nationalist Discourse*. New Delhi: Oxford University Press, 2011.

Nandy, Ashis. 'The Politics of Secularism and the Recovery of Religious Toleration'. In *Secularism and Its Critics*, edited by Rajeev Bhargava. New Delhi: Oxford University Press, 2010.

Narayan, Kirin. *Storytellers, Saints, and Scoundrels: Folk Narrative in Hindu Religious Teaching*. Philadelphia, PA: University of Pennsylvania Press, 1989.

Nicholson, Andrew J. *Unifying Hinduism: Philosophy and Identity in Indian Intellectual History*. New York: Columbia University Press, 2010.

Noorani, A. G. *The Muslims of India: A Documentary Record*. New Delhi: Oxford University Press, 2003.

Olivelle, Patrick. *The Āśrama System: The History and Hermeneutics of a Religious Institution*. New York: Oxford University Press, 1993.

Pandey, Gyanendra. 'Rallying Around the Cow: Sectarian Strife in the Bhojpur Region, c. 1888–1917'. In *Subaltern Studies: Writings on South Asian History and Society*, Vol. 2, edited by Ranajit Guha. Delhi/New York: Oxford University Press, 1983.

Pandey, Dhanpati. *Swami Dayanand Saraswati: Builders of Modern India*. New Delhi: Publications Division, Ministry of Information and Broadcasting, Government of India, 1985.

Parekh, Bhikhu. *Gandhi's Political Philosophy: A Critical Examination*. New Delhi: Ajanta Publications, 1995.

Parekh, Bhikhu. *Debating India: Essays on Indian Political Discourse Debating India: Essays on Indian Political Discourse*. New Delhi: Oxford University Press, 2015.

Parosons, William B. 'Psychoanalytic Spirituality'. In *Spirituality and Religion, Psychoanalytic Perspectives*, edited by Jerome A. Winter and James William Anderson. Chicago, IL: Mental Health Resource, 2007.

Pinch, W. *Peasants and Monks in British India*. Berkeley, CA: University of California Press, 1994.

Pingle, Vibha, and Ashutosh Varshney, 'India's Identity Politics: Then and Now'. In *Managing Globalization: Lessons from China and India*, edited by David A. Kelly, Ramkrishen S. Rajan and Gillian H. L. Goh. Singapore: World Scientific Publishing Co Pte Ltd, 2006.

Pradhan, Rajesh. *When the Saints Go marching in': The Curious Ambivalence of Religious Sadhus in Recent Politics in India*. New Delhi: Orient BlackSwan, 2014.

Puniyani, Ram. *Communalism: What is False, What is True*. Bombay: Sarvodaya Friendship Centre, 2005.

Radice, William, eds. *Swami Vivekananda and the Modernisation of Hinduism*. New Delhi: Oxford University Press, 1998.

Rajagopal, A. *Politics After Television: Religious Nationalism and Reshaping of the Indian Public*. Cambridge: Cambridge University Press, 2001.

Rajagopal, A. 'The Public Sphere in India: Structure and Transformation'. In *The Indian Public Sphere*, edited by A. Rajagopal. New Delhi: Oxford University Press, 2009.

Ram, P. R. *Hindutva Offensive: Social Roots and Characterization*. Mumbai: Centre for Study of Society and Secularism, 1996.

Ramdev, Swami. *Jeevan Darshan*. Haridwar: Divya Prakashan, 2008.

Raychaudhuri, Tapan. 'Shadows of the Swastika: Historical Perspectives on the Politics of Hindu Communalism'. *Modern Asian Studies* 34, no. 2 (May 2000): 259–279.

Robinson, Francis. *Separatism Among Indian Muslims: The Politics of the United Provinces' Muslims, 1860–1923*. London: Cambridge University Press, 1974.

Roy, Rajat Kanta. *Exploring Emotional History, Gender, Mentality and Literature, in the Indian Awakening*. New Delhi: Oxford University Press, 2001.

Roy, Olivier. *Holy Ignorance: When Religion and Culture Part Always*. London: Hurst & Co, 2010.

Sadguru. *Ancient Technology for the Modern Mind*. Coimbatore: Isha Foundation, 2008.

Sadhguru, and Cheryl Simone. *Midnights With The Mystic*. Mumbai: Jaico Publishing House, 2012.

Sampurnanand. *Congress Ideology and Programme in Memories and Reflections*. Bombay: Asia Publishing House, 1962.

Sanyal, Hitesh Ranjan. *Social Mobility in Bengal*. Calcutta: Papyrus, 1981.

Sarkar, Sumit. *Writing Social History*. New Delhi: Oxford University Press, 1997.

Sarkar, Sumit. 'Educating the Children of the Hindu Rashtra: Notes on RSS Schools'. In *The Sangh Parivar: A Reader*, edited by C. Jaffrelot. Oxford: Oxford University Press, 2006.

Savarkar, V. D. *Hindutva: Who is a Hindu*? Bombay: Pandit Bakhle Publications Division, 1923 (1999 edition).

Sen, Amiya. P. *Swami Vivekananda*. New Delhi: Oxford University Press, 2000.

Sharma, Mukul. *Green and Saffron: Hindu Nationalism and Indian Environmental Politics*. New Delhi: Permanent Black, 2012.

Sharma, Jyotirmaya. *Hindutva: Exploring the Idea of Hindu Nationalism*. New Delhi: HarperCollins, 2015.

Sheldrake, Philip. *Spirituality: A Guide for the Perplexed*. New York: Bloomsbury Academic, 2014.

Singh, Kirti. 'Women's Rights and the Reform of Personal Laws'. In *Hindus and Others*, edited by Gyanendra Pandey. New Delhi: Viking, 1993.

Sinha, Mrinalin. *Colonial Masculinity: The Many Englishman and the Effeminate Bengali in the Late Nineteenth Century*. Manchester: Manchester University Press, 1995.

Sivaraman, Krishna. *'Introduction' in Hindu Spirituality: Vedas Through Vedanta*, edited by Krishna Sivaraman. New Delhi: Motilal Benarasidas, 1995.

Smith, M. L., L. Miller-Kahn, W. Heinecke, and P. F. Jarvis. *Political Spectacle and the Fate of American Schools*. New York: Routledge Falmer, 2004.

Srinivas, S. *In the Presence of Sai Baba: Body, City, and Memory in a Global Religious Movement*. Leiden/Boston, MA: Brill, 2008.

Srinivasan Vasanti. *Hindu Spirituality and Virtue Politics*. New Delhi: SAGE Publications, 2014.

Stutley, M., and J. Stutley. *A Dictionary of Hinduism*. London: Routledge, 1977.

Taylor, Charles. *A Secular Age*. Cambridge: Harvard University Press, 2017.

Thapar, Romila. *Cultural Transaction in Early Idea, Tradition and Patronage. History and Beyond*. New Delhi: Oxford University Press, 2002.

Tripathi, Bansidhar. *Sadhus of India*. Bombay: Popular Prakashan, 1978.

van der Veer Peter. 'Spirituality in Modern Society'. *Social Research* 76, no. 4: 1097.

van der Veer Peter. *Religious Nationalism: Hindus and Muslims in India*. Berkeley, CA: University of California Press, 1994.

Vanik, Achin. 'Communalization of the Indian Polity'. In *India's Political Parties*, edited by Peter Ronald deSouza and E. Sridharan. New Delhi: SAGE Publications, 2006.

Vasanthi, Srinivasan. *Hindu Spirituality and Virtue Politics*. New Delhi: SAGE Publications, 2014.

Vergati, Anne. 'The Construction of Tradition: The Cult of the God Rama in Rajasthan, North India'. *History and Anthropology* 15, no. 3 (2004): 263–271.

Verma, Vishwanath Prasad. *The Political Philosophy of Mahatma Gandhi and Sarvodaya*. Agra: Lakshmi Narain Agarwal, 1972.

Voix, Raphaël. 'Social Services, Muscular Hinduism and Implicit Militancy in West Bengal: The Case of the Bharat Sevashram Sangha'. In *Cultural Entrenchment of Hindutva: Local Mediations and Forms of Convergence*, edited by Daniela Berti, Nicolas Jaoul, and Pralay Kanungo. London/New York: Routledge, 2011.

Warrier, M. 'The Seva Ethic and the Spirit of Institution Building in the Mata Amritanandamayi Mission'. In *Hinduism in Public and Private: Reform, Hindutva, Gender and Sampraday*, edited by A. R. H. Copley. New Delhi/New York: Oxford University Press, 2003.

Watt, C. A. *Serving the Nation: Cultures of Service, Association, and Citizenship in Colonial India*. Oxford: Oxford University Press, 2005.

Weber, Max. *The Protestant Ethics and the Spirit of Capitalism*. New York: Charles Scribner's Sons, reprint 1958.

Weiner, Myron. *Party Politics in India: The Development of a Multi-Party System*. Princeton, NJ: Princeton University Press, 1957.

White, G. *The Alchemical Body, Siddha Traditions in Medieval India*. Chicago, IL, 1996; *Sinister Yogis*, Chicago, 2009.

Wilkinson, S. I. Votes *and Violence: Electoral Competition and Ethnic Riots in India*. Cambridge: Cambridge University Press, 2009.

Zavos, John, Pralay Kanungo, Deepa Reddy, Maya Warrier, and Raymond Brady Williams, eds. *Public Hinduisms*. New Delhi: SAGE Publications, 2012.

Zizek, Slavoj. *The Ticklish Subject: The Absent Centre of Political Ontology*. London: Verso, 1999.

Published Papers and Digital Sources

Adcock, Cassie, and Radhika Govindarajan, 'Bovine Politics in South Asia: Rethinking Religion, Law and Ethics'. *South Asia: Journal of South Asian Studies* 42, no. 6 (2019): 1095–1107.

Anderson, Edward. '"Neo-Hindutva": The Asia House M.F. Husain Campaign and the Mainstreaming of Hindu Nationalist Rhetoric in Britain'. *Contemporary South Asia* 23, no. 1 (2015): 45–66.

Anderson, Edward, and Arkotong Longkumer, 'Neo-Hindutva': Evolving Forms, Spaces, and Expressions of Hindu Nationalism'. *Contemporary South Asia* 26, no. 4 (2018): 371–377.

Ali, Sharib A. 'Clean Chits, Deaths, Acquittals: The Unending "Tricks of Fate" in Saffron Terror Cases'. *Economic and Political Weekly* 53, no. 17 (28 April 2018): 1–7.

Alter, Joseph S. 'Somatic Nationalism: Indian Wrestling and Militant Hinduism'. *Modern Asian Studies* 28, no. 3 (1994): 557–588.

Balagopal, K. 'An Ideology for the Provincial Propertied Class'. *Economic and Political Weekly* XXII, nos. 36, 37 (5–12 September 1987): 1544–1546.

Banningan, John A. 'The Hindu Code Bill'. *Far Eastern Survey* 21, no. 17 (3 December 1952): 173–176. [Published by Institute of Pacific Relations.]

Beckerlegge, G. 'Seva (service to humanity): A boundary issue in the study of recent and contemporary Hindu movements'. In *Man in India: A Quarterly International Journal of Anthropology* 91, no. 1 (2011): 54–55.

Berger, P., and R. Hefner. 'Spiritual Capital in Comparative Perspective'. Paper prepared for the Spiritual Capital Planning Meeting 2003. http://www.metanexus.net/spiritual capital/pdf/Berger.pdf (accessed 29 March 2006).

Bhargava, Kusum. 'Rajasthan Politics and Princely Rulers: An Analysis of Electoral Processes'. *The Indian Journal of Political Science* 33, no. 4 (October–December 1972): 413–430.

Bhattacharya, Sabyasachi. 'Secularism and the State'. *Frontline*, 5 February 2016. https://frontline.thehindu.com/politics/secularism-and-the-state/article8123816.ece

Bhuvi Gupta, and Jacob Copeman. 'Awakening Hindu Nationalism Through Yoga: Swami Ramdev and the Bharat Swabhiman Movement'. *Contemporary South Asia* 27, no. 3 (2019): 313–329.

Bidwai, Praful. 'End of Social Engineering'. *Frontline* 22, no. 26 (17–30 December 2005), https://frontline.thehindu.com/columns/article30207860.ece

Bidwai, Praful. 'Understanding a Political Chameleon'. *India International Centre Quarterly* 32, no. 1 (Summer 2005): 131–137.

Bidwai, Praful. 'Confronting the Reality of Hindutva Terrorism'. *Economic and Political Weekly* 43, no. 47 (22–28 November 2008): 10–13.

Bilgrami, Akeel. 'Secularism: A Genealogical Analysis'. *American Book Review* 39, no. 5 (July/August 2018): 11, 15.

Burghart, Richard. 'Renunciation in the Religious Traditions of South Asia'. *Man* (New Series) 18, no. December 4, Royal Anthropological Institute of Great Britain and Ireland, 1983.

Chaturvedi, Shashank, David N. Gellner, and Sanjay Kumar Pandey. 'Politics in Gorakhpur Since the 1920s: The Making of a Safe "Hindu" Constituency'. *Contemporary South Asia* 27, no. 1 (2019): 40–57.

Chatterjee, Angana. 'Hindutva's Violent History'. *Tehelka Magazine* 5, no. 35 (13 September 2000).

Cohen, Lawrence. 'Science, Politics, and Dancing Boys: Propositions and Accounts'. *Parallax* 14, no. 3 (2008): 35–47.

Dasgupta, Koushiki. 'Textualing Women as "Hindu": The Bharat Sevashram Sangha Perspective on Hindu Women in Twentieth Century'. *The Indian Historical Review* 44, no. 2 (2017): 270–284.

Datta, Dvijadas. 'Moksha, or the Vedántic Release'. *The Journal of the Royal Asiatic Society of Great Britain and Ireland*, New Series 20, no. 4 (October 1888): 513–539.

Desai, Radhika. 'Cultureless and Contemporary Right: Indian Bourgeoisie and Political Hindutva'. *Economic and Political Weekly* 34, no. 12 (20–26 March 1999): 695–712.

Dimitrova, Diana. 'The Development of Sanatana Dharma in the Twentieth Century: A Radhasoami Guru's Perspective'. *International Journal of Hindu Studies* 11 (2007): 89–98.

Dumont, Louis. *Homo Hierarchicus*. Paris: Gillimard, 1966.

Dyson, Esther, George Gilder, Jay Keyworth, and Alvin Toffler. 'A Magna Carta for the Knowledge Age'. *New Perspectives Quarterly* 11, no. 4 (1994): 45, 46.

Emmons, R. A., and R. F. Paloutzian. 'The Psychology of Religion'. *Annual Review of Psychology* 54 (2003): 377–402.

Freitag, Sandria B. 'Sacred Symbol as Mobilizing Ideology: The North Indian Search for a "Hindu" Community'. *Comparative Studies in Society and History* 22, no. 4 (1980): 597–625.

Gatade, Subhash. 'The Ideological and Institutional Incorporation of Dalits into Hindutva Maelstrom'. *South Asia Citizens Wire*, 27 January 2009.

Gondhalekar, Nandini, and Sanjoy Bhattacharya. 'The All India Hindu Mahasabha and the End of British Rule in India, 1939–1947'. *Social Scientist* 27, no. 7/8 (July–August 1999): 48–74.

Gopalakrishnan, Shankar. 'Defining, Constructing and Policing a "New India": Relationship Between Neoliberalism and Hindutva'. *Economic and Political Weekly* 41, no. 26 (30 June 30 to 7 July 2006): 2803, 2805–2813.

Gopalakrishnan, Shankar. 'Neoliberalism and Hindutva: Fascism, Free Markets and the Restructuring of Indian Capitalism'. *Radical Notes*, 29 October 2008.

Gordon, R. 'The Hindu Mahasabha and the Indian National Congress, 1915 to 1926'. *Modern Asian Studies* 9, no. 2 (1975): 145–203.

Gould, William. 'Contesting Secularism in Colonial and Post-Colonial North India Between the 1930 and 1950s'. *Contemporary South Asia* 14, no. 4 (2005): 481–494.

Guha, Ramchandra. 'Elections in 1951–1952, Not Much Difference'. Columns, *Hindustan Times*, 20 April 2019, https://www.hindustantimes.com/columns/elections.html

Habermas, Jürgen, 'Secularism's Crisis of Faith: Notes on a Post-Secular Society'. *New Perspectives Quarterly* 25, no. 4 (2008): 17–29.

Hansen, Thomas B. 'Recuperating Masculinity: Hindu Nationalism, Violence and Exorcism of the Muslim Other'. Critique of Anthropology 16, no. 2 (1996): 137–172.

Hatcher, Brian A. 'Bourgeois Vedanta: The Colonial Roots of Middle-Class Hinduism'. *Journal of the American Academy of Religion* 75, no. 2 *(2007): 298–323.*

Heehs, Peter. 'Bengali Religious Nationalism and Communalism'. *International Journal of Hindu Studies* 1, no. 1 (April 1997): 117–139.

Jaffrelot, Christophe. 'Hindu Nationalism: Strategic Syncretism in Ideology Building'. *Economic and Political Weekly* 20, no. 12–13 (March 1993): 517–524.

Jaffrelot, Christophe. 'Hindu Nationalism: Strategic Syncretism in Ideology Building'. *Economic and Political Weekly* 28, nos. 12/13 (20–27 March 1993): 517–524.

Jaffrelot, Christophe. 'Composite Culture Is Not Multiculturalism: A Study of the Indian Constituent Assembly Debates'. In *India and the Politics of Developing Countries: Essays in Memory of Myron Weiner*, edited by Ashutosh Varshney. New Delhi: SAGE Publications, 2004.

Jaffrelot, C., and I. Therwath. 'The Sangh Parivar and the Hindu Diaspora in the West: What Kind of "Long Distance Nationalism"?' *International Political Sociology* 1, no. 3 (2007): 278–295.

Jha, Dhirendra K. *RSS and the Akharas*, 8 March 2019, https://fountainink.in/reportage/rss-and-the-akharas

Kanungo, Pralay. 'Hindutva's Entry into a "Hindu Province": Early Years of RSS in Orissa'. *Economic and Political Weekly* (2 August 2003): 3293–3303.

Karat, Prakash. 'The Rise of Narendra Modi: A Joint Enterprise of Hindutva and Big Business'. *The Marxist* XXX, no. 1 (January–March 2014).

Kasturi, M. 'Asceticising Monastic Families'. Ascetic Genealogies, Property Feuds and Anglo-Hindu Law in Late Colonial India'. *Modern Asian Studies* 43, no. 5 (2009): 1039–1083.

Kasturi, M. Sadhus. '*Sampradaya,* and Hindu Nationalism: The Dasnamis and the Shri Bharat Dharma Mahamandala in the Early Twentieth Century'. NMML, Occasional Paper, History and Society, New Series, 79.

Lucia, Amanda. 'Innovative Gurus: Tradition and Change in Contemporary Hinduism'. *International Journal of Hindu Studies* 18, no. 2 (August 2014): 221–263.

Manchanda, R. 'Militarized Hindu Nationalism and the Mass Media: Shaping a Hindutva Public Discourse'. *Journal of South Asian Studies* 25, no. 3 (2002): 301–320.

Mathur, D. C. 'The Concept of Action in the Bhagvad-Gita'. *Philosophy and Phenomenological Research* 35, no. 1 (September, 1974): 34–35.

McLeod, H. *Religion and the People of Western Europe, 1789–1990*. Oxford: Oxford University Press, 1997.

McLeod, H. 'The Religious Crisis of the 1960s'. *Journal of Modern European History* 3, no. 2. Christian Churches and Religion in the 20th Century, 2005.

Mukhopadhyay, Nilanjan. *The Demolition. India at the Crossroads*, 214. New Delhi: Indus, 1994.

Mukta, Parita. 'The Public Face of Hindu Nationalism'. *Ethnic and Racial Studies* 23, no. 3 (2000).

Nair, P., and M. Bano. 'Faith-based Organisations in South Asia: Historical Evolution, Current Status and Nature of Interaction with the State' (Working Paper 12, Birmingham School of Religions and Development, 2006).

Namboodiripad, E. M. S. 'Adi Sankara and His Philosophy: A Marxist View'. *Social Scientist* 17, no. 1/2 (January–February 1989): 3–12.

Niekerk, Brimadevi van. 'Religion and Spirituality: What are the Fundamental Differences?' HTSTeologieseStudies/TheologicalStudies,/Users/Intel/Downloads/Religion_and_spirituality_What_are_the_fundamental.pdf, p. 10 (accessed 22 February 2019).

Pandey, Gyanendra. 'Rallying Around the Cow: Sectarian Strife in the Bhojpur Region, c. 1888–1917'. In *Subaltern Studies: Writings on South Asian History and Society*, Vol. 2, edited by Ranajit Guha. Delhi/New York: Oxford University Press, 1983.

Pandya, Samta, P. 'Seva in Mata Amritanandamayi Mission: Social Service as a Public Face of Faith'. *Implicit Religion* 19 (2016): 401–423.

Panigrahi, Saswat. 'When Will Swami Lakshmanananda's Killers Be Brought To Justice?' 25 August, 2016, https://swarajyamag.com/politics (accessed 12 December 2017).

Pantham, Thomas. 'Indian Secularism and Its Critics: Some Reflections'. *The Review of Politics* 59, no. 3, Published online by Cambridge University Press, 5 August 2009, https://doi.org/10.1017/S0034670500027704

Parel, Anthony. 'The Political Symbolism of the Cow in India'. *Journal of Commonwealth Political Studies* 7, no. 3 (1969): 179–203.

Ramdev, Swami. 'Vedas—The Proponent of World Fraternity'. *Yog Sandesh*, January 1.5, (2004): 14–19.

Reddy, D. 'Hindutva as Praxis'. *Religion Compass* 5, no. 8 (2011): 412–426.

Reghunath, Leena Gita. 'The Believer: Swami Aseemanand's Radical Service to the Sangh'. *Caravan*, 2014, http://www.caravanmagazine.in/reportage/believer

Rao Tarte, Narayan. *Vishva Hindu Parishad Ki Kalpana* (Formation of Vishva Hindu Parishad), Hindu Vishva, Silver Jubilee Issue, 1989–1990.

Richards, Glyn. 'Gandhi's Concept of Truth and the Advaita Tradition'. *Religious Studies* 22, no. 1 (March 1986): 1–14.

Rudert, Angela. 'Research on Contemporary Indian Gurus: What's New About New Age Gurus?' *Religion Compass* 4, no. 10 (2010): 629–642.

Sharma, Arvind. 'On Hindu, Hindustān, Hinduism and Hindutva'. *Numen* 49, no. 1 (2002): 1–36.

Sheldrake, Philip. *Spirituality: A Guide for the Perplexed.* Bloomsbury Academic, 2014, https://www.bloomsburycollections.com/book/spirituality-a-guide-for-the-perplexed/

Sen, Amiya P. *Hinduism and the Problem of Self Actualisation in the Colonial Era: Critical Reflections*. South Asia Institute Papers, South Asia Institute, Heidelberg Unive: sity, no. 1, 2015, www.sai.uni-heidelberg.de (accessed 12 December 2019).

Som, Reba. 'Jawaharlal Nehru and the Hindu Code: A Victory of Symbol over Substance?' *Modern Asian Studies* 28, no. 1 (February 1994): 165–194.

Tuteja, K. L., and O. P. Grewal. 'Emergence of Hindu Communal Ideology in Early Twentieth Century Punjab'. *Social Scientist* 20, no. 7/8 (July–August 1992): 19.

Udupa, Sahana. 'Enterprise Hindutva and Social Media in Urban India'. *Contemporary South Asia* 26, no. 4 (2018): 453–467.

Valantasis, Richard. 'Constructions of Power in Asceticism', *Journal of the American Academy of Religion* 63, no. 4 (winter, 1995).

van der Veer Peter. '"God Must Be Liberated!" A Hindu Liberation Movement in Ayodhya'. *Modern Asian Studies* 21, no. 2 (1987): 402–422.

van der Veer Peter. 'Secularism and National Development in India and China'. *Third World Quarterly* 13, no. 4 (2012): 721–734.

Varshney, Ashutosh. 'Contested Meanings: India's National Identity, Hindu Nationalism, and the Politics of Anxiety'. *Daedalus* 122, no. 3, Reconstructing Nations and States (Summer 1993): 227–261.

Walter O. Kaelber. 'Asceticism', in *The Encyclopedia of Religion*, edited by Mircea Eliade. New York: Macmillan, 1987.

Warrier, Maya. 'Guru Choice and Spiritual Seeking in Contemporary India'. *International Journal of Hindu Studies* 7, no. 1/3 (February 2003): 31–54.

Watt, C. A. 'Education for National Efficiency: Constructive Nationalism in North India, 1909–1916'. *Modern Asian Studies* 31, no. 2 (1997): 339–374.

Weber, Max. *The Protestant Ethic and the Spirit of Capitalism*. New York: Scribner, 1930.

Weber, Max. *The Theory of Social and Economic Organization*. New York: Free Press, 1947.

Webster, Travis D. 'Secularization and Cosmopolitan Gurus'. *Asian Ethnology* 75, no. 2 (2016): 327–357.

Yang, Anand A. 'Sacred Symbol and Sacred Space in Rural India: Community Mobilization in the "Anti-Cow Killing" Riot of 1893'. *Comparative Studies in Society and History* 22, no. 4 (1980): 576–596.

Zavos, John. 'Searching for Hindu Nationalism in Modern Indian History: Analysis of Some Early Ideological Developments'. *Economic and Political Weekly* 34, no. 32 (7–13 August 1999): 2269–2276.

Zavos, John. 'Defending Hindu Tradition: Sanatana Dharma as a Symbol of Orthodoxy in Colonial India'. *Religion* 31, no. 2 (2005): 109–123.

Zavos, John. '"Stamp It Out!" Disciplining the Image of Hinduism in a Multicultural Milieu'. *Contemporary South Asia* 16, no. 3 (2008): 323–337.

PhD Thesis

Alder, Ketan. 'Arenas of Service and the Development of the Hindu Subject in India'. Unpublished PhD thesis, University of Manchester, School of Arts, Languages and Culture, 2015.

Lutgendorf, Philip. 'The Life of a Text: Tulsidas' Ramcaritmanas in Performance'. PhD diss., University of Chicago, 1987.

Shridhar, Paras. 'The Guru Disciple Relationship in Diaspora'. Unpublished PhD thesis, Derby University, 2005.

Thachil, Tariq. 'The Saffron Wave Meets the Silent Revolution: Why the Poor Vote for Hindu Nationalism in India'. Faculty of the Graduate School of Cornell University, 2009.

Tucker, Emily. 'Identity, Religion and Dialogue: The Rearticulation of Hinduism in America'. BA thesis, Radcliffe College, Harvard University, 1993.

Zavos, John. 'Sangathan: The Pursuit of a Hindu Ideal in Colonial India: The Idea of Organisation in the Emergence of Hindu Nationalism 1870–1930'. PhD thesis, University of Bristol, Department of Theology and Religious Studies, September 1997, pp. 49–50.

About the Author

Koushiki Dasgupta works as Vidyasagar Chair Professor at the Department of History, Vidyasagar University, West Bengal. Her most recent publications include *Electoral Politics and Hindu Nationalism in India: The Bharatiya Jana Sangh, 1951–1971*, (Routledge, London, 2020). She has received the Charles Wallace Research Grant in the United Kingdom and UGC (University Grants Commission) Resource Associateship at IIAS (Indian Institute of Advanced Study), Shimla, and has worked as a Visiting Scholar at SOAS, London. She has extensively published works on different aspects of Bengal politics, gender studies, diaspora studies and post-independence Indian politics and is a regular speaker at national and international conferences. Her interests include writing poetry, singing classical music and playing the guitar.

Index